'Steven's book adds an excellent and wi[illegible] debate on the future path for our country.'

Chris Liddell, CFO, Microsoft

'The survival of Maori as a people, Te kakano i ruia mai i Rangiatea – has grown from a legacy we inherited from the entrepreneurial spirit and enduring strength of our ancestors. In this book, Steven Carden reflects how Aotearoa in 2007 brings together that base of Maori innovation along with the skills and talents of other New Zealanders, to create an emerging and distinctive sense of nationhood. It is well worth a read!'

Tariana Turia, MP, Co-leader of the Maori Party

'Steven Carden's is a fresh, invigorating and thoughtful perspective. I commend it.'

Dr John Hood, Vice-Chancellor, Oxford University

'This book is a gutsy and inspiring pronouncement of the challenges facing New Zealand as we engage in a rapidly changing world. Steven invokes science, philosophy and history to tell a story of how great we can be if we are courageous enough to use our nation's size, creativity and flexibility to maximum advantage. A welcome contribution to the national conversation; honestly appraising an unpredictable future and offering optimism about our potential place in it.'

John Key, MP, Leader of the National Party

'Steven Carden has done us a great service by providing an illuminating guide to the ideas and trends that will shape the world in which New Zealand will operate in over the coming decades – and how New Zealand ought to think about responding.'

Dr David Skilling, Chief Executive, The New Zealand Institute

'What Steven has written is a penetrating analysis of who we are and where New Zealand can go if we have courage and determination. This is a book worth reading.'

Sir Paul Reeves, former Governor General

'Steven Carden's New Zealand Unleashed *integrates new insights from technology, psychology, biology and history into an important challenge for New Zealand: absorb ideas, innovate and master change. It is refreshing, provocative and should stimulate much needed debate. In today's rapidly changing world, this is a challenge we must rise to meet. As an emerging New Zealand thinker, Steven Carden has helped us to do just that.'*

Hon. David Cunliffe, MP, Minister of Immigration

'Through an insightful weaving together of historical examples with modern scientific theories, New Zealand Unleashed provides a thought-provoking look at New Zealand's past and, most importantly, our future. Carden challenges all New Zealanders – at home and abroad – to reflect on the global issues facing our nation and to take action in shaping our future society.'

Dr Karen Willcox, Associate Professor of Aeronautics and Astronautics, MIT

NEW ZEALAND UNLEASHED

the country, its future and the people who will get it there

STEVEN CARDEN

with Campbell Murray

RANDOM HOUSE
NEW ZEALAND

A catalogue record for this book is available
from the National Library of New Zealand.

A RANDOM HOUSE BOOK
published by
Random House New Zealand
18 Poland Road, Glenfield, Auckland, New Zealand
www.randomhouse.co.nz

Random House International
Random House
20 Vauxhall Bridge Road
London, SW1V 2SA
United Kingdom

Random House Australia (Pty) Ltd
20 Alfred Street, Milsons Point, Sydney
New South Wales 2061, Australia

Random House South Africa Pty Ltd
Isle of Houghton
Corner Boundary Road and Carse O'Gowrie
Houghton 2198, South Africa

Random House Publishers India Private Ltd
301 World Trade Tower, Hotel Intercontinental Grand Complex
Barakhamba Lane, New Delhi 110 001, India

First published 2007

ISBN 978 1 86941 858 8

Design: IslandBridge
Cover illustration and design: Katy Yiakmis
Printed in Australia by Griffin Press

Steven Carden

Steven Carden is an Engagement Manager at the manag-ement consulting firm, McKinsey and Co., in New Zealand. Prior to returning home to New Zealand in 2006, Steven worked for three years in McKinsey's New York office. Steven is the founder of the First Foundation, a non-profit organisation that provides New Zealand's most talented, but financially-disadvantaged secondary school students with work, mentoring and funding from New Zealand's largest companies. Steven holds an MBA from Harvard Business School, where he received a Knox Fellowship and was awarded a Fulbright Scholarship. He holds an LLB and a BA from the University of Auckland. In 2005, Steven was picked by the Sir Peter Blake Trust as one of New Zealand's five emerging leaders.

To Kristin

Contents

Preface 9

Acknowledgements 11

Introduction 15

Part 1 The end of certainty

1 A complex, crazy world 25

2 New Zealand's unknown future 40

3 A world of uncertainty 68

Part 2 How to build a successful society

4 Energy, entropy and rats 87

5 Two laws and adaptation 103

6 What Peter the Great learnt from the Dutch 121

Part 3 New Zealand's DNA

7 Maori 1 – a crash course in survival 149

8 New Zealand and the crazy 1870s 166

9 Maori II – a new world 180

Part 4 A few ideas for a more adaptable New Zealand

10 Unstoppable creativity 205

11 A sponge for ideas 232

12 Finding the willingness to change 261

Endnotes 287

Index 307

Preface

The purpose of this book is to contribute to the debate about New Zealand's future, and the best way to get us there. It is written from a perspective that I hope people find both new and thought-provoking. My hope is to sketch out some ideas, and to present those ideas as being plausible enough to encourage others to engage with them further.

The genesis of this book – the initial research and writing – began when I was living overseas. It was completed after I returned to New Zealand. The book, therefore, encompasses both perspectives: that of an outsider as well as that of someone living and breathing the daily life of the nation. Being outside New Zealand helps you see the country in a broader context, as with anything viewed from a distance. But living here provides a feel for the vibe of the country, and a reality-check on what will and will not work.

A 300-page book on New Zealand necessarily represents a mile-high view of this country. Such perspectives on our country are rare but, I think, important. Inevitably, however, an elevated vantage point means glossing over some of the intimate detail. I've indicated sources in the endnotes for those interested in digging deeper into the nuances of the ideas and concepts considered.

Finally, while information and insights are gleaned from around the world, this is a book about New Zealand, for a New Zealand audience. I've used local data and research wherever possible, but these have not always been available. So you'll see references to various overseas statistics and studies, particularly American. They may not provide a perfect proxy, but I've used them where I think they're indicative of, or relevant to, the New Zealand context.

Acknowledgements

The jury is out on this book. When the verdict is returned, I'll happily credit those mentioned below with its successes and accept full responsibility for any failings and errors.

Firstly, Campbell Murray, a partner in this project from the outset, has been a valuable contributor to the book. His insights, ideas, and research have played an important part in the book's final form.

My employer, McKinsey & Company, was gracious enough to provide a leave of absence to allow me to work on the book full-time. Needless to say, any opinions expressed in the book are my own, and not those of my employer.

Rachael Germann and Paul Ryan were the backbone of the research effort, spending more time in libraries than any undergraduate ever should.

My thanks to the Sir Peter Blake Trust for its belief in, and financial support of, this project.

A number of very busy people were prepared to read and comment on the book during the writing phase. Hazel Petrie, Amokura Kawharu, Gary Bartlett, Patrick Snedden, Derek Aframe, and Malcolm Paterson all gave highly insightful comments on selected chapters. Dr Andrew Leigh, Georges Baron van Tuyll van Serooskerken, David Madden, Dr David Skilling, Ian Narev, Professor Alan Davidson, Sarah O'Brien, MacGregor Duncan and Clinton Lawgun all provided very helpful comments on the entire manuscript as it was approaching completion. Peter Tynan reviewed in detail various drafts of the manuscript and made substantial suggestions.

My brother, Dr Craig Carden, had the unenviable task of reading the first full draft of the book. That's a task you give to someone you both respect and trust. His diplomatic, constructive suggestions came at a pivotal time.

Random House took a gamble on an unknown, first-time author when it agreed to publish this book. Jenny Hellen has managed the process from start to finish with great patience and experience. Her guidance throughout has been invaluable. My editor, John MacKinven, worked hard to smooth out the prose. My thanks also to Nic McCloy and Sarah Thornton and the rest of the team at Random House.

I might have completed the project in half the time were it not for my young son Lucas, who came up with far better uses for my time than writing.

Finally, it's no exaggeration to say that this book would never have been completed were it not for the help and support of my wife, Kristin. She was unfailingly encouraging and carried the burden of everything but the book itself for the countless days I locked myself away to write. On top of that, her astute insights and merciless red editing pen helped shape my writing in numerous ways. This book is dedicated without reservation to her.

Don Juan: I, my friend, am as much a part of Nature as my own finger is a part of me. If my finger is the organ by which I grasp the sword and the mandoline, my brain is the organ by which Nature strives to understand itself . . .

The Devil: What is the use of knowing?

Don Juan: Why, to be able to choose the line of greatest advantage instead of yielding in the direction of the least resistance. Does a ship sail to its destination no better than a log drifts nowhither? The philosopher is Nature's pilot. And there you have our difference: to be in hell is to drift: to be in heaven is to steer.

Man and Superman, George Bernard Shaw

Introduction

The Lenox Globe, today in the collection of the New York Public Library, is one of the oldest globes in the world. Constructed around 1507, a mere fifteen years after Christopher Columbus made landfall in the Americas, it is a wonderful example of how obscure the world was to Western eyes a mere five centuries ago.

Allow your eye to follow the indentations in the copper globe and it's easy to make out most of Western Europe and the outline of the Mediterranean. This territory looks much as it does on today's map. But the further your eyes travel around the globe from Europe, the hazier the geographic detail and the less familiar the world appears. Africa looks like New Zealand's South Island on speed. The Pacific looks narrow enough to canoe across in an afternoon. In place of North America there are scattered islands, one of which, located near *Terra de Brazil*, oddly enough bears the name Japan.

On the east coast of Asia is a rather intriguing inscription: *hic sunt dracones* (here be dragons). In the early days of exploration by Europeans, nautical maps often bore the image of a sea serpent over any area that remained unknown to the mapmaker. This was uncharted territory. A place of the unknown: *terra incognita*. A place of adventure and peril, and perhaps of mermaids.

'Here be dragons' inscriptions and pictures of terrifying sea creatures are conspicuously absent from modern maps. Uncharted territories no longer exist, at least on the earth's surface. We know where Japan is. Even New Zealand, the last major landmass on earth to be 'discovered' by Europeans, has found its way onto most maps. Satellites criss-cross the skies, taking photographs of every square kilometre of the Earth's surface. The result is an end to ambiguity about which landmasses go where on a globe.

Yet while we may have charted the Earth's surface in detail, the future remains as ambiguous and uncertain today as it would have done to the map-makers of the sixteenth century. In fact, it may seem even more uncertain.

Back then a mapmaker might hope at best to draw a few maps, dodge various diseases and the odd war, and perhaps make it into his thirties. The narrative of his life was mirrored in the lives of the generations before him. That isn't the case any more. The world of today is very different from that of even fifty years ago. What the next fifty, even twenty, years will bring is equally uncertain.

To many of us in New Zealand, 'Here be dragons' might be an apt description of how we feel about the future. It's unknown and a little scary. It is certainly a future filled with its share of metaphorical dragons. China, the yellow dragon to the north, will feature very prominently in the lives of every New Zealander. Exactly how is unclear, but its influence will certainly extend well beyond the shelves of cheap electronics, toys and shoes at The Warehouse. Advances in genetic manipulation are such that there's no saying what dragon-like life forms may yet emerge – not from the world's oceans, but from its scientific laboratories.

Whether we envisage the dragons in New Zealand's uncharted future as threatening or magnificent or something else altogether, one thing is clear – we can't avoid facing them. Unlike the sailors of old, we don't have a choice about whether we set off for these uncharted territories or not. The future is coming. The question is: are we ready for it?

That's what this book is about. It's a look at what sort of society New Zealand will need to become in order to tackle successfully an unpredictable future. It is about how New Zealand can thrive in an uncertain future, rather than fearing and resisting it.

I think this is a very important issue. New Zealand is small, isolated, and vulnerable. We feel the effects of change more than most. So we need to be thinking seriously about what sort of society is going to handle the waves of change rolling our way. That's not something for politicians alone or other leaders in society to be thinking about. It's an issue for every New Zealander.

That's why this exploration of New Zealand and its future won't be an exercise in policy formulation. Interest rate movements and overseas debt levels and business regulation and budget surpluses and small-business competitiveness and tax rates and productivity growth and trade agreements and so on are all important. Vital, in fact. I'm just not going to talk about them much in this book. Discussion of them already goes on in our newspapers, our magazines and over our airwaves. We're faced with a daily barrage of opinions, reports and analyses where these topics are concerned. This is the territory of think tanks and lobby groups. Our government also employs hundreds of highly skilled people to sit in the Beehive and Bowen House to think about such matters. For better or worse, this book won't add to that deluge.

Instead, our quest to understand New Zealand and its struggle to master the future will take a different route. The economics historian Thomas Sowell once said that, 'What is truly needed is not a blueprint to be imposed from on high but an understanding of what does and does not produce prosperity.'[1] In that vein, the task I've set myself in this book is not to outline in great detail exactly what New Zealand should *do*; but rather to talk a lot about how New Zealand should *be*.

The final section does offer some thoughts on what I think New Zealand can 'do' to succeed in the future – in a book of this sort it would be disingenuous of me not to throw out a few ideas. But you'll be disappointed if you expect a laundry list of policy prescriptions. This book is not a policy manifesto in disguise. Instead, it's more a discussion about the type of society that will most successfully face an uncertain future, with a few thoughts thrown in on how New Zealand can become more like that.

To accomplish that we will meander into some rather unusual places for a book of this sort: biology labs, physics departments, and psychologists' offices. We're also going to dip our toes into New Zealand's history, dabble in the murky past of a few other nations, peek occasionally through the windows of the business world, and peer around the blackboard at our nation's schools.

Of course, trying to figure out what New Zealand will need to be like to prosper in an uncertain future is no easy task. This eclectic range of topics could quickly become a confusing jumble to even the most committed reader. So, in the spirit in which I started this introduction, let me provide a map of how we're going to proceed.

A blueprint for the road ahead

This book is divided into four parts, and there is a primary question that we're aiming to answer in each.

Part One – The end of certainty
Why does the pace of change seem so rampant today, the future so uncertain, and why does that unnerve us so much?

Part Two – How to build a successful society
What are three traits that successful societies have used to cope with the complex and the unpredictable?

Part Three – New Zealand's DNA
Has New Zealand exhibited these three traits in the past, and what does that tell us about our ability to cope with change and uncertainty in the future?

Part Four – A few ideas for a more adaptive New Zealand
How can New Zealand nurture these three key traits to help build a stronger country in the future?

Let me say a little about each of these parts now before we dive into the first of them.

We begin our journey by examining the complexity of modern-day life in New Zealand, and the uncertainty of its future. Modern-day life offers more prosperity than we've ever experienced in the past. But the by-product of that prosperity is a life more complicated and faster paced than ever before. Our sense of control over our lives has never felt weaker.

This is particularly important given the shroud of uncertainty hanging over our future. Chapter Two outlines a host of the major changes that will affect our way of life. And there are many of them. Our newspapers are already filled with stories of remarkable (and, let's admit, slightly alarming) scientific breakthroughs. In just the last few years, for instance, we've cracked the very code of life itself, and now we're starting to manipulate it in ways only science fiction has anticipated. Today's science is on the verge of the genetic manipulations of humans that seemed so extreme in the 1997 movie, *Gattaca*.

It's not just barely comprehensible scientific breakthroughs that have us eyeing the future with uncertainty. Suddenly it seems as though countries everywhere are working full tilt to gain the advantage over New Zealand. The Chinese, Indians and Romanians are no longer satisfied to be the global suppliers of rice, curries and dill pickles. Their path to prosperity is a high-tech one and they're quickly building the skill set to beat New Zealand to the loose ball. The result of this quickly globalising, competitive world is that New Zealand has grown relatively poorer over the past three decades, and it's beginning to show. As New Zealanders, it's easy to feel as though our place in the sun is disappearing before we've really had a chance to bathe in it.

Of course, New Zealand's future doesn't have to be gloomy. Not by a long shot. The increasingly fast-moving world of tomorrow could provide ever greater opportunities for small, agile, flexible nations to excel. The point is simply that our world is changing quickly. We can't afford to be complacent about that. Whether the future presents great opportunities for New Zealand or horrible headaches depends on what kind of society we become.

Acknowledging that the world is changing quickly and that the future is uncertain doesn't make it any easier to accept. Chapter Three helps us understand why. It explores where our love of certainty comes from and why it permeates the way we view the world. It goes on to explain why our usual way of viewing the world in a mechanistic, predictable fashion doesn't prepare us for a highly unpredictable future. Our 'cause and effect', 'action and reaction' way of interpreting things doesn't always work. The world is more unpredictable than that. All of which explains our seeming inability to 'fix' recurring problems like economic underperformance, or crime, or health system woes. We will continue to be disappointed if we think that any one policy or combination of policies today will completely sort out the New Zealand of tomorrow. The days of establishing a target, making a plan and setting off are over, if they were ever here. It's on that slightly disconcerting note that we end Part One.

Part Two looks at how societies handle the uncertainty and complexity outlined in Part One. We begin in Chapters Four and Five by exploring a relatively new branch of science called complexity theory. In the last couple of decades, a growing number of scientists have been trying to understand the way highly complex, unpredictable systems in nature – like an ant colony or an ecosystem – actually work. Until recently scientists thought the way they operated was somewhat of a mystery. But now they've discovered that the seeming complexity and randomness of a termite colony or ecosystem, for example, are in fact guided by a series of simple rules. These rules help explain why a termite colony works like a well-drilled army, despite the fact that no termite is in charge. They explain why an ecosystem suddenly disintegrates when one species disappears but is unaffected by the loss of another.

What happens in a termite mound may seem completely unrelated to the topic of this book: New Zealand and its future. But it isn't. Because the very same rules that govern a complex system like a termite colony also play a pretty major role in human society – another complex system. It's these rules that enable the beehive or ecosystem or society to adapt to changes in its environment. That's really important because the need for adaptation is hard-wired into the way this world works. We see it in the survival of species. And if we look back over time, we see it in the survival of societies. Adaptation means changing the practices, strategies or ways of thinking that were successful in the old environment but not in the new. This book argues that societies that can adapt well will best handle the complex, fast-changing world of the future.

Chapter Six concludes Part Two by looking at three traits that fuel a society's adaptability. First, lots of new ideas need to be generated – I'll call that creativity. Creativity fuels innovation. It needs to be nurtured and encouraged. Second, the ideas of others need to be absorbed. Being a sponge for these ideas can help New Zealand retain the vibrancy needed to adapt. Third, an adaptive society needs to be willing to change. By having a high tolerance for change, New Zealand can make the hard decisions necessary to keep adapting.

In Part Three, we take this theory and apply it to New Zealand's experience. That involves taking a fresh look at slices of our brief past by examining New Zealand's own experience at adapting to change. If history is any guide, we should be quietly confident. Our small island nation, young as it is, has already experienced periods of rapid change. Maori in pre-European and colonial times operated in a highly adaptive manner, and as a result were able to leverage European technologies and ideas to build remarkable trading relationships around the world as well as forcing the world's most powerful empire into a stalemate in the New Zealand Wars. The foundations of modern-day New Zealand were also laid during a dynamic period of change in the late nineteenth century. Adaptation, it would seem, is built into New Zealand's DNA.

That's encouraging news, but no reason for New Zealand to be complacent about the future. And it's the future we turn to in the fourth and final section of the book. This section discusses how New Zealand can weave the three attributes of adaptive societies – generating lots of new ideas, absorbing the ideas of others, and demonstrating a willingness to change – into its social fabric. There is no miracle cure, and these chapters don't pretend to offer one. The solutions, we'll discover, are to be found in the way we think as much as in the way we act, in our attitudes as much as in our actions.

That's the game plan. Like any author, I hope my arguments stand the test of time. More importantly, I hope they inspire dialogue, discussion and perhaps even follow-up by those who think they can do better.

These are important times for New Zealand. We can't afford to be blasé about the challenges they bring nor underestimate the opportunities they offer. I hope this book helps you think about New Zealand and its future in a new light.

Part 1

The end of certainty

1

A complex, crazy world

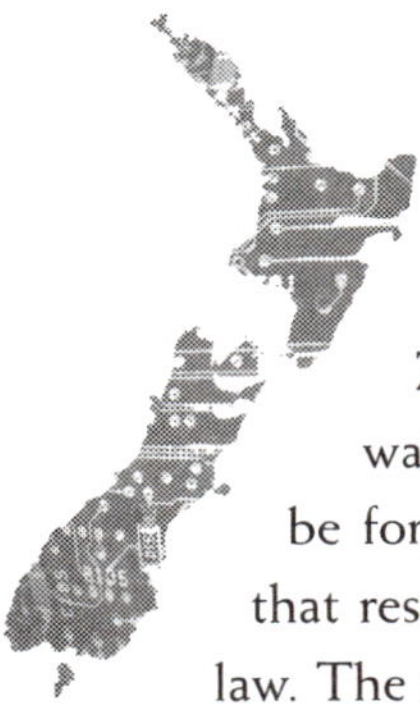

Driving a car used to be a waste of time in New Zealand. In the late 1890s, cars travelled no faster than walking pace. While the Auckland driver of today could be forgiven for asking what's changed, it wasn't traffic jams that resulted in walking-paced car rides back then; it was the law. The speed limit was officially walking pace. And, if getting overtaken by a jogger wasn't humiliating enough, you had to have at least one man walking ahead and another walking behind the vehicle to warn others of your impending approach.

William McLean, a Wellington businessman and MP, didn't think these restrictions were going to cut it. He had just imported two Benz vehicles and found that under these road restrictions it would take him three days to get his son from Naenae to cricket practice in Lower Hutt.

So, like any enterprising MP, McLean sought to have the law changed. To accomplish this he went to great lengths to convince fellow politicians of the worthiness of the motor car. He obtained permission at one point to take two Wellington city officials for a ride through Newtown.[1] Things were going smoothly until he crashed into a water channel while trying to avoid a horse. It was New Zealand's first motoring accident. Worse was to follow. The Mayor of Wellington decided to take one of McLean's cars for a spin. Struggling with the adjustment from reins to a steering wheel, the mayor smashed the car into the Basin Reserve fence and broke his nose.

Despite these mishaps, the McLean Motor-car Act was passed in 1898. It allowed, for the first time, the use of motor vehicles on New Zealand roads at speeds up to a terrifying twenty kilometres an hour. New Zealand's love affair with the car had begun.

It was a tentative affair to begin with. The combination of unreliable engines, poor suspension and pot-holed roads reduced the car to more novelty than practical value. By 1905 there were only about five hundred cars on the roads. But as the reliability of the car improved and the roads grew smoother, the practicality of motor vehicle travel became more and more apparent. By 1920 the number of motor vehicles in New Zealand had grown to 50,000.[2] Five years later, that number had doubled.

The horse and buggy industry had no chance. When the horse was put out to pasture, so were all the industries that supported it. Blacksmiths disappeared, manufacturers of watering troughs and saddles went out of business, stables were torn down, and people who curried horses looked for work elsewhere. An entire network of industries that depended on the horse rapidly collapsed in what the economist Joseph Schumpeter once called a 'gale of destruction'.[3] He cheerfully labelled this process 'creative destruction', but for those whose livelihoods depended on horse-powered transportation there can't have been anything cheerful about it.

The complexity of the motor car required a complex infrastructure to support it. Where once stables stood, service stations sprang up. Roads were paved. Traffic courts, traffic cops and traffic lights came into being. Someone began selling fluffy dice. Each invention opened up new niches for future inventions, and components from one invention have often been recycled into new forms. A whole new network of goods and services began to grow, each one filling a vacancy created by the goods and services that came before it.

As this car-driven system has become more complex, ever more diverse and specialised organisations have emerged. Someone has to make the personalised number plates, the antenna balls, the racing-seat covers, the bullet-hole stickers, the speed radars, the roof racks and the car tents. Then there are all the people who provide services for your vehicle, from the car-washing outfit down the road to the specialist mechanics. All of these groups, whether big or small, have their own set of relationships with hundreds of suppliers for the parts and services they need.

A simpler technology (the horse and buggy) was replaced by a more complex technology (the car). A more complex technology spawned the creation of whole new industries, products, services and jobs. The explosion of the use of the car and its impact on New Zealand is a microcosm of a broader phenomenon we can see in New Zealand today: the move towards greater and greater complexity in our society.

This matters to all of us because it directly affects what the future will look like and how we can deal with it. That's why we begin this book by seeking to understand what's behind this growth in complexity and what that means for the way we think about the future.

A world of increasing complexity

Let's begin by stating what to some will be the obvious: our lives are a lot more complicated today than they used to be. Eric Beinhocker, in his recent book *The Origins of Wealth*, illustrates this by comparing the average income of the Yanomamo, a stone-tool-making hunter–gatherer tribe from Brazil, with that of a person from the West.[4] While average incomes between the two differ by a factor of about four hundred, what is truly remarkable is the difference in the variety of things that wealth can purchase. Increase the wealth of the average Yanomamo and he can improve his hut, buy some clay pots and attain the finest cuisine. But that's about it.

By contrast, the number of economic choices available to the average westerner is staggering. The Borders store in Auckland carries over two hundred thousand titles. There are over twelve hundred restaurants in Auckland alone. Beinhocker estimates that the number of types of products (the stock-keeping units, or SKUs) available to the New York shopper is somewhere around 10^{10} (in other words, tens of billions). Thus, Beinhocker argues, the most dramatic difference between the Westerner and the Yanomamo is the hundred-millionfold, or eight orders of magnitude, difference in the complexity and diversity of their respective economies.

Of course, we all lived like the Yanomamo 15,000 years ago. But look across those 15,000 years, and it's apparent that the growth in complexity of the modern economy really only took off in the last two hundred and fifty years. Beinhocker quotes analysis conducted by Berkeley economist J. Bradford DeLong which suggests that world gross domestic product

(GDP) merely doubled between 15,000 BC and AD 1750. Over the last two hundred and fifty years, all hell has broken loose. Global wealth took off, increasing thirty-sevenfold. Economic historian David Landes puts it another way: 'The Englishman of 1750 was closer in material things to Caesar's legionnaires than to his own great-grandchildren.'[5]

The sheer increase in complexity of our lives even in the space of a single generation has been astonishing. In New Zealand forty years ago, my father was paid, in cash, every week. He had a quarterly electricity bill from the only electricity provider. Should he wander down to the grocery store, he would be confronted with about three different breakfast cereal options and two varieties of bread. The cleaning options on his electric wringer washing machine were 'on' or 'off'. He had one TV channel available to him – black and white of course.

Look at us now. My financial documents occupy an entire drawer in my house. We have seven power companies to choose from in Auckland alone. Our living room is overflowing with electronic entertainment options, from multiple channels on the television to DVDs to PlayStation to the Internet to tailored albums on my iPod. We have forty different types of toothpaste to choose from at the supermarket. The myriad coffee combinations at Starbucks are overwhelming. It's complicated all right.

It's no wonder we're becoming smarter. In the mid-1980s, New Zealand psychologist James Flynn, from the University of Otago, made a startling discovery: average IQ scores have increased significantly over the last century.[6] There has been a rise of twenty-four points in the US since 1918, twenty-seven points in Britain, and comparable rises in other countries, including New Zealand.[7] That effectively means a person whose IQ placed him in the top ten per cent of the American population in 1920 would today fall in the bottom third.

Scientific opinion is divided over what has caused this increase in IQ. Some point to better nutrition. Others to smaller families. Still others to better education. Flynn himself has suggested that one of the things that has been lifting IQs since our grandparents' time is the much richer and more challenging environment our minds must deal with. Our gadgets are more complicated; we do more intellectually difficult work. And, of course, we just have far more stuff to cope with.

Some have even suggested that popular culture contributes to the complexity. In *Everything Bad Is Good for You*, Steven Johnson argues that what is making us smarter is precisely what we are told is making us dumber: popular culture.[8] Video games, television shows and movies have become increasingly complex, requiring greater levels of brain power to process. For example, a typical episode of *The Dukes of Hazzard*, in the 1970s, was pretty basic. Two characters were engaged in a single storyline, moving towards a high-octane conclusion. A single episode of *Shortland Street*, by contrast, might follow four narrative threads, involving a dozen characters who weave in and out of the plot. Apparently it takes more brain power to keep track of who's gossiping about whom. It's no wonder our IQ is increasing.

The ephemeralisation phenomenon

This extraordinary growth in complexity begs a question: how did it happen? What's behind this seemingly relentless drive towards more and more complexity in our lives? Many believe it has a lot to do with the rise of computers.

In the mid-1960s, Gordon Moore, a leading inventor of integrated circuits and later chairman of the microchip manufacturer, Intel, observed that every twenty-four months twice as many transistors were being squeezed onto a microchip. He termed this phenomenon Moore's Law, and the phrase has become a byword for the increasing power of computers. The world's most powerful integrated circuit in 1965 contained sixty-four transistors. By 2000, Moore's sixty-four-transistor chip had evolved into the Pentium 4 processor's forty-two million transistors.[9]

Squeezing more transistors onto the microchip has resulted in an exponential growth in the power of computers. That's why the desktop computer you use at home to send emails and browse the Internet is a lot more powerful than the combined processing power of the computers aboard the spaceship Apollo 11 as it made its way to the moon in 1969.

This huge boost in computing power is a key driver behind the increase in the efficiency of just about everything. *Ephemeralisation* is a term coined by Buckminster Fuller, the American designer, architect, and inventor, to refer to the tendency for current technology to be replaced by much smaller, lighter, and more efficient technology. Author Stewart Brand, in his book *The Clock of the Long Now,* describes Fuller's concept as 'doing more with less'.

To illustrate the concept of ephemeralisation, Fuller pointed to satellites that weigh just a few hundred kilos, yet functionally replace some 680,000 tonnes of transatlantic cable. Our cars travel further on less fuel, while their speed, power and comfort have increased. Better techniques, such as irrigation, crop improvement, fertilisers, pesticides, and harvesting machines, produce more yield per acre than they used to. As a result, the price of food in real terms has declined seventy-five per cent over the last half-century.[10] A hundred years ago it took about sixty per cent of the workforce of the US to supply that country's agricultural food needs. Today, about three per cent manages to accomplish it.

Ephemeralisation is equally apparent in the spectacular gains that have occurred in the transmission of information.[11] Two hundred years ago, people communicated over long distances via letters carried by couriers on horseback. Assuming that a letter contained 10,000 bytes, and that a journey took one month, the average speed of information transmission was 0.03 bits per second. Today, the most powerful long-distance connections, using fibre optic cables, transmit billions of bits per second. In a mere two hundred years, the speed of information transmission has increased some one hundred billion times.

The collection and processing of information has become much easier as a result of ephemeralisation. It took more than a century to populate the planet with one billion telephones. The second billion took only five years. By 2010, two billion people will own not just phones, but phones with Web browsers. At the end of 2005, over one billion people were using the Internet and sending over nine trillion emails to each other a year. That same year, the research company Gardner estimated that 936 billion text messages were sent, a number expected to grow to 2.3 trillion messages by 2010.

The scientific community is using the enhanced flow of data to good effect. Peer review no longer takes months, only weeks. The rate of scientific progress is increasing. More than six million articles are published in scientific journals each year. Still more incredibly, eighty to ninety per cent of all the scientists who have ever lived are alive now, and an overwhelming majority of all scientific work ever published will be achieved in a contemporary scientist's lifetime.[12] On a worldwide scale, scientific and technical literature *grows* at a rate of about sixty million pages per year.[13]

Powerful computers, heightened information flow and scientific research have led to a flood of new technologies, innovations and products. The general effect of ephemeralisation is that things which used to be scarce or difficult to obtain have become abundant. Ephemeralisation is why the real price of everything from a can of coke to a car has dropped so drastically over the last fifty years. It's why we can fill the inside of our houses with more stuff, and surround the outside of them with more cars and boats and swimming pools. It's why our lives are filled with eight orders of magnitude more things than those of the Yanomamo.

The death of friction

The drop in the cost of producing almost anything is wonderfully convenient for a small country like New Zealand. Someone once said that being a New Zealander is about walking into an Irish pub for a Belgian beer while wearing an Italian suit, then travelling home in a German car, grabbing an Indian curry or a Turkish kebab on the way, to sit on Australian furniture and watch American shows on a Japanese TV. As a small nation that can't possibly produce all the products on the shelves of our stores or make the shows that fill our television screens, we've been notable recipients of the benefits of ephemeralisaton. It has tied us as never before to the rest of the world, and we're constantly reminded of this dependence by the enormous trade deficits we clock up.

Our lives and our environment are filled with 'stuff' because we've overcome most of the physical constraints that used to slow down the accumulation of products in the past: duration, distance, energy, raw materials, communication. All those constraints are ebbing away. To put it another way, there's less and less friction in the system.

Let's take an example, and we'll stick with the motor vehicle theme with which we began the chapter. You might have seen the US docu-reality television programme *American Chopper* where this big guy with a handlebar moustache and his fast-talking team construct incredible custom-built motorbikes. The bikes are real head turners – enormous frames, handlebars that reach the stars and fancy paintwork with flames.

Now let's imagine you'd like to order a custom-made machine of your own, to be sent to you in New Zealand. Would that have been possible fifty years ago? In theory, sure. But it would have taken a long time, and cost a lot. Settling on the design, specifications and price alone would have taken months as letters and plans bobbed their way across the oceans. Transacting payment would have been a cumbersome affair involving wire transfers.

Assuming the money had finally reached the right hands, and the design had been accurately determined, just constructing the machine alone would have taken months. Aside from the antiquated drilling and welding machinery, simply getting hold of parts from elsewhere would have added aeons to the process. Shipping the completed bike would add more months. By the time the bike arrived you'd have been lucky if you were still in a fit state to ride it.

What's more, the bike would have cost a fortune. Most of the cost wouldn't have been in the labour, as it is today, but in the materials. The real price of most physical resources (e.g. copper, steel) has been constantly falling over the past century and is insignificant now as a fraction of the income we spend on consumption. Today's electricity is infinitely cheaper and more ubiquitous. That might explain why a 1997 Ford Taurus, for example, loaded with such features as air-conditioning and a CD player, cost seventy per cent less in real-dollar terms than a Model T did seventy years earlier.

So if it's possible to get a custom-built chopper delivered to your home in a matter of weeks, your problem becomes one of choice rather than access – deciding *what* you want out of the millions of possibilities available. Would you choose lounging on a Fijian beach over a visit to London, or a romantic weekend in Melbourne over tramping in the Southern Alps? A guided tour along the Great Wall of China, perhaps? Which of these one hundred channels would you like to watch in the next thirty minutes? Which of these two hundred courses appeal for your arts degree? Could I tempt you with one of our hundreds of different types of lipstick? Whatever kind of activity or consumption you are considering, the death of friction has made our options almost limitless.

On top of that, ephemeralisation has changed our concept of time. As James Gleick notes in his bestseller *Faster: The Acceleration of Just About Everything*, the compression of time characterises modern living.[14] We live in an age of lose-not-a-minute torment. Pruning seconds has become an obsession. Certain things and places symbolise this impatience of ours: notorious intersections; waiting on hold; doctors' 'waiting' rooms; the well-worn DOOR CLOSE button in the elevator; speed-dial buttons on telephones. We substitute a quicker activity (that ten-minute abs-of-steel workout) for a slower one (playing tennis for two hours). We prefer temporal precision ('I'll see you at 12.30') to approximation ('Come any time around lunchtime'). Our busyness is a sign of our importance. Going at a slower pace can feel like being left behind.

And what are we doing with all this time we are saving? We're having sex for an average of four minutes a day. New Zealanders spend forty-eight minutes grooming themselves and eight minutes playing organised sport (thus demolishing a stereotype or two about the average New Zealander).[15] Internet users wait nine minutes daily for their websites to materialise. Sixteen minutes are dropped into the black hole of looking for lost objects.[16] The average New Zealand male between thirty-four and forty-five spends only about twenty minutes a day thinking, reflecting, relaxing, resting and planning.[17] We brag about how little time we have as if the more time we have on our hands, the less meaning our lives have.

We've built our lives around the pace that ephemeralisation allows. We have chosen speed and we thrive on it – more than we'd care to admit. As writer Mark Helprin observes:

> Your life is lived with the kind of excitement that your forebears knew only in battle . . . They, unlike you, were the prisoner of mundane tasks. They wrote with pens, they did addition, they waited endlessly for things that come to you instantaneously, they had far less than you do, they bowed to necessity, as you do not. You love the pace, the giddy, continual acceleration.[18]

Admit it. We do! Instant-aneity rules: instant coffee, instant dating, instant replay and instant gratification. Stewart Brand goes so far as to say that 'civilization is revving itself into a pathological short attention span.'[19]

Even Aldous Huxley, in his *Music at Night*, written back in the early 1930s, foretells our obsession with speed: 'Speed provides the one genuinely modern pleasure.' And he wasn't talking about the injected kind.

Our lives become balanced on a knife edge. We lose electricity for a few hours and all hell breaks loose. We lose our cellphones and we feel like recluses until they're replaced. So a massive industry has emerged to deal with our unending frustration, our need to get what we want, when we want it – the infamous call centre. We've built an industry complete with Dickensian working conditions for those hapless souls prepared to put up with the rantings of an ephemeralisation-driven society. Welcome to hell . . . would you hold, please?

Getting what we don't want, faster

Ephemeralisation may be great if you want custom-made motorbikes delivered to your doorstep. But fancy motorbikes are not the only things being moved around faster. The same process that brings us cheap bananas from Ecuador also brings us strains of bacteria from Bolivia. An *Escherichia coli* epidemic spread throughout five states in the US in a matter of days thanks to a truckload of dodgy lettuces. The avian flu virus spread person to person throughout Asia and into Canada in weeks. We're connected electronically, so digital viruses too have a field day. The 2004 Mydoom virus was released onto an unsuspecting wired world on a Monday and by Thursday it had infected one out of every twelve emails sent, accounting for thirty per cent of all email traffic.

If our lives are not being derailed by computer viruses, they're being crushed by the sheer weight of information floating around. Emphem-eralisation has led to a glut of useless information. We're drowning in information. We have so much data flying around because the bar for what qualifies as communicable information has been set pretty low. Throughout most of history, information has been a scarce resource. It was difficult both to acquire and transmit. Consider the effort involved in sending a letter: find a piece of paper, laboriously write the note by hand, find an envelope and a stamp, locate the mailing address, then make it to the nearest post box. With that much effort, you wanted every word to count.

It's a different story today. Anyone can type an email in five minutes and with a single command send it to thousands of people. The result is an explosion in irrelevant, unclear and simply erroneous fragments of data. This overabundance of low-quality information has been called data smog.[20] This smog chokes our brains. We can no longer tell the good from the bad. Millions of amateurs have taken over from thousands of professionals, posting their opinions on blogs in every corner of the Web. What constitutes an authoritative source any more?

Some of you will, no doubt nostalgically, remember the time when nothing but quiet reflection disturbed the hours between the TV Kiwi going off to bed and the delivery of the next morning's newspaper. Now, says American journalist Jeff Greenfield, the whole thing has been caught in this maelstrom of semi-informed, uninformed windbaggery. From infomercials to endless cable and satellite TV broadcasts, we're swamped with news and views.

Ironically, the abundance of information compels us to gather more information. Our increasingly intricate world, where an event in one part of the world has ramifications everywhere else, broadens the scope of information gathering. Scientists in Japan discover that the use of a certain type of vitamin decreases the chances of getting colon cancer. The response: I think I have a colon, so I'd better learn more about that. Or a study from Australia might report that baby girls travelling in SUVs can experience bouts of post-traumatic stress in later life. Well, the thinking goes, I have neither an SUV nor a baby girl, but I may have one or both eventually, so I should read on. Although we may wish to limit our intake of information, ephemeralisation forces us to pay attention to ever more data.

This avalanche of information wouldn't be a problem if our brains could handle it. Unfortunately, they can't. We have what scientists call *bounded rationality*. Back in the 1950s, psychologist George Miller showed that people can keep no more than seven items at once in their working memory.[21] One estimate calculates our brain's maximum processing capacity at one hundred and twenty-six bits per second.[22] While our long-term memory can store millions of concepts, it is short-term memory that we use to think, decide, and solve problems in real time. That's the part of our brain ticking over at one hundred and twenty-six bits per second, about the speed of a clunky 1960s computer. So our brains have a pretty rudimentary ability to handle the avalanche of information and images we're confronted with each day.

The practical effect of these limitations is that at a certain stage, people will be confronted with more information than they can effectively process: that's information overload. Gloria Mark, a professor at the University of California, Irvine, has been studying attention overload and multitasking among workers in a financial services office. She has found that the average employee switches tasks every three minutes, is interrupted every two minutes and has a maximum focus stretch of twelve minutes.[23]

The brain's way of handling this overload is not to blue-screen, but to start exhibiting stress. About three-quarters of the people in the United States, Australia, Canada, France, Germany, Italy, South Korea and the United Kingdom say they experience stress on a daily basis, according to a 2006 survey.[24] In *Dying for Information? An Investigation into the Effects of Information Overload in the UK and World-wide* – a big report based on a survey of 1313 junior, middle and senior managers in the UK, US, Australia, Hong Kong and Singapore – forty-three per cent of the senior managers surveyed suffered from ill health as a direct consequence of stress associated with information overload. And that report was completed in 1996, before a key information overloader – email – really took off.

As David Kirsh, professor of Cognitive Science at the University of California at San Diego, notes, the upshot of all this is an environment of increased complexity, saturated with multitasking, interruption, and profound information overload.[25] The growing mountain of information that needs to be processed to keep up in today's fast-paced world has to be scaled by human brains with a limited capacity to process it all.

The result is a growing sense of anxiety that we're losing control over our lives. It seems that the biggest problem facing present-day society is not that there is too little progress, but rather too much of it.

Back in the 1970s the world's most famous futurologist, Alvin Toffler, made a detailed study of the acceleration of change in society.[26] In his famous book, *Future Shock,* he developed the idea that many aspects of our world are undergoing accelerative change. The book has become an extremely influential and widely accepted description of our times.

Toffler spoke of the death of permanence, a situation where jobs, friends, spouses, homes, belongings, and everything else that gives human life stability have become unstable, transient, disposable, and exchangeable. The exponential curve of growth and change has become the most pervasive icon of our times. But for many the pace of change can be overwhelming – the paralysing sense of helplessness that Toffler called future shock.[27]

The rise of anxiety is a modern-day phenomenon of Western society. Jean Twenge, then a PhD student at Case Western Reserve University, conducted two analyses of anxiety published in the December 2000 issue of the *Journal of Personality and Social Psychology*.[28] Twenge found that thirty per cent more young Americans, as compared with their peers in the 1960s and 1970s, now believe their lives are controlled by outside forces rather than their own capacity for action.[29] Twenge is reported as saying: 'Many kids feel like they can't make a difference. Most feel that luck is a stronger determinant of their future than their own power to make things happen.'[30] In another poll, half the British people surveyed said they frequently or sometimes felt life was beyond their control.[31]

This anxiety is enhanced when we start doubting the ability of those who are *meant* to have the answers. Increasing complexity and the rate of change can lead to a loss of confidence in institutions, such as governments, police, law, and private companies, all of which may be seen to fail in their function of controlling these complexities. In 2006, only thirty-six per cent of New Zealanders had confidence in the tertiary education system, and only half of the public had confidence in the police force.[32]

It's the loss of confidence in the government that is most alarming. In 1985, only 8.6 per cent of New Zealanders had 'a great deal' of confidence in the government.[33] By 1998 that figure had fallen to a dismal 2.5 per cent. Over the same period, the number of people who were 'not at all' confident in the good intentions of their government doubled from eleven per cent to almost twenty-two per cent. According to a State Services Commission report, confidence in Parliament fell from over thirty per cent in 1975 to ten per cent by the mid-1990s.[34]

Yet while we're often critical of government performance, we continue turning to the government to address our every need. In a 2000 study reported with the headline 'Americans Distrust Government, But Want It to Do More', only twenty-nine per cent of respondents said they trusted the federal government to do what was right.[35] Yet a majority wanted the government to do more in almost ever area of life, from looking after the elderly to protecting the environment, to reducing poverty, to promoting values and morality.

Another American survey asked people their opinions about the roles government should play in the future, and only fifteen per cent said the government should play a less important role.[36] This despite the fact that only twenty-five per cent believed the government pursued the people's agenda and sixty-three per cent said that government serves vested interests. It seems as though governments everywhere have their work cut out for them.

But then perhaps we're just expecting too much of our governments. In an increasingly complex, fast-paced world, isn't it asking too much of any government, organisation or individual to expect them to have the the answers to all society's ills? The bureaucrats valiantly trying to make sense of a fast-changing world face the same problems we do. Mountains of data, and not enough time to process it. Unpredictable shocks, bad or incomplete models, bad or incomplete data, the ever-branching results of action and reaction, and all performed at an increasingly fast pace. Who can get it right through all of that?

It was difficult enough a hundred years ago to figure out how new technologies like the motor car would change the country. Today the job for the government is infinitely more difficult given the infinitely greater amount of complexity it must confront. And that forces square pegs into round holes. As the physicist Freeman Dyson notes, 'legislators act as if the future was predictable. They legislate solutions to technological problems, and they make choices between technological alternatives before the evidence upon which a rational choice might be based is available.[37]

But it's not the government's fault . . . it *has* to act as if the future was predictable to some degree. The government has to work on the basis of a world that is generally orderly and predictable. A country's courts, and ultimately its people, demand certainty and clarity from its law makers. The system works on predictability.

Here is the crux of the problem we face. As we've seen in this chapter, we're living in crazy, complex times. Yet the very institutions we've looked to for solutions to society's problems in the past are struggling to cope today. The government is constrained by annoying technicalities like elections, select committee hearings and public submissions. Its hands are tied when it comes to moving with the speed necessary to keep pace with the changes it sees occurring.

That's why no society can depend on the government for all the solutions it needs. It simply doesn't have the bandwidth to develop the range of ideas and options a fast-moving world requires. This is how Singapore's then Deputy-Prime Minister, Lee Hsien Loong, put it: 'Our world has become more uncertain. Technology is advancing relentlessly, markets are changing unpredictably, and we can no longer take our prosperity and security for granted. The Government has no monopoly of knowledge and ideas. To understand and tackle our challenges fully and vigorously, we need to draw on the expertise and resources of all our people.'[38]

Governments don't have a monopoly on new ideas because they're not in the business of generating them. As the conservative economist and philosopher Friedrich Hayek says: 'The successful politician owes his power to the fact that he moves within the accepted framework of thought, that he thinks and talks conventionally. It would be almost a contradiction in terms for a politician to be a leader in the field of ideas. His task in a democracy is to find out what the opinions held by the largest number are, not to give currency to new opinions which may become the majority view in some distant future.'[39]

The government's role is as important today as it's ever been. The structure and security it provides have never been needed more. As we will see later, a government's investment in education, and its financial support of science and engineering, are critical in developing an innovative, creative society. But it can't do it all. Ultimately – and this is the theme we will return to again and again – the mechanisms for coping with the rapid pace of change in an increasingly complex world will be determined as much by the ideas and attitudes of the New Zealand people as by any combination of government policies.

As such, we need to rethink where we go looking for solutions to tomorrow's problems. Because as we're about to discover in the next chapter, the future promises a treasure trove of changes. And the rate of change could make that of the last thirty years look snail-paced.

2

New Zealand's unknown future

We've all had a brush or two with the future. It's that 'this is big' moment that comes along every now and then. For some of you, witnessing Jean Batten's plane touch down at Mangere after her record-breaking flight from England in 1936 would qualify. For others, the protest at Bastion Point in 1977–78 that signalled the dawn of an era of settled Treaty of Waitangi grievances. For some the 'brush with the future' moment may be slightly less dramatic: your first microwave meal; the notes vibrating through the headphones of your first cassette walkman; the hum of electric windows in your car.

For me, it was my first game of computer chess (yes, I was *that* kid at school.) The year was 1982. I must have been eight or nine at the time and my mechanical opponent was 'Chess Challenger'. Nothing fancy about this machine – you even had to key in your moves once you made them. It was still just chess, but there was something cool about playing a machine.

What a remarkable moment. Ever since chess emerged from India around the sixth century, humans have only played against other humans. For 1400 years, you would look up from the chessboard and rest your eyes on a human opponent seated opposite. It was brain against brain. Then, all of a sudden, it was brain against microchip. My regular chess opponent, four-foot-six Tony from school, had been replaced by a one-inch square chip, a processor and a few blinking lights.

And it wasn't just poor old Tony who was shunted aside. Computers, in the next few years, began replacing people everywhere. ATMs began to replace bank tellers. Automated attendants took over from bored human ones in parking buildings. Automated car-washes became standard at service stations. They were all driven by pretty simple computers, for sure, but they represented the vanguard of a revolution: more and more powerful machines replacing more and more human activities. Here I was witnessing my own piece of a process that continues today as relentlessly as ever.

But the rise of the computer wasn't the only piece of history encapsulated in my chess-playing computer. The machine, while purchased in the US, was made in China. As such, it was the product of an economy that looks set to remake New Zealand's in the future. And by sitting playing a computer game, I was at the forefront of a revolution in recreational lifestyle that is today redefining the meaning of both 'community' and 'big boned'. Heck, playing that machine was virtually like looking into a crystal ball.

This chapter will involve some crystal-ball-gazing at some major trends shaping New Zealand's future. In the last chapter we discovered how the process of ephemeralisation is increasing the complexity and pace of life for most New Zealanders. In this chapter we explore how the country is on the threshold of some startling, and perhaps alarming, changes.

Dean Kamen, the multimillionaire 'inventrepreneur', is responsible for such inventions as the stair-climbing wheelchair and the Segway stand-up scooter. From his vantage point on the scooter, he can see some major changes marching over the horizon towards us. 'People tend to overestimate the changes likely in the next five years,' he says, 'but dramatically under-estimate changes that will take place in the next twenty-five years. In the short term we will be disappointed, in the long run we will be amazed.'[1] You'd best hold on. We're about to enter the bizarre world of nano battle-suits and hospital reception robots.

Humanity takes on the computer and loses

Of course, back in 1980 I didn't realise the significance of what a computer chess game represented. The computer was simply a good excuse to avoid doing homework. Soon the novelty of this chess-playing computer began to fade. For one thing, it soon became clear that Chess Challenger wasn't going to be much help in a cul-de-sac cricket match.

The worst thing about the machine, though, was that it messed with my head. After I'd spent minutes figuring out a pawn to G5 move that reeked of Bobby Fischer-like genius, the computer would smack back its response in a millisecond. The machine lacked the human decency to at least pretend to contemplate my move. It psyched me out in the end. I became fixated with trying to get the computer to 'think' for at least a couple of seconds. In the end my entire strategy boiled down to making the most unpredictable moves possible, hoping to surprise the computer. It didn't work. Its cold, emotionless responses got into my kitchen and began making eggs. Ten moves into the game and I was an emotional wreck. Suffice to say, I never succeeded in gaining the computer's respect and shortly thereafter I skulked off to regain Tony's friendship.

Humanity's quest to gain the respect of chess-playing computers obviously didn't end with my sulky encounter a few decades ago. In the years that followed, chess would come to exemplify the battle of human against machine. Chess Grandmaster clashes against the world's best chess-playing machines became humanity's last stand to retain its dignity. A showdown was inevitable between the world's best human and computer chess players.

In 1997 that showdown happened. World chess champion Garry Kasparov, considered by many to be the greatest chess player of all time, took on IBM's 1.36 tonne Deeper Blue computer in a six-game series at the Equitable Center in downtown Manhattan. Over three hundred members of the press covered the event. It was promoted as the ultimate test of man against machine. *Newsweek* magazine's cover story for the clash was titled 'The Brain's Last Stand'. Never before has so much hung on the moves of a couple of white bishops and black knights.

Humanity breathed a sigh of relief in the first game when Kasparov won easily. He never looked troubled. But in game two, Deeper Blue caused a stir by winning. An overwhelmed Kasparov said the machine 'played like God', and had left a scar on his memory.[2] In game six, Kasparov made a fatal blunder early on in the match and was defeated a mere nineteen moves later – the fastest loss in his career. Deeper Blue went on to win the series 3.5–2.5. Chess buffs hailed it as a moment to rank with the 1969 Moon landing as a milestone in human history. It was a small move for the computer, but a giant leap forward in a computer's use of artificial intelligence.

The news of a computer's chess victory over the best player in the world may not have rattled your cage, but perhaps you've noticed that computers seem to be doing a lot of leaping forward these days. They are no longer just handing out notes at cash machines or raising barriers in car park buildings. Now they're performing surgeries and flying planes.

We'll get to just how powerful computers are becoming shortly, but let's begin our look into the future by examining two scientific fields that seem set to change our lives. It has been the improvements in computing power that have enabled the remarkable breakthroughs in genomics and nanotechnology – breakthroughs that look set to transform, amongst other things, healthcare.

Healthcare as we've never known it before

Hard as it may be to believe after a visit to your GP, the fundamental tenets of medicine have changed little in the last three thousand years. Young doctors still learn the art of medicine in a fashion that the father of medicine himself, Hippocrates of Cos, would have recognised. Diseases are classified by the organ system affected, a classification known as gross pathology. You have lung cancer, heart disease, kidney failure, and so on. The mantra of location, location, location is as meaningful as it is for real estate agents.[3] An accumulation of knowledge over the centuries allows the medical profession to treat each patient with a generic set of tried and tested treatments.

But here's the problem . . . we're different. Each one of us. And that's where the gross pathology system struggles a bit. The current standard of care is based on the average effect of the therapy. But patients invariably do better or worse based on their genetic make-up. So the medical treatment for one lung cancer patient can be completely inappropriate for the guy sitting next to him with the same condition. It's like going to an optometrist and getting lenses that match the average New Zealander's eyesight.

The result is treatments less effective than we'd like. In the US in 2002, for example, about $110 billion (or forty per cent of the total) was spent on drugs that either did not help, or actually harmed the individual.[4] Seven per cent of patients sustained serious drug-related injuries or died, while another one-third were simply not helped at all.[5] Comparing medicines to a more mundane consumer product, refrigerators, a *Nature Medicine* article suggests that 'if new refrigerators hurt seven per cent of customers and failed to work for another one-third of them, customers would expect refunds'.[6] The good news is that in recent years we've become a lot smarter in our understanding of how our bodies work. These breakthroughs could revolutionise medicine.

Many thought the definitive breakthrough had occurred when the genome was sequenced to great fanfare at the turn of this century. At a White House ceremony on 26 June, 2000, President Bill Clinton announced the decoding of the three billion chemical letters of the human genome.[7] These letters (TCTAGAAACA . . .) are abbreviations for the molecules making up the individual's DNA. It was an exciting day. The world finally had the 'book of life' in its hands. Everything from our personality to our future medical history was thought to be encoded in this book. The dawn of a new age was upon us.

Not so fast. Look beyond the hyperbole and a less exciting story emerges. As impressive a feat as the sequencing of the human genome was, it doesn't actually help us that much by itself. It won't tell us, for example, whether an individual will get Parkinson's or lose their hair or drop dead at seventy.

That's because decoding the human genome meant that we now simply had an inventory of the human cell's parts. It's like disassembling your car, reducing it to thousands of car parts in your backyard. There is the car, in its simplest form. The problem, of course, is that the parts are useless on their own. If you ever want to see that car running again you need a map telling you how to assemble it.

The same applies to the different cells in our bodies. And what makes the job of assembling the pieces even more difficult is that not all the parts are used in every cell (and many parts are duplicated). So it's more like dismantling five or six slightly different cars and then trying to work out which carburettor goes in which car. As long as the original mechanic of the human body keeps the map to Himself, we'll need to work out how the genes fit together from scratch.

That's where the field of genomics comes in. Genomics refers to the scientific discipline of mapping, sequencing, and analysing genomes. Unfortunately, it's a little more easily said than done. Part of the problem is that about ninety-eight per cent of our DNA doesn't code for proteins (i.e. doesn't instruct proteins to build different parts of our bodies). Until recently scientists thought that this part of our DNA was evolutionary scrap material and referred to it as 'junk DNA'. Life is never that simple. Now they realise that this junk DNA is in fact the administrative centre for the remaining two per cent of our DNA (kind of like a massive bureaucracy). It controls how the instructions in the genes are translated – basically, how we turn out. It is a large part of what makes humans look different from chimpanzees, even though the actual difference in genes between humans and chimps is relatively small. Until scientists figure out how this regulatory code works, we can't do as much as we might like with our knowledge of our genes.

The other part of the problem is that the human body is highly influenced by its environment. Scientists have discovered that different environments can produce different traits from the same genotype. A study conducted in Dunedin found that men with the so-called violent form of the MAOA gene were no more likely to grow up to be antisocial or violent than the majority of men with the non-violent form of the gene, unless they had also been abused or neglected as children.[8] So even if we can link a particular genotype with a certain behaviour or sickness, we also have to understand what role the environment plays in how that genotype will affect an individual. It's nature *and* nurture.

But the potential of doing so is enormous. Genomics will allow drugs to become a lot more effective at curing disease. It'll take the chance out of drug discovery. Rather than testing and hoping, as conventional pharmaceutical research often does, this new intelligent drug discovery will mean actually creating drugs molecule by molecule to fit targets. That's the equivalent of getting contact lenses prescribed by the optometrist specifically for your eyes. It will be possible to develop drugs that are so fine-tuned and precise that they affect only the malfunctioning cells, leaving the healthy cells alone. In the hit-and-miss world of medicine, that's big.

Put another way, genomics could do for medicine what the Rosetta Stone did for Egyptian archaeology. Up until the nineteenth century, archaeologists had the parts of the ancient Egyptian script – all the pictures and symbols – but no idea how they linked together to form a language. The position changed in 1792, however, when the Rosetta Stone was discovered. This stone had text in Greek and in Egyptian hieroglyphics. By 1822 the stone had been translated, and archaeologists could finally understand how to link the parts – the hieroglyphs – together. That's what genomics will do – link the parts of our genetic code into an understanding of how they interact with one another.

Scientists are using this knowledge to figure out how an individual's genetic inheritance affects the body's response to drugs. If successful, this would mean a quantum leap in the effectiveness of new drugs.[9] The number of new drug development targets is expected to leap from five hundred in 1995 to five thousand by 2010. Suddenly genomics makes us a whole lot better at identifying potential drug candidates.

Take malaria as an example. Currently a million people lose their lives each year to the mosquito-carried disease. But now scientists have sequenced the genome of the *Anopheles gambiae* mosquito and the malaria parasite. Add that to the growing knowledge of genetic factors that influence a person's response to malaria, and suddenly the chances are greatly improved that a powerful new malaria treatment could soon be available.[10] Go, science.

If little Billy gets a sore throat, a blood sample will allow the chemist to prepare an antibiotic that will take out only the organism that makes Billy's throat hurt. No more broad-spectrum antibiotics that kill all bacteria, harmful or not, in his body. Goodbye to Billy's sore throat. Goodbye to Billy's excuse for a few days home from school playing Xbox. And goodbye to antibiotic-resistant strains of bacteria. The era of personalised medicine will soon be upon us.

Could we be moving towards an age in which entering nature's genetic lottery is no longer seen as a desirable way to bring a child into the world? Worldwide, around one child in sixteen is born with a mental or physical disability due to a genetic defect, and most of us probably carry gene variants that predispose us to serious illnesses later in life. Might natural conception even come to be thought of as irresponsible, as bad as smoking while pregnant? Sex for fun, IVF for children? Then once we're done screening out the bad things, how about screening in the good? Will those who can afford it select genes for intelligence, memory, a good side-step and rugged good looks? Sure, it sounds a bit like a Hollywood movie, but it is increasingly becoming more science than fiction.

Then when the baby is born, a cell sample from its cheek will be taken and the genome sequenced. People could visit their doctor and have their genome sequenced to investigate a predisposition to heart disease. Any diseases or metabolic imbalances that need to be rectified will be. Any time one of us has a medical problem, a tissue sample will be taken and analysed at a molecular level to determine what's broken. No more prodding, pricking, or tapping the knee with a hammer. In twenty years' time, a tissue sample won't even be necessary as modified advanced MRI scanners will be able to detect whether molecular imbalances exist in your body. Inject some stem cells and the worn-out or damaged tissue will be as good as new. It'll be personalised medicine. Drugs will be approved that are effective for only ten per cent of the population and potentially lethal for everybody else.

A mountain of ethical issues is likely to be raised. For example, should genetic information be kept strictly private, and should patients receive special legal protection against discrimination in employment and insurance? Will the benefits of genomics be distributed fairly throughout society or concentrated in the hands of a privileged few? How will our health system choose between paying for treatments for the ailing elderly and preventing ailments in the young? These are tough questions, but New Zealand has little choice but to confront them.

Scientific discoveries continue relentlessly, changing the impossible to the possible. As a society we'll need to be good at adapting to the changes these discoveries bring. That's no easy task. In her study of the frailties of human action, German-American philosopher Hannah Arendt examined the fundamental paradox of our time: 'as human powers increase through technological progress, we are becoming less and less well equipped to control the consequences of our actions.'[11] And she was writing that back in 1958.

Sausages in Petri dishes

Step away from healthcare for a minute and we can see gene manipulation techniques creating other startling changes for New Zealand. The controversy over potential manipulation of organisms through genetic engineering is only the tip of the iceberg. Over-sized tomatoes? Extra-tasty apples? Those are only for starters. Try pest-repellent plants that produce their own insect-killing toxins. Scientists are creating mosquitoes in Africa that will inject a vaccine into cattle. Consider slow-ripening fruit and vegetables that will allow developing-world farmers to get more produce to market before it rots. So-called golden rice enriched with vitamin A offers a solution to nutritional deficiency that causes blindness among some two million children per year. Researchers in India are now developing a protein-rich potato that can help combat malnutrition. The Australians are developing drought-resistant crops. In China, the largest cotton producer, over fifty per cent of cotton production is in pest-resistant genetically modified varieties. In the US, the second largest cotton producer, that number is nearer the seventy-five per cent mark.

It doesn't stop at super rice or mega-nutritious potatoes. What about growing meat from scratch? Scientists at the University of Utrecht in the Netherlands are trying to make minced pork from cultured stem cells with the backing of Stegeman, a sausage company. It could be used in sausages, burgers, and sauces. It could also be made healthier by adjusting its composition – introducing heart-friendly omega-3 fatty acids, for example.[12] Researcher Morris Benjaminson, at the Touro College School of Health Sciences in New York, is working on removing living tissue from fish, and then growing it in culture.

Scientists in Australia and New Zealand are actively experimenting with the production of wool by utilising genomic technologies. SheepGenomics is a major A$30 million initiative of Meat and Livestock Australia and Australian Wool Innovation Ltd, supported by ten leading research organisations in Australia and New Zealand. It aims to discover genes that influence economically important traits in sheep. By using discoveries made within SheepGenomics' research programme, sheep producers will be able to start breeding for a wide range of wool traits (water resistance, durability, extra lightness, and so on).

But to Drew Endy, a professor at Massachusetts Institute of Technology, all the great breakthroughs of the past thirty years in biotechnology were mere tweaks.[13] Wonders such as mass-produced insulin, cancer-fighting drugs, pest-killing crops and glowing fish – they're simply the result of moving a single gene from one organism to another. Endy and colleagues constitute a new breed of scientists known as synthetic biologists.[14] If these scientists are to be believed, in the years to come we'll begin to see the first custom-crafted biomachines: devices that could be engineered, for example, to hunt down and kill tumour cells. Christopher Voigt, a biochemist at the University of California, San Francisco, has already built a device from biological parts: a bacterium programmed to seek out cancer tumours.[15] These micromachines will guard against disease, create new fuels and manufacture chemicals. Voigt's *E. coli* bacteria are still years away from being anything other than a research tool, but the potential of this technology is incredible.

It's exciting and yet deeply unsettling at the same time. It sounds like a world full of promise, but the risks to New Zealand are palpable. Setting aside the host of ethical and environmental concerns, the prospect of artificially created meats and crops is a very real threat to the largest segment of New Zealand's economy. A great climate and hard work, mixed with superior farming techniques and cutting-edge research, have been the backbone of New Zealand's agricultural success in the past. Whether this remains the case as the bio-sciences leap forward will be a key determinant of New Zealand prosperity in the years ahead.

Nanonano

All of this gene manipulation is occurring at a miniscule level. We're tinkering with the very molecules that make up our cells. But it's not just in biology that this small-world manipulation is happening. The exploration of the super-small is occurring across fields as remote from each other as clothing and TV screens.

Back in 1959, Nobel physicist Richard Feynman gave a speech at the annual meeting for the American Physical Society, entitled 'There's Plenty of Room at the Bottom'. The speech opened the eyes of many to the notion that the only thing preventing us from working at the nanoscale is . . . us. Or more specifically, our technology. It just wasn't good enough in the 1950s. Nor for that matter in the sixties, the seventies, the eighties, or much of the nineties. That's now changed. Today, technologies that allow for fine-grain control and construction at a very small scale are here.

Nano derives from the Greek word for dwarf, and means a billionth. One nanometre is one billionth of a metre. Put another way, there are one million nanometres in one millimetre.[16] Or, if this helps, a nano is the width of five carbon atoms. They're small. Nano-sized materials and devices are built from the 'bottom up', atom by atom. If you can start building atom by atom, the possibilities are staggering. As someone once said of nanotechnology: 'In the past we grew a tree, cut down the tree and made the table. In the future we will grow the table.'[17]

Nanotechnology is finding its way into consumer products. Toray Industries, a Japanese electronics parts manufacturer, has used nanotechnology to develop a polyester resin that, when applied to glass, makes it resistant to the hardest strike of a hammer. Apply the film to LCD or plasma display panels and soon you have very light widescreen TVs.[18] L'Oréal has developed a line of cosmetics that contain nanocapsules. These nanotools are capable of guiding the active ingredients to the right place in the skin. You can buy scratch-free polymer-coated sunglasses, packaging with antimicrobial agents keeps food fresh, while the easy-to-clean heat-resistant surfaces found in the latest kitchens are all products of nanotechnology.

And that's just the start. Look beyond the lightweight TVs and skin creams, and the future of nano is startling. For example, the Massachusetts Institute of Technology (MIT) in the US is producing nanoscale fibres and devices that can be woven into clothing. If you think your wrinkle-free trousers are impressive then check out the Pentagon-financed MIT research: nano battlesuits. These are not very small items of clothing, but textiles made of nano particles.

When this research is finished, the American soldier of tomorrow could find himself running around in an outfit like that of a scuba diver. Though they'll inevitably have to endure crude jokes about the size of their weapons, American soldiers may have the last laugh. These battlesuits will be able to neutralise chemical poisons, treat wounds, and hydrate soldiers by recycling body fluids (they probably won't mention that part). The fabrics will be able to monitor heart rates, deliver drugs and sustenance, repair and clean themselves, change shape in response to temperature, and even change colour for chameleon-like camouflage.[19] If bleeding occurred, the fabric would contract at strategic points to apply a tourniquet, or stiffen to support a broken leg.[20]

Nanotechnologies go well beyond the manipulation of clothing fibres. It's now possible to make super-small computers. In 2005 the smallest computer structures measured about eighty nanometres, about 10,000 times thinner than a strand of hair. You can imagine how often you'd misplace that computer around the house. These nano computers include technologies that can purify even the most polluted water, while nanotechnologies are at the forefront of hydrogen fuel cell development for water-powered motor vehicles.

Magnetic microparticles injected into the bloodstream could help pinpoint a virus. Nanomaterials might be used to help create inexpensive solar panels that could be painted on any flat surface. The longer-term play in nanotech is to create nanofactories, or auto-assemblers: tiny robots the size of cells which would be programmed to collect raw material from the natural world (atoms, molecules) and convert it (slowly, piece by piece) into the building blocks of the desired product.[21] These nanobots might repair damaged cells in people stricken with cancer, or unclog plaque-filled arteries.

New Zealand has dipped its toe into this world of very small things. Since 2002 the government has been writing a cheque for about $5 million annually and sending it to the MacDiarmid Institute for Advanced Materials and Nanotechnology. This amount is small change compared to the $20 billion invested elsewhere – a mere 0.02 per cent in fact. It's a nano-like stab at a new scientific field. Nonetheless it pays for over one hundred researchers wearing very thick glasses.[22] What breakthroughs they'll discover is anyone's guess, but they're spinning off companies to commercialise their discoveries all over the show. Nano Cluster Devices Ltd, for example, is trying to produce nanowires that could find employment in miniscule circuit boards, or hydrogen fuel cells.[23]

At the end of his 1959 lecture on nanotechnology, Richard Feynman startled the audience by throwing out a challenge. He offered $1000 prizes for whoever was first able to create a couple of atomic structures. One was a tiny motor. Perhaps to his dismay, the challenge was quickly solved through the MacGyver-like use of a toothpick, a lathe and a microscope. The other challenge proved more difficult. The task was to write a page one twenty-five-thousandth of its normal size. This was not achieved until

1985 when a very small version of the immortal opening page of *A Tale of Two Cities* was produced.

The delay in solving his second challenge proved Feynman's point. The hindrance to exploring and manipulating nano-sized objects had always been a technological one. To work magic at the nano level requires more than just exceptionally good eyesight. You really need darn powerful computers. And as we've seen, computers have been getting more powerful quickly thanks to the Moore's Law phenomenon – exponential increases in the computing power of the microchips every few years. The recent surge in computing power has made possible many of the scientific breakthroughs discussed above.

Yet the growth in computing power has only just begun. Anticipated increases in computing power over the next few decades are set to make your current laptop look as antiquated as an abacus.

The super computer

During World War II the Americans built their first computer, the ENIAC. This monster of a machine was bigger than an eighteen-wheel truck, weighed more than seventeen mid-sized cars and could execute up to 5000 basic arithmetic operations per second. Buy a reasonable desktop computer today and it will contain a microprocessor the size of a postage stamp that weighs less than a sugar packet, and can execute two billion instructions per second. Computer performance has come a long way in the last sixty years.

The world's fastest computer in 2005 was a machine at Lawrence Livermore National Laboratory in the US that has reached more than a hundred and thirty-six trillion operations per second, or 100,000 times the speed of a fast desktop personal computer. That means that the world's top supercomputers can produce data at a rate equal to putting out one United States Library of Congress every few seconds.

With that sort of grunt, they're being used to forecast weather, design more fuel-efficient cars, map DNA, and explore the cosmos. The US company Procter & Gamble uses them to design sturdier plastic laundry soap bottles. The Riverside Casino in Iowa has one to manage thousands of electronic slot machines and keep track of millions of bets. The Italian police use them to analyse clues at murder scenes. They're even being used to assess the aerodynamic features of potato chips on the manufacturing line to ensure they don't go flying off.

As impressive as all that sounds, we ain't seen nothing yet. If the advances in computing technology anticipated for the next twenty years materialise, the improvement from the ENIAC to the modern computer over the last sixty years will seem like child's play. 'The age of computing has not even begun,' says Stan Williams, a research scientist at Hewlett-Packard. 'What we have today are tiny toys not much better than an abacus. The challenge is to approach the fundamental laws of physics as closely as we can.'[24]

When computer manufacturers start saying things like 'approaching the fundamental law of physics', a lot of computer geeks start salivating. If computers are to continue up the curve of greater and greater capability, humanity will have to figure out how to manipulate the brain-bending rules of a place scientists call the quantum realm. It's the move from the silicon-based circuitry of today to the subatomic circuitry of tomorrow. We've now entered the era of the mega-tiny.

The primary application of subatomic circuitry is magnetoresistive random access memory (MRAM). Unlike conventional high-speed memory devices, MRAM uses magnetism instead of electrical charges to store data – making it, in a sense, a back-to-the-future technology based on the same laws of physics that enabled the creation of audio and videotape recorders as well as hard drives.[25] Often described as the holy grail of memory, MRAM will allow faster start-up times for computers (on like a light), reduced data loss, shorter waits for data to load and increased battery run time. That's all very cool, but it hardly sounds earth-shattering, right?

Fair enough. It's the technology behind MRAM that's making the computer geeks salivate. MRAM gets its speed from something called the giant magnetoresistive effect, or GMR. In essence, GMR is all about spinning electrons in opposite directions to create magnetic resistance. If they can do this, they have moved computer technology into the molecular realm. When you've moved into this realm you've begun to manipulate particles, even if they're trillions of miles apart – a phenomenon Albert Einstein described as 'spooky action at a distance'.[26] With molecular-level chips, a quantum laptop could have more computing power than trillions of today's supercomputers. To put it another way, it would take a supercomputer about ten billion years to factor a four-hundred-digit number, whereas a quantum computer could get the job done in thirty seconds.

Such computer power isn't as far away as you might think. In 2006, IBM and the Swiss Federal Institute of Technology in Lausanne announced the launch of the Blue Brain Project, an attempt to model the electrical circuitry of the human brain using a supercomputer based on IBM's Blue Gene design. The research is based on the discovery by Nobel Prize-winner Torsten Wiesel of Rockefeller University that the fundamental neurological units of mammalian brains are neocortical columns.[27] Neocortical columns are one of the key distinctions between the brains of mammals and reptiles. In humans, each column is just two millimetres high and half a millimetre in diameter, but contains some 10,000 cells connected by five kilometres of fibres. The columns are similar in other mammals, but the human brain is crammed with more of them. Indeed, it was the need to accommodate more columns that forced the human brain into its walnut-like, wrinkled shape.[28]

The Blue Brain Project involves building a Blue Gene supercomputer with 8000 processors that can trundle along at an impressive 100 trillion calculations a second. Each processor will be used to simulate one or two neurons. If they stopped now, the machine would be one of the five fastest supercomputers in the world. Expected to take ten years, IBM researchers will begin by simulating 60,000 neurons in the human neocortex.[29] The human brain contains ten billion neurons, so the scale of Blue Brain will still only be a fraction of the real thing. But inevitably that will change as Blue Brain's capacity increases.

If quantum computing turns out to be viable, the typical computer of 2020 could be a hundred million times more powerful than the computer of 2003.[30] Think about it this way. Today $1000 buys a computer with the speed and capacity of an insect brain (that's more impressive than it sounds). Futurologist Ray Kurzweil estimates that to equal the power of the human brain a machine will need to be capable of around 10 quadrillion calculations a second.[31] By 2030, $1000 would likely buy a computer that has such processing power – that of a human brain. By 2060, a $1000 computer might well be equal to all human brains combined.[32] Granted, that amount of computer power feels like a bit of a waste for a few games of solitaire, some online gambling and the odd email, but that's how much computing power you could have at your finger tips a few decades from now.

Harnessing this power means being able to tackle some pretty meaty problems. Protein folding (understanding protein functions and malfunctions as seen in diseases as diverse as cancer and Alzheimer's), gene design, controlling very complex systems such as Auckland's traffic pattern or Wellington's weather system, modelling the climate, and even reaching the goal of artificial intelligence – all seem to contain too many variables to model successfully with today's computers. Quantum computers would change that.

Manipulating small objects (electrons) in order to boost the power of computers sounds like a fairly handy strategy. But computers so powerful they can tie their own shoelaces raises the frightening prospect of mechanical monsters with the ability to wrestle control of the planet from humanity. This is a notion that has kept Hollywood scriptwriters employed for decades. The artificial intelligence ability of computers is improving all the time. In a major survey of Internet leaders, analysts, and activists, by US think tank the Pew Institute, forty-two per cent were pessimistic about our ability to control the technology of the future, believing that dangers and dependencies will grow beyond our ability to stay in charge.[33]

Regardless of whether we'll have *Terminator*-like problems on our hands in twenty years, one thing is certain: computers will become increasingly capable of doing the jobs we perform today.

The work we do

In 1987 Kasparov boasted: 'No computer can ever beat me.'[34] As we saw, advances in modern technology have humbled him somewhat since then. In 2003, he lamented: 'I give us only a few years. Then they'll win every match, and we may have to struggle to win even a single game.'[35]

Kasparov had made the classic John Henry mistake. John Henry was a symbol of the might of the American workforce in the nineteenth century.[36] He worked on teams building railroads, and could drive steel faster and more powerfully than any man alive. He was the epitome of the brute human strength that tamed much of the colonial world .

One day, the tale goes, a new steam-powered drill arrived at the workers' camp. John Henry scoffed at the idea that a machine could beat manpower, so he proposed a man against machine rock-demolition contest. While the machine took the early lead, John Henry rallied and as granite flew in all directions, he finally managed to pull ahead at the very end, clinching the victory. His workmates cheered. Humanity, it appeared, was safe. John Henry then collapsed and died. His demise became a parable of the industrial age as machines replaced men's backs. Then the increasing sophistication of robotics on the assembly line had machines replacing human hands. Now, Deep Blue has shown that machines are increasingly replacing men's brains.

Management guru Tom Peters once said that for knowledge workers, 'Software is a forklift for the mind'. As computers become more powerful, these forklifts won't need human drivers. Any job that depends on routines that can be reduced to a set of rules, or broken down into a set of repeatable steps, is at risk. As a 2006 report by a high-powered commission looking at the future of the US workforce notes, 'If someone can figure out an algorithm for a routine job, chances are that it is economic to automate it. Many good, well-paying, middle-class jobs involve routine work of this kind and are rapidly being automated.'[37]

For example, computer scientist Vernor Vinge notes that the routine functions performed by computer programmers are increasingly being turned over to machines.[38] A British engineering company called Appligenics has created software that can write software, and at extraordinary speeds. Where a typical human programmer can write about four hundred lines of code a day, Appligenics' software can do it in less than a second – and without bugs.

As Adam Kessler points out, doctors face the same dilemma. Radiologists are being replaced by computer-aided detection. Ophthalmologists are being shut out by laser surgery. Pharmacists dispensing statins for those with high cholesterol will be replaced by cheaper-in-the-long-run plaque-removing procedures. Dieticians will step aside for minimally invasive stomach stapling surgery. Robots are performing a wider range of surgeries. High-precision optical machines have been trained to recognise suspicious lumps by scanning in thousands of mammograms from breasts with cancer. The machine is being taught to think like a radiologist.[39]

Not even the receptionist in the hospital is safe. High-tech Japan is well known for shooting its own labour pool in the foot.[40] It has done it again at Aizu Central Hospital, which now has robots that provide information, guide patients to their rooms and carry bags. One robot sits on its shiny metal backside at a reception desk. A slimmer green robot (looking like a metallic Stewie Griffin from *Family Guy*) is tasked with roaming the halls and lugging around visitors' bags.[41] No one's envisioning boarded-up hospitals just yet, but few can deny the impact technology will have on healthcare. As the practice of healthcare changes, so will all the jobs associated with it.

You've seen this movie before. Not the Stewie hospital robot movie, necessarily, but the technology replacing humans movie. ATMs came along, and all of a sudden, lots of bank tellers no longer had jobs. Technology went around tellers and squeezed many of them out. We miss the smile of the teller, but now we can access our cash twenty-four hours a day, and on Sunday too. 'Heck,' as Dogbert says to an office colleague in a *Dilbert* cartoon, 'you work in a cubicle while your routers and servers have their own climate-controlled offices . . . the machines have taken over.'

Technology is democratising every industry you can think of. A website can transform a travel agent's knowledge into a series of clicks and mouse movements. Increasingly sophisticated chips embedded in cars are taking a mechanic's knowledge and diagnosing the cause of that strange thumping noise. Scanning devices that in eight seconds can take data from 200,000 points on your body are creating clothes tailored not to your size, but to your exact body shape.

Add the advances in computer power anticipated in the next twenty years, and the job market will invariably be changed again in ways we can barely imagine. That's serious stuff. Especially for New Zealand. As a small country with relatively few industries, our workforce doesn't have the luxury of being blasé about the threat technology poses to our livelihoods. Scoff at technology if you must. Just don't do a John Henry.

Unfortunately the threats to the New Zealand worker don't end with the computer keyboard. If QuickTax doesn't swipe your comfortable accounting job, then a $500-a-month Chinese chartered accountant will.

If a RAD machine doesn't take your lucrative radiology job, a $2000-a-month radiologist in Bombay will. The drums of globalisation are beating, and the noise is only going to get louder.

Lots of new workers ...

In the September 2006 edition of *National Geographic*, there is a story about the rise of the Manchuria district of China. One particular photo shows a middle-aged couple sitting in the plush living room of their home. The caption reads as follows: 'In Changchun, policeman Zhao Gingyan and his wife, businesswoman Jin Liming, sit proudly at home in a new development called Up East Side Manhattan. A recent vacation to New Zealand helped Zhao appreciate his China. "We visited the homes of some middle-class people, and the homes there are not as good as ours."'

Once upon a time, New Zealanders travelled abroad and returned home feeling upbeat about how wealthy their country was. Now Chinese, it would seem, have started going to New Zealand for the same reason. Is New Zealand becoming a rung against which developing countries compare themselves as they rocket up the ladder of economic progress? In the future, will a Chinese tourist ski some private slopes in the Southern Alps that only foreigners can afford? They're questions every New Zealander should be asking.

The rise of China (and following close behind, India and a host of other developing nations) is well known. Certainly we hear the facts often enough. The Yellow Dragon is home to close to 1.3 billion people. Many of these people live in the one hundred and sixty cities with populations of one million or more (the US by contrast has nine, and New Zealand has one).[42]

That's a lot of people. And a lot of workers. Today the words 'Made in China' are a universal slogan: the nation sews more clothes and grows more crops than any other. China is also the world's largest manufacturer of consumer electronics, pumping out TVs, DVD players and cellphones.[43] China's economy is developing into a manufacturing powerhouse of low-cost products.

Next time you're in a Warehouse store, take time to look at the toy, clothing or shoe sections, and you'll see first-hand what China's low-cost manufacturing economy is doing. By mid-2006, eleven per cent of New Zealand imports were from China, making it New Zealand's fourth largest trading partner.[44] But a whopping thirty per cent of imported consumer goods came from China, including a massive seventy-four per cent of clothing imports. The Warehouse's equivalent in the US, the mega-retailer Wal Mart, the world's largest company, imports so many products from Chinese manufacturers (seventy per cent of its products) that it accounts for ten per cent of China's exports, making it China's fifth largest export partner ahead of Germany, Italy and the UK.[45] In fact, a few years ago, Wal Mart alone accounted for a staggering 1.5 per cent of China's entire GDP.[46]

China joined the World Trade Organisation in 2000 and injected seven hundred and fifty million workers into the global economy. China currently has two hundred and twenty million 'surplus workers' in its central and western regions alone, almost sixty per cent more than the entire number of workers in the US.[47]

But China and company are not just churning out millions of factory workers. The pool of talent in these markets is increasingly becoming better qualified. And the pool is Olympic-sized. In 2003 China had roughly 9.6 million young professional graduates with up to seven years' work experience and an additional ninety-seven million people who would qualify for support-staff positions.[48] It has twice as many computer scientists as the US, and 1.6 million young engineers. In 2003, universities in India produced 167,000 students with science and engineering degrees, nearly two-thirds more than the US. India and China together turn out one-fifth of all doctoral students in science and engineering. The thirty-three million university-educated young professionals in developing countries constitute more than double the number in developed ones.

Back in the 1980s, campaigns such as 'Buy New Zealand Made' sprang up to urge people to shun imports and protect local jobs. But the reality of today's New Zealand consumer is that they prefer to buy cheap goods. So what does the manager of a New Zealand company do? Go where the labour is cheapest. Because labour accounts for, on average, about two-thirds of the cost of producing most goods and services, she will have a widget made in China or Vietnam, or a software program written in Russia or Estonia, or a centre for processing calls or managing a back office set up in India. At a time when workers at German car manufacturer Volkswagen are negotiating a twenty-five- to thirty-four-hour work week, there are equally skilled workers in many countries around the world prepared to do twice the hours at half the price.

According to Dan Pink's book *A Whole New Mind*, there are some scary off-shoring projections coming out (well, scary if you're in the West):[49]

- One in four IT jobs in the US will be off-shored by 2010. Such is the demand, India is having difficulty producing enough IT professionals to fill the jobs at the large off-shoring IT facilities
- According to Forrester Research, 'at least 3.3 million white-collar jobs and $136 billion in wages will shift from the US to low-cost countries like India, China, and Russia' by 2015
- The UK alone will lose some 25,000 IT jobs and upwards of 30,000 finance positions to India and other developing nations in the next few years. By 2015, Europe will lose 1.2 million jobs to offshore locations. Faced with the very same pressures, New Zealand may experience some similarly scary job losses.

But there's a silver lining to the looming cloud of the developing world worker. As the workers of China and India capture more of the global economic pie, their income rises. As their income rises they begin demanding better clothes, widescreen TVs and trips to New Zealand. So big markets await the New Zealand exporter.

... But also lots of new consumers

Almost a billion new consumers will enter the global marketplace in the next decade as economic growth in emerging markets pushes them beyond the threshold level of $5000 in annual household income – the point when people generally begin to spend on discretionary goods.[50] In the decade from 2006 to 2015, consumer spending power in emerging economies will increase from four trillion dollars to more than nine trillion – nearly the current spending power of Western Europe.

During periods of its not-too-distant past when China struggled to feed itself, the country's huge population was considered a burden. Now, as the country's wealth increases, that enormous mass of people has becomes the world's largest consumer market. Upwards of two hundred and fifty million Chinese have recently moved up the income ladder and reached the middle-class rung.

While a middle-class household in China will make less money each year in New Zealand dollar terms than a New Zealand middle class household, from a purchasing parity perspective they enjoy the same relative wealth. By 2008 there will be ninety-five million high-income households in China, up from forty-nine million in 2003. Whereas in years past they could barely afford the rice to feed themselves, these consumers are now buying software from Microsoft, wearing shoes made by Nike, driving stylish Volkswagens and opening accounts with Citibank.

India is only a few steps behind. For the past quarter of a century, India's GDP has grown at an average annual rate of six per cent, making it one of the fastest-growing economies in the world. As a result, India's middle class has more than tripled in size to two hundred and fifty million people. It adds another twenty-five million to its middle class each year, almost a whole Malaysia or Thailand, and by 2025 over half of India's population will fall into this category.

The growth and potential of these markets is obviously not going unnoticed by the world's largest companies, who are either eager to tap into such extraordinary potential markets or who have little choice but to use them as a source for low-cost production. General Motors expects the Chinese automobile market to exceed the US market by 2025 with seventy-four million families able to afford a car. Already China sucks up over four billion dollars worth of New Zealand exports, having climbed quickly to become New Zealand's fourth largest export market by 2006.[51]

This newly emergent middle class is powering the growth of a super economy. In 2005, China's GDP was US$2.25 trillion.[52] By that measure, China was the seventh-largest economy in the world. On a purchasing power parity basis it is even higher, estimated to be at closer to $8.8 trillion.[53] China already accounts for ten per cent of world trade, up from four per cent in 2000.

Equally remarkable is the speed of the country's economic growth.

Growing at over nine per cent for a generation, China's economy has doubled nearly three times over – a surge that has no equal in modern history.[54] By contrast, it has taken New Zealand over forty years to double the size of its economy.

This growth has created a huge demand for energy, which has been rising by a staggering twelve per cent every year.[55] China is hurriedly building enormous energy-generating infrastructure to cope. Take the Three Gorges Dam, due to become fully operational in 2009. It will easily be the largest hydroelectric dam in the world. At almost two hundred metres high and over two kilometres long, the dam will be more than five times the size of the Hoover Dam – a mammoth structure in itself. The 600-kilometre long reservoir (over half the length of the North Island of New Zealand) will, at completion, have submerged 635 square kilometres of land. When its twenty-six turbines become operational in 2009, the dam will have a capacity of more than 18,000 megawatts – fifty per cent bigger than the next largest hydroelectric power dam in the world, Itaipu, in Brazil.[56] And yet for all its size and impressiveness, it will cater for just eighteen months' worth of rising electricity demand.

What these numbers mean is that the productive might of China's vast low-cost manufacturing machine, along with the swelling appetites of its billion-plus consumers, has turned China's people into what is arguably the greatest natural resource on the planet.[57] And soon you can add India, Indonesia, and a whole raft of other rising economies to that list. The developing world, or at least big chunks of it, is catching up to us here in the West. Globalisation, for all its controversy, is shifting wealth from the developed to the developing nations.

New Zealand is sitting on the wrong side of the growth equation. Our economy is growing more slowly than many in the developing world. They're catching up. And as they do, our place in the world will change – in more ways than one. The downside is the impact it will have on our standard of living. As other countries become wealthier they'll demand products we'd also like. Imports will increase in cost. Those Nike shoes, flatscreen Sony TVs and BMW 7 Series we import will become more expensive to the New Zealand consumer. We'll have more and more visits from the likes of Zhao Gingyan and friends, but we'll have a tougher time being able to afford to visit them.

The good news is that while New Zealand is becoming relatively smaller, our geographic isolation is also decreasing. What was once the tyranny of distance is becoming less tyrannical. The world's marketplaces are moving closer to New Zealand. In 1998, of the thirty-eight countries which together made up eighty-five per cent of world's economic engine, New Zealand was the most remote. But the growth of other economies, particularly in South East Asia, means that since 1950 New Zealand has been moving closer to more of the world's GDP. We're still remote, sure – just a little less so.

With China's economy going gangbusters, and with India and the other South East Asian countries powering along behind, New Zealand's location at the bottom of the South Pacific (or, if you prefer, north of Antarctica) has never looked better.

Our changing bodies – older and heavier

But before you crack open a bottle of champagne and toast the rise of the Asian tigers, there is another problem. In years to come we'll have relatively fewer people working to take advantage of our increasingly lucrative location. The reason, of course, is that a fair chunk of our workforce is retiring. Like the Europeans, the North Americans and the Japanese, our nation's hair will become increasingly grey over the next forty years.[58]

Statistics New Zealand anticipates that the average New Zealander will live six years longer in 2051 than they do today. However, for many people, it will be more like ten or fifteen years. For some, it could be more like thirty. The number of people aged over sixty-five will almost triple to 1.3 million by 2050.[59] So out of every four New Zealanders standing in the checkout line at the supermarket, one will be over sixty-five. Even more remarkable is that one out of every ten will be over eighty-five.

This greying of our society is pretty common knowledge by now. But what of the implications? Not only will average driving speeds fall (I'm speculating on this one), so will the relative size of the workforce. For every person over sixty-five in 2005 there were just over five and a half workers toiling.[60] By 2051, there will be just over two workers.[61]

But that's making a big assumption. For many who reach that age, sixty-five won't feel old at all. Certainly not a natural time to retire. You can't just play golf for the next twenty years (or can you?). The assumption that one is too old for many activities – from work to sports to travel to sex to further education – is being more and more widely challenged. No matter how naughty, life doesn't begin at forty. Sixty is more like it.[62]

But a prerequisite of that challenge is access to improved healthcare. Part of what the two workers will be paying for will be the bed, doctors, nurses and equipment to keep each elder in good health. By 2051, the New Zealand Treasury predicts, the over-sixty-fives will account for a whopping sixty-two per cent of healthcare expenditure (while those aged under fifteen will account for a mere five per cent of all health expenditure).[63] In fact, in 2050, the expenditure on healthcare for the over-sixty-fives will easily exceed the entire education budget.[64]

New medical technology is likely to further inflate future costs for the elderly. While some of the proposed technologies, such as cancer vaccines and better treatments for acute stroke, are expected to increase elderly healthcare spending by less than one per cent, other innovations will be more expensive. For example, researchers at US think tank the Rand Corporation estimate that the cost of expanding use of implantable defibrillators – devices implanted in patients' chests that show promise in treating heart attacks and heart failure – would increase expenditure on these treatments for the elderly in the US by seventy per cent between 2015 and 2030.[65] A preventive treatment for Alzheimer's or new cancer-fighting drugs could each increase spending on the elderly by eight per cent, and anti-aging compounds – an area of active research in biomedicine – could drive up costs from fourteen to seventy per cent. Of course we'll want these treatments available. We just have to find a way of paying for them. Otherwise, we face some awkward choices.

But if the ailments of the elderly don't crush our health system, then our collective weight will. Between 1989 and 2003, the percentage of adults over the age of fifteen considered obese in New Zealand jumped from eleven per cent to twenty-one per cent – almost doubling in just fourteen years.[66] Our kids are struggling as well. Thirty-one per cent of them are considered obese or overweight (including, tragically, sixty-five per cent of Pacific Island children). These 'fat stats' put New Zealand twenty-third out of twenty-nine countries in obesity prevalence in 1999–2003. We may not be the world's biggest country, but we're quickly becoming the heaviest.

We can take some comfort in the fact that we're not alone. It's a global problem. Not just the West, but the whole world. Far more Filipino adults are now overweight than underweight. In China, one in five adults is too heavy, and the rate of overweight children is twenty-eight times higher than it was two decades ago. In Thailand, Kuwait, and Tunisia, obesity, diabetes, and heart disease rates are soaring.

It's the poor's problem. A study in Vancouver, Canada, found that preschoolers in food-insecure households were twice as likely as other kids to be overweight or obese. In New Zealand, forty-seven per cent of Pacific Island women and twenty-seven per cent of Maori women are obese.[67] The wealthy have organic food, gyms, and personal trainers. The poor have Burger King and KFC. When money's tight, you feed your kids at McDonald's.

And that's just the diet side of the equation. Before modern technology, adult men would expend about 3,000 calories a day. Now they expend about 2,000. In China, households with a car have an obesity rate eighty per cent higher than their peers.

New Zealand's statistics show us to be more passive than we'd care to admit. According to Sport and Recreation New Zealand, almost a fifth of our adult population is not active for more than thirty minutes on any day of the week.[68] (This must include the twenty-five per cent of adults who, according to the survey, somehow manage to avoid participating in any walking). Our children are also less active than they used to be – almost thirteen per cent of them now have what Sport and Recreation New Zealand consider a 'sedentary lifestyle', up from eight per cent in 1997.

The implications for New Zealand's future are worrying. The healthcare costs of an overweight population are sizeable. The rates of type 2 diabetes, strongly linked to obesity, are climbing dramatically. Costs for diabetes will grow from $250 million in 2001 to over $1 billion by 2012.[69] In 2001, that extra weight we're carrying added about $135 million to our health bill – a number that floats to upwards of $700 million if we reach the upper end of World Health Organisation obesity cost estimates. The WHO estimates the costs of obesity at between two and seven per cent of the annual health budget. We'll have plenty to choose from for the All Black front row, sure, but . . .

So what to do?

It's impossible to deny that a myriad changes are going to affect New Zealand, from new technologies, to demographic trends, to big shifts in the global economy – and that's without even touching on potentially massive climate change. In the words of former Massachusetts Institute of Technology president Charles Vest, 'This is without question the most exciting period of human history in science, technology and engineering.' Exciting, yes, but also – I'd be the first to admit – a little scary.

Of course, you don't have to be a highly regarded academic to form an opinion of what the future holds. That's why in 2006, four hundred and fifty New Zealand ten-year-olds were asked what they thought we would be using to keep in touch with each other in the future. Their answers sound like a cross between *Star Trek* and *The Jetsons*: teleportation, mind reading, computers for the wrist, jets, flying letters, flying robots and holograms. Fertile imaginations, our ten-year-olds have. But who knows? Perhaps their predictions are more accurate than we might think. In fact, they might have hit the nail on the head. But how can we know if they're right or not? We can't.

To understand why, let's return to where we started this chapter: chess. Most people think great chess players have become really good by being able to think many moves ahead. But contrary to popular wisdom, chess masters don't. In fact, they usually think just a few moves ahead.[70] When asked how many moves ahead he typically looked, the grandmaster Richard Reti replied: 'One – the right one.'

Instead, grandmasters rely heavily on a technique called pattern recognition. Simply put, it's the ability to leverage their experience of previous scenarios to anticipate how their current match will play out. In other words, they've been there, done that, on many occasions. Chess is a game of patterns with interesting names like pawn chains, weak squares, and knight forks. Studies have shown that Kasparov was able to play within a hundred points of his best even in exhibition matches where he was placed under severe time constraints, suggesting he uses pattern recognition extensively. Chess is very much more science than art, more experience than genius (although a big dollop of neural horsepower is required to be really good).

The reason chess masters don't try to think too far ahead is simple: the information is too uncertain. Deeper Blue had the ability to identify two hundred million possible moves – per second! That's impressive.[71] But not impressive enough. Because even for a computer, chess is a fiendishly complex game. From any average position on a chess board, there are thirty-eight possible moves. To analyse all the implications of just six turns by each player would require considering nine billion billion possible combinations of moves – more than any current computer can handle.[72] Even at Deeper Blue's analytical speed of over two hundred million moves per second (let alone Kasparov's two or three), it would have taken the machine over 1400 years to figure out the optimal set of any six moves near the beginning of the match.[73]

Anticipating the outcome of move, counter move, counter-counter move and so on, is too unpredictable. The future is too uncertain. Chess is about controlling the situation at hand. You want to determine your own future. You certainly don't want your opponent to determine it for you. But for that you need clarity about the type of future that might exist, not clairvoyance.

The problem is that we all want clairvoyance. In a world of such complexity, moving at such a fast pace, faced with such remarkable changes in the future, it's natural to want clairvoyance. It's understandable to want a map for navigating the future ahead of us. It would give us some certainty about what to do today. But as we'll now discover, this quest for certainty about our lives and about our future is an illusory one.

3
A world of uncertainty

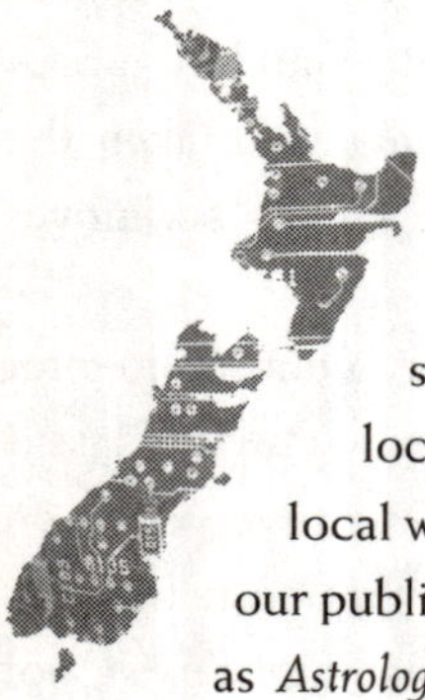

Being lousy at predicting the future doesn't mean people don't try. For a highly sceptical country, we still seem to place a lot of faith in the stars. Most of our locally produced magazines have horoscopes, as do our local weeklies and our major newspapers. Books purchased by our public libraries in the last few years have included such gems as *Astrology and Love: Techniques for Harmonious Personal Connections*; *Astrolove* (a similar concept, one assumes); and *Don't Blame Me, I'm a Gemini!: Astrology for Teenagers*.

Some believe that Sir Isaac Newton, the illustrious seventeenth-century English physicist and mathematician, was a secret astrologer as well. At his death, Newton's library is said to have contained no fewer than four books on the subject. Legend has it that when the astronomer Edmond Halley (the guy who named the somewhat anti-climactic comet that last shot across our skies in 1986), once spoke disparagingly on the subject of astrology, Newton is said to have berated him with the remark: 'Sir Edmond, I have studied the matter, you have not!'

But history does not remember Newton as a defender of astrology. Instead he is most famous for his Laws of Motion. Like a new Moses bringing truth to the people, these falling-apple-inspired equations were able to predict the tides, the orbits, or the movements of any object that could be seen or felt. Every action begat a reaction. Output equalled input. The universe, Newton's laws led us to believe, was like some giant clock, its parts acting in concert, precisely, predictably. Modern-day life has been built on this fundamental view of the world.

But the future is anything but predictable. In this chapter we'll discover that the universe is a lot less certain than Newton's laws led us to think. The functioning of a cell or the organisation of an ecosystem or the workings of an economy are not quite as predictable as the advances in all of these fields over the last three hundred years would lead us to believe. For a New Zealander living at the beginning of the twenty-first century, on the cusp of the big changes we discussed in the previous chapter, that can be a little unnerving.

Newton and the laws of certainty

From the time Newton was donged on the head by an apple in the late seventeenth century right through until the early twentieth century, his Laws of Motion and other linear, mechanical principles dominated the understandings of science and filtered down through every aspect of the Western world. They underpinned the Industrial Revolution. The principles of mechanics inspired Frederick the Great to organise the Prussian Army as an assemblage of standardised parts and equipment.[1] Over time, this view of reality came to dominate our education system, our culture, our language, our organisations, our understanding of economics and our management practices to such an extent that it was universally taken for granted.

This view of life predetermines how we've interpreted much of what goes on in the world around us. We see nature as ordered and reasoned in the same way as we perceive the human mind to be. Ever since Newton established cause and effect as a central premise of physics, humanity has believed it inhabited a world of lineal order, regularity and stability. We have found an intense satisfaction in the ordered nature of the universe.[2]

This confidence in the mechanics of nature found its voice in positivism. Positivism is the belief that science and the scientific method can ultimately understand physical reality in its entirety, and use that understanding to predict and guide the future. This presumption led the influential French enlightenment intellectual Pierre-Simon Laplace to make his famous claim that, given enough facts, we could not merely predict the future but retrodict the past.[3] As Steven Weinberg expresses it in his book of the same name, it is the 'dream of a final theory'.[4]

This search for fundamental laws is found in the ideal of *reductionism*. Understand the parts of the car, the reductionist belief maintains, and you can understand the car itself. Economic and social phenomena are to be explained in terms of human behaviour. In turn, that behaviour is to be explained in terms of biological processes, which likewise are to be explained by chemical processes, and they in turn by the laws of physics. Traditional science puts things under a more and more powerful microscope. In biology, for exapmle, the investigations go from classifying organisms to functions of organisms, then organs themselves, then all the way down to protein, metabolic pathways, and DNA. This is finer and finer reductionist thinking at its finest.

As science moved into the twentieth century, various discoveries began to undermine the sense of certainty. In deep space, as Einstein's Special Theory of Relativity showed, the Laws of Motion utterly broke down. Quantum theory suggested that at the subatomic level, time sometimes went backwards. Heisenberg's uncertainty principle, the decoding of DNA – these began to free science from the conviction that the world was and governed by universal mechanical laws. Much of what was machine-like and objective and determinate at the start of the century was by mid-century unpredictable and indeterminate – the motion of currents, the growth of plants, the course of a storm.

As the British physicist, astronomer, and mathematician Sir James Jeans said back in the 1930s, 'Today there is a wide measure of agreement . . . that the stream of knowledge is heading towards a non-mechanical reality: the universe begins to look more like a great thought than a great machine.'[5] What had defined science at the start of the century – its power to predict – no longer defined it at the end. In the century just past, Newton's calculus lost its mojo.

Equilibrium in our economy

While science was beginning to welcome the unpredictable, the mechanistic view of the world was becoming entrenched in areas outside the science labs. The image of a uniform, mechanical and ultimately predictable universe not only shaped the development of science and technology, it also became the dominant metaphor in politics, economics, organisations and education. The industrial age was built on the theories that pictured the entire universe as a machine.

Our Westminster parliamentary political system finds equilibrium through a series of checks and balances; economic theory analyses trends and develops supply and demand models designed to bring the economic system into equilibrium; organisations are studied according to the science of industrial engineering, which analyses the system to fine tune operations based on the tweaking of strict organisational hierarchies.

The very notion of business planning itself began in the coal mines of France in the late nineteenth century, when a manager named Henri Fayol began equating men to tons and projecting the outcome five and ten years into the future.[6] This was a big plus: by deconstructing the future, a manager knew how many resources its fulfilment required. In the first half of the twentieth century, scientific management reduced everyone to a cog.

As *The Wall Street Journal*'s Thomas Petzinger explains in his book about the transformation of the modern workplace, by the 1950s and 1960s, planning had become entrenched in massive flow charts and mindnumbing textbooks, 'creating a generation of corporate and government leaders whose influence persisted for thirty years . . . Career advancement, product development, project management – all occurred according to plan'.[7] Our organisations were simply big machines, to be tweaked by management for maximum productivity.

Today we've built our companies around the framework of organisation charts, with executives on top, through layers of middle management, down to the factory-floor worker. We have job descriptions, responsibilities and duties to ensure the predictability of the people we work with. We devise a gamut of methods to control the behaviour of employees, from wages to bonuses to promotions to assembly lines to time sheets to dress codes.

This fuels an economy we've come to interpret as one of order. Back in the eighteenth century, Adam Smith, the father of modern economic theory, enshrined order in his book *The Wealth of Nations*. The selfish interests of the individual, he asserted, were guided as if by an invisible hand to the common interest of all. We inherited the thinking that the economy is no more than a massive machine; that if we merely controlled its parts, we could guide the whole.

Beinhocker notes that since the late nineteenth century, the organising paradigm of economics has been the idea that the invisible hand's economy is an *equilibrium system*, essentially a system at rest.[8] He describes traditional economic theory as viewing the economy as like a rubber ball rolling around the bottom of a large bowl. Eventually the ball will settle at the bottom of the bowl, to its resting – or equilibrium – point. The theory states that if we know the economic forces at work we can predict where the ball will come to rest in the bowl: the prices set, the quantities produced, and the profitability of firms, all under equilibrium.

Today we're ensconced in this mechanistic view of our economy. It's a big machine, where the Reserve Bank governor, like some all-powerful puppeteer, tweaks interest rates to control the rate of economic growth. We eagerly await word of what the Official Cash Rate is, and then hold our breath for the economy to speed up, slow down or about-turn as predicted.[9] It's comforting to know that our economy works in such a mechanistic fashion, especially so we can blame someone or something when it goes wrong.

The joy (and importance) of certainty

We crave certainty and we demand control of our lives. Order and regularity in the world give people a feeling of security. We all claim to be spontaneous, crazy individuals, but deep down we crave certainty and predictability. We live lives of routine. Sure, we moan about that at times. But step out of routine for too long and soon we're craving a return to predictability. From international institutions, through the state and the government, on to cities, communities, organisations, and all the rich variety of forms into and through which we organise our lives, we are continually creating structures that promote order in our lives.

Linear order, regularity, reliability and predictability *do* all exist in this world, and for that reason our understanding of the world has been immeasurably enhanced by Newton's cause-and-effect approach. Many phenomena do change in an orderly, linear way, so that we can anticipate outcomes. Give a ball a small nudge, and it will move a short distance. Give the ball a punt and it will fly further. That's a world we know, understand and use to defeat Australian sportspeople on a regular basis.

It's also a world of certainty. Small differences in initial conditions will not have a major effect later. Take the fertiliser we add to our vegetable gardens.[10] If we didn't add any to the garden, growth would be negligible or non-existent. Empty the whole bag on the vegetable patch, and we'd likely kill every living organism on that chunk of earth.

But small differences in the amount of fertiliser we apply would likely have no effect. We can live our lives in a rational manner when we know that most of the things we deal with are not too sensitive to small differences in their initial state. A mechanical contraption like a pendulum, a small electrical circuit – as long as these systems can be reduced to a few perfectly understood, deterministic laws, their long-term behaviour will be stable and predictable.

Science built itself on this principle of insensitivity to small differences. Here's how James Gleick describes it:

> This assumption lay at the philosophical heart of science. As one theoretician liked to tell his students: 'The basic idea of Western science is that you don't have to take into account the falling of a leaf on some planet in another galaxy when you're trying to account for the motion of a billiard ball on a pool table on earth. Very small influences can be neglected . . . [they] don't blow up to have arbitrarily large effects.'[11]

Classically, the belief in approximation worked well. Gleick notes that a tiny error in fixing the position of Halley's Comet in 1910 would only cause a tiny error in predicting its arrival in 1986, and the error would stay small for millions of years to come. Approximately accurate input gives approximately accurate output. It's a principle that computers rely on to guide spacecraft. And if it's good enough for spacecraft hurtling around in outer space, it's got to be good enough for us.

But Houston, we have a problem. Insensitivity to small differences is not always the case. Behind the veneer of order and predictability we've constructed, something chaotic is going on.

A world of things that don't behave predictably

There was once a woman named Phoebe Moses. Phoebe was a performer in Buffalo Bill's Wild West Show, a gun-fighting and horsemanship show that toured the United States in the 1880s.[12] Phoebe was reputed to have been able to shoot the head off a running quail by the age of twelve. In the show she would shoot the flame off a candle wick, and the corks off wine bottles. But it was her grand finale that she was famous for. Each night of the show, she would shoot the end off a lit cigarette held in a man's mouth. She would ask for a volunteer from the audience and, not surprisingly, no one would ever dare to raise their hand. So her husband, Frank, had the unenviable task of being planted in the audience and volunteering each night.

In 1890, Buffalo Bill and crew were touring through Europe when, legend has it, a person at one show actually did answer the call for a volunteer – a young man named Frederick. To everyone's amazement he strode onto the stage, lit a cigarette, placed it in his mouth and waited. Phoebe's trepidation at this unexpected turn of events was exacerbated by the fact that she had spent the previous night at a local beer garden.[13] With a trembling hand she lined up the cigarette in the sights of her gun, closed her eyes, squeezed . . . and hit the target. Frederick returned to his seat, probably lighting another cigarette to calm his nerves. Backstage, Phoebe no doubt did the same.

The young man was none other than the Prussian prince Frederick Wilhelm II. He would later become Kaiser and lead Germany into World War I. The risky behaviour of this young prince has led to some intriguing speculation about just how close the world came to an alternative course of history. Could it be argued that if Phoebe's aim had been just slightly off, World War I would never have happened? That would have saved the lives of 8.5 million soldiers and thirteen million civilians. Hitler, it could be argued, would never have risen to power on the back of a humiliated Germany, and Lenin would not have overthrown an exhausted Russian government. In fact, the entire course of twentieth-century history might have been changed by the merest twitch of Phoebe's hand at a critical moment.

Scientists have labelled moments such as Phoebe's brush with Prussian nobility a *frozen accident* – a tiny event that decides the path history takes. But there's a lesson here beyond the obvious caution of volunteering to have a hung-over woman shoot a cigarette out of your mouth. The nature of our world is such that although an event might be small, divergence in the paths history takes can be huge. Small events *can* have big impacts, consequences we have no hope of predicting.

This idea is encapsulated in the popular phrase, the butterfly effect. The phrase refers to the idea that a butterfly's wings might create tiny changes in the atmosphere that ultimately cause a tornado to appear. In a nutshell, the flapping wing represents a small change in the initial condition of the system, which causes a chain of events leading to some big event. Had the butterfly not flapped its wings, the big event might never have happened or been totally different. This sensitivity implies that the details of exactly how the butterfly flapped its wings would have to be known to infinite precision in order to predict the result.

The person who came up with the notion of the butterfly effect was Edward Lorenz, a meteorologist at the Massachusetts Institute of Technology. One day in the early 1960s he was working on his primitive computer to solve a number of equations that modelled the Earth's atmosphere. He took a coffee break in the middle of his calculations. When he returned, he ran his calculations again. Before his break his calculations were run to an accuracy of six decimal points. After the caffeine boost, he ran them to three decimal points accuracy. The difference between the before and after calculations amazed him. The tiny difference involving three numbers after the decimal point had resulted in completely different solutions.

Since Lorenz's fortuitous coffee-break discovery, there have been many attempts at accurate long-range weather forecasting. Both the Americans and Europeans have invested billions of dollars in sophisticated models. These churn out long-range weather forecasts using thousands of variables. But beyond two or three days the world's best forecasts are still very speculative. That's because for small sets of weather conditions, any prediction deteriorates rapidly. Errors and uncertainties multiply, cascading upward through a chain of turbulent features, from dust devils and squalls up to continent-size eddies that only satellites can see. In technical terms, it's known as *sensitive dependence on initial conditions*. In reality, it means leaving home without an umbrella the day a big storm arrives in town.[14]

But if small input differences only yield small output differences, why should this tiny variation in the forecast matter? What Lorenz was seeing was an example of a system (in this case, weather patterns) that does not change in linear, predictable ways. When they change they are extremely sensitive to tiny initial differences, which in the process of repetitive change are blown up apparently out of all proportion. A quivering finger changes the course of history. A small kick of the ball somehow sends it soaring away. Our conventional cause-and-effect take on the world can't explain it.

Look around and you'll see many things that don't behave in a linear fashion. Taking ten aspirin won't reduce the headache tenfold. Two neighbouring societies with almost identical conditions at the outset can evolve completely different norms. The Athenians built a completely different society from that of the neighbouring Spartans. Identical twins can end up developing completely different personalities. Two seemingly identical shots in snooker send the balls on the table in wildly different directions. The smallest differences, magnified again and again, create vastly different outcomes.

This lesson of all this for New Zealand is that there is a limit to what we can control about our future. If the non-linearity of our world makes it impossible to predict weather with any accuracy more than three or four days out, how can we peer into New Zealand's future with any accuracy? We can anticipate a certain future, based on what we're seeing today, and what we've witnessed in the past, but it could well end up very differently. Small actions – whether, say, an amendment to the law on how fast cars may travel or a modest investment in a fledgling biotech company – can end up having big, unintended consequences down the road. These consequences are not necessarily negative, they're just unintended and unplanned for. Realising this will be important in later chapters when we cover how New Zealand can prepare for an uncertain future.

Accepting the reality of a complex, unpredictable world

In 1972, the future Nobel Prize-winning physicist Philip Anderson published an article in the journal *Science* – titled 'More Is Different'.[15] Dr Anderson was exploring what happens when a number of elements – molecules, cells, ants, people – interact with one another. Interactions lead to messy interdependence, ratcheting up the difficulty of understanding what goes on and why.

Learn all you want about the structure and properties of a single water molecule, for example, and you still have no clue that a collection of them will be a liquid at one degree Celsius and frozen at minus one degree Celsius. This abrupt change in state involves no alteration of the molecules themselves, but rather a change in the organisation of their interactions. Something called *emergence* occurs, when the activity of the parts does not add up to the activity of the whole. Interrupt a game of chess and it is impossible to get a sense of who's winning simply by adding up the value of the pieces on the board.

Similarly, the stability of an ecosystem cannot be ascertained merely by studying the biology of lions and elephants in isolation. Scientists know lots about neurons in the brain, but little about consciousness. We could learn everything there is to know about how a computer works, but we'd be no closer to explaining the growth pattern of the World Wide Web, or the nature of virtual communities like MySpace.

Just seeing the world as a bunch of molecules or particles or ants or computers isn't enough in itself. They interact, and when they do they become a system. In essence, a complex system consists of many dynamically interacting parts or particles. In such systems the interactions of the parts or particles at a micro level lead to the emergence of behaviour at the macro level. For example, a water molecule, in and of itself, isn't particularly interesting (not to me, anyway). Combine billions of them together, however, and you get water (slightly more interesting). Add energy to it, like our pot of soup earlier, and it simmers, gurgles, bubbles and steams (downright fascinating). You cannot have water with a single H_2O molecule; rather, water is a collective, or what scientists call emergent, property of the system itself. It is in the behaviour of a system that things really start getting interesting. As complexity economics author Eric Beinhocker notes, the biological world comprises 'a massive hierarchy of systems: molecules interact in cells, cells interact in organisms, and organisms interact in ecosystems'. The human body is a highly complex collection of systems, like the brain and circulatory system, interacting with other systems, like the nervous system or the immune system. If you took away the systemic structure of the human body, 'we would each be nothing more than a small box of chemicals and half a bathtub of water.'[16]

Beinhocker then points out that human society is a complex series of interconnecting systems. There is the physical kind – 'the earth is girdled by roads, sewers, water systems, electrical grids, railroad tracks, gas lines, radio waves, television signals and fibre-optic cables. These provide the highways and byways for the matter, energy and information flowing through the open system of the economy.' Then there are the virtual systems: people interact in companies, companies interact in markets, and markets interact in the global economy. Just as in biology, the networks of the economic world are arranged in hierarchies – networks within networks.[17]

As Beinhocker notes, 'the interactions of millions of people, making decisions, engaging in strong reciprocal behaviour, acting out their cultural norms, co-operating, competing, and going about their daily lives, creates an emergent phenomenon that we call society.'[18] What emerges from the swirl of human activity is in some ways greater than its constituent parts.

So seeking to understand the parts – whether they are molecules, cells or people – is important, but inadequate. The ability to reduce everything to simple fundamental laws does not imply the ability to start from those laws and reconstruct the universe.[19] Reductionism doesn't get us to the finish line – something modern science is coming to recognise. In a special section of *Science* on complex systems, entitled 'Beyond Reductionism', the editors noticed that 'The much-used axiom that scientists "know more and more about less and less" may have an element of truth' and that 'perhaps there is something to be gained from supplementing the predominantly reductionist approach with an integrative agenda'.[20]

In the course of the twentieth century, scientists have come to recognise that most phenomena in the universe are far from resting in equilibrium.

They are dynamic and complex. They never settle into a state of rest. In the twentieth century, science came to accept the uncertain and the indeterminate.

There goes the future

But accepting the uncertain and the indeterminate doesn't do much to help a society like New Zealand prepare for a complex, fast-moving future. How can we explain *that* in a science textbook, let alone structure our world around the random and the emergent? How does a company plan for the future? How does a government set policies to account for the unpredictable?

As we've seen, the non-linearity of much of the world makes it impossible to anticipate what the future will look like. Consider remarkable coincidences or random events – say, the lahar from Mt Ruapehu that wiped out the Tangiwai bridge in 1953, or a hanging chad here or there that decided the 2000 presidential election in the US – that are magnified into history-changing outcomes. As the physicist Freeman Dyson noted, 'Whenever things seem to be moving smoothly along a predictable path, some unexpected twist changes the rules of the game and makes the old predictions irrelevant.'[21]

Yet it is so easy to fall into the trap of making predictions about the future. Take one of our brightest, Ernest Rutherford, the man who figured out the structure of the atom and who now adorns our hundred-dollar note. Nobel Prize winner and towering figure of atomic and nuclear physics that he was, he nonetheless confidently stated that the potential usefulness of nuclear energy was 'all moonshine'. Yet only a year after Rutherford's death in 1937, Otto Hann and Fritz Strassman demonstrated nuclear fission. This prompted Albert Einstein to send his famous letter to President Roosevelt, opening the stage for the atomic bomb and nuclear energy. The rest is a happy historical saga filled with mushroom clouds, Chernobyl and the *Rainbow Warrior*.

These sorts of blunders rightly lead many to throw scorn on attempts to accurately plot the future. Management guru Peter Drucker, among the most perceptive of trend spotters, once declared emphatically:

> I don't speculate about the future. It's not given to mortals to see the future. All one can do is analyze the present, especially those parts that do not fit what everybody knows and takes for granted. Then one can apply to this analysis the lessons of history and come out with a few possible scenarios . . . Even then there are always surprises . . . So all I am willing to say is: here are today's realities and what they imply for the next 20 years, and here are the probabilities based on the lessons of history. Everything else is quackery.[22]

We all make the mistake of imagining the trends of the past can be extrapolated in a linear way into the future. We're conditioned into seeing the world as a plodding machine, predictable and controllable. Our minds construct a view of the world that's fixed in this point in time. This is how the French political philosopher Bertrand de Jouvenal puts it:

> [We tend] to postulate that tomorrow will be the same as today; likewise, when we are aware of movement, we assume that tomorrow will differ from today in the same way as today differs from yesterday . . . The lifespan of man has become longer; it will become longer still. The number of work hours in the year has decreased; it will decrease yet further . . . The sharper our awareness of a past movement, the stronger our conviction of its future continuation.

Today's world is the world we know, and it's that view of the world that we'll use to picture the future.

But life is not like that. The future we face at the dawn of the twenty-first century is, as Virginia Postrel describes it in *The Future and its Enemies*, 'emergent, complex messiness'.[23] Its messiness lies not in disorder, but in an order that is unpredictable, spontaneous, and ever shifting, a pattern created by millions of uncoordinated, independent decisions. Trying to build ordered plans in the midst of all that messiness is a recipe for disaster, as the old Soviet Union found with its infamous five-year plans.

That emergent complex future will be constructed by all the variegated aspects of life. As Postrel points out, people will create and sell products or services, adopt new fashions of dress, choose partners and select home towns, make medical decisions and seek new forms of art, explore the universe and search for spiritual insights.[24] These actions shape a future no one can anticipate, a future that is inherently unpredictable.

All of this is more than a little alarming to our order-seeking minds. For the last two hundred years we've spent a lot of time and effort trying to boil the world down to simple laws, and then to build structures to reflect it. The idea that there is a world of unpredictability beneath the veneer of order and stability is an uncomfortable one. Here's how Brigham Young University professor of Management Margaret Wheatley describes it in the context of an organisation:

> While we have lusted for order in organizations, we have failed to understand its true nature. We have seen order reflected in the structures we erect, whether they be bright mirror-glass buildings or plans started on paper napkins. These structures take so much time, creativity, and tinkering attention that it is hard not to want them to be permanent. It is hard to welcome disorder as a full partner in the search for order when we expended so much effort to bar it from the gates.[25]

Disorder has infiltrated our stable, equilibrium-loving view of the world, and it is here to stay.

That's why I am the first to acknowledge that much of what's written in Chapter Two could prove quite wrong. We can project trends based on the current state of technology, but the world is a fickle, unpredictable beast. Advances in nanotechnology will heighten our ability to manipulate the very small, but whether this becomes a billion- or trillion-dollar opportunity is impossible to tell. Genomics will be significant in the future, but the who, what and when of its impact on healthcare and agriculture depend on a host of safety, technological and societal factors. China's role in the life of every New Zealander will inevitably grow, but what that actually means for Mrs Smith in Te Awamutu twenty years down the track is very difficult to say in any tangible way.

But that conclusion doesn't help Mrs Smith very much. She, along with the rest of us, may not be happy sitting back and waiting for the future to hit her. We want to plot a path from the present to the future. Doing so would provide some comfort. At least there would be a plan. We want the organisations that we depend on for our jobs to know exactly where they're going in the future.

Likewise, we expect the government to have a plan for navigating us through the turbulent waters ahead: invest in the right technologies, form the right trade partnerships, attract the right overseas investors, recruit the right immigrants, train students in the right academic disciplines, and so on.

We need our governments and institutions to make decisions and set policies for the future. The governmet's role in setting the strategy for our nation is more important than ever. Its job in equipping the nation to prosper – by developing strong schools, by investing in new research, by providing the right incentives for individuals and organisations, by developing strong trading relationships, by maintaining the health and security of its people, and so on – will only become more important.

But it's not enough on its own. And with the centrality of the government in the public discourse it is easy to forget that. For even the best government policies will only take us so far. Because it's impossible to plan with great certainty far into the future, it's therefore very difficult for any government to set policy for it. For that reason, New Zealand will have to be very good at doing something else: changing or adapting. Changing policies that don't work. Adapting to new circumstances. Being flexible. Developing new ideas. Responding quickly. It's the people, not the government, who ultimately determine a nation's response to an uncertain future.

Getting comfortable with uncertain, complex things

That's what this book is about: why it is important to be a society good at adapting, and how New Zealand can become better at it.

How good we are at adapting depends on what sort of society we have. Our attitudes. Our ability to generate innovative ideas. Our skill at absorbing new ideas from elsewhere. Our willingness to confront tough choices and change. It's the extent to which these characteristics are found in our culture, in our 'New Zealandness', that will determine just how effective we are at adapting to the crazy, complex, unpredictable, uncertain world we have been discussing. I'm going to talk more about these characteristics of our culture in more detail shortly.

But to understand why these characteristics are important for New

Zealand, we first need to understand why adaptation is important. And to do that we need a better idea of how complex, unpredictable systems – like New Zealand society – work. Fortunately the advent of powerful computers over the last three decades has helped scientists gather new insights into the way com-plex, unpredictable systems work. That's why a host of eminent biologists, physicists, sociologists, mathematicians, anthropologists, computer scientists and even some economists have started to get excited about a relatively new field of academic research called *complexity science*.

Complexity science provides some insights into how a society can cope with the unpredictable, the indeterminate and the uncertain – put another way, how New Zealand can adapt effectively.

That is what the next section of this book is about.

Part 2

How to build a successful society

4

Energy, entropy and rats

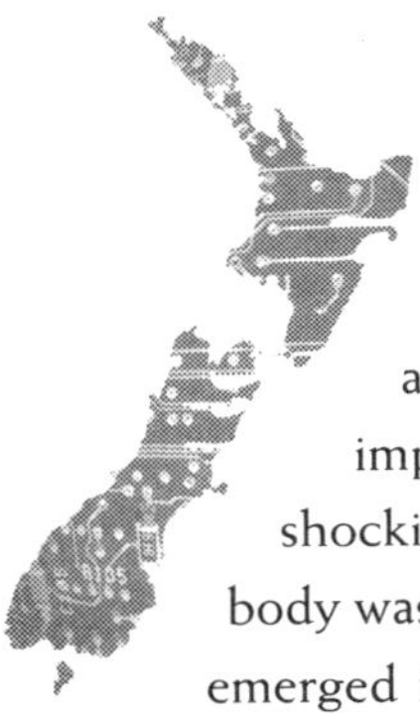

In May 1900, a Mr Keely, of Upper Queen Street, Auckland, died of a mysterious disease.[1] Lacking a health department at the time, the government improvised by sending a veterinarian to investigate. His shocking discovery of Black Plague-like welts on the deceased's body was confirmed shortly afterwards when a huge pack of rats emerged from the bush at Awakino, swam across the river and promptly died, en masse, near the town of Mokau. Thankfully the Black Plague's visit to our shores was brief and claimed the lives of only two humans and a few hundred rats.

Five hundred and fifty years earlier, Europe hadn't been so fortunate. In late 1347, twelve Genoese ships arrived in the Sicilian port of Messina. They had just come from the trading port of Caffa on the Black Sea (today, the city of Feodosiya in southern Ukraine). Besieged by the ferocious Mongols, Caffa had gradually been worn down by a tight blockade.

The war had, however, taken an unexpected turn when Mongol soldiers began dying. Their general, Khan Janibeg, ordered the corpses of his dead to be flung over Caffa's walls in the hope they would infect the city – biological warfare at its most basic. As the city began to fall under the curse of the disease, the Genoese merchants decided it was high time to flee in their ships. Below decks, hundreds of rats also prepared for the journey.

The Genoese (and, one assumes, their rats) had little time to rest upon arrival at Messina. Soon after the ships docked, locals began exhibiting similar symptoms to those of the sick soldiers. Word spread quickly. Panic began to set in. Suspecting the recent arrivals from Caffa, the city expelled the ships. As word spread of the disease-carrying Genoese ships, other ports refused them entry, firing flaming arrows to ward them off. Eventually the ships out-sailed their bad press and found safe harbours further afield. With only rudimentary navigation equipment and limited fresh provisions, most trading vessels of the period tended to stick close to the coastline, docking every three or four days. As each ship from Caffa docked, the plague spread from port to port. The Black Plague had reached Europe.

As we will see shortly, the Black Plague changed Europe in numerous ways. European society had to adapt to survive. The last chapter ended with a claim that adaptation is key to a society's ability to respond to change. This chapter begins my explanation of why that's the case, and why that's particularly important for complex systems like fourteenth century Europe and twenty-first-century New Zealand.

Europe and the Black Plague

Responsible for more than twenty-five million deaths from 1348 to 1352, the Black Plague ended up killing about a third of Europe's population. Spread in two ways – bites from plague-carrying fleas and respiration (coughing, sneezing) – the plague spread quickly and was lethal. A person could go to sleep at night feeling fine and be dead by morning. In other cases, a doctor could catch the illness from one of his patients and die before he had collected his fee.[2] While this lowered the patients' medical bills it did little for their peace of mind.

Given its potency, the plague left a path of destruction. Entire towns were depopulated. Barely a single family was left unscathed. In Norway, the story is told of a ship from England that drifted offshore for months before it ran aground with its cargo of dead crew. Lawyers refused to witness wills, doctors refused to tend the sick, priests did not hear confessions, and husbands deserted their wives. These were difficult times indeed.

The response of Europe's governments was, well, disappointing. The majority of monarchs responded to the crisis by hightailing it to the hills. From remote castles they tried to impose some semblance of control by issuing laws in a desperate attempt to check the plague's progress. In a questionable response to such a sweeping pandemic, one such law passed at the time outlawed large-scale fishing.

The wealthy and poor alike were struck down.[3] Very soon the cemeteries were filled, so the Pope consecrated the likes of the Rhone to allow the citizens to pitch their dead into the river. Initially, priests rushed around hearing confessions. Soon, however, laypeople were authorised to conduct the last rites as the disease took a particularly heavy toll on the clergy. Of the one hundred and forty Dominican friars at Montpellier, only one man survived. In 1349, an Irish monk, describing these matters, wrote that he was leaving his record 'in case anyone should still be alive in the future'.

If ever we wanted an example of a society struggling with upheaval, we'd need to look no further than plague-ravaged Europe. Like a stone cast into the still waters of a pond, the plague sent ripples of change through society, altering it in inconceivable ways. Society in fourteenth-century Europe was slow to change, almost static, its institutions and ways of life evolving only in small, almost unseen ways from one generation to the next. The epidemic acted as a catalyst for some remarkable adaptations as each society attempted to cope with a radically different post-plague world. The speed and enormity of its impact was such that few traditional pillars of medieval society escaped. Almost every facet of fourteenth-century life in Europe was turned on its head.

The Catholic Church certainly was. At least forty per cent of the parish clergy died prematurely as a result of the plague, either because they tended to the sick or because of the close living quarters in monasteries. Fronting a recruitment drive, the Pope relaxed age requirements for joining the clergy, with priests ordained at twenty rather than twenty-five. Monastic vows could be administered to adolescents at fifteen rather than twenty.[4] University graduates, suddenly in demand in the post-Death years, disturbed the surviving older generation of church officials by bargaining for higher pay and free gym memberships. Radical sects, such as the Lollards led by John Wycliffe, pointed to the inexperience of parish priests as the rationale for the establishment of counter-churches.

Beyond staffing headaches, a more fundamental problem emerged for the Church. The flock began losing confidence in the Church itself. Unable to cure or even explain the disease, the Church was found wanting.

Its hold on much of Europe loosened.[5] At a time when even the boiling of an egg was timed according to how long it took to say a prayer, that was no trifling matter. Five universities were closed during the plague years, but fifteen were created shortly afterwards as the drive for knowledge spread beyond the clutches of the Church. The stage was set for the Renaissance and the rise of Europe.

The plague changed the medical and sanitary practices of the time. The practice of alchemy as medicine (in the form of chemical concoctions), up until that time the norm for most doctors, began to wane as the cures offered by many alchemists appeared to hasten, rather than delay, the demise of the afflicted. That said, alcohol, a medicine the alchemists supplied which didn't actually poison people, was commonly used as a remedy for the Black Death. While it is unclear whether the alcohol actually cured anyone, or just stopped them from caring, the consumption of liquor in Europe rose dramatically after the plague.

The changes bought about by the plague didn't stop there. Peasants took advantage of the critical labour shortage to demand steep increases in wages from landlords. While the French Peasants' Revolt of 1358, the Florentine Ciompi Revolt in 1378 and the Peasants' Revolt of 1381 in England were eventually crushed, the labour momentum couldn't be stopped. Many labourers won better pay and were able to buy land – the middle class was on the rise.

The shortage of labour induced a flurry of innovation in labour-intensive sectors of society, like agriculture. The invention of the light one-stilt plough may not seem like a big deal today, but it substantially increased the productivity of workers in the fields in the fourteenth century. Landlords spent more on capital to assist the productivity of their labourers, purchasing oxen to aid the peasants in ploughing, and increasing their supply of fertiliser.[6] The demise of the large teams of monastic copyists, the backbone of the handwritten book publication industry, spurred the introduction of Johann Gutenberg's printing press in 1453.[7]

As the balance of power shifted further in favour of the workers, landlords began pursuing less labour-intensive industries. Only one or two shepherds are needed to look after hundreds of sheep, while a small army of tillers and harvesters is required to cultivate wheat.[8] This trend in turn aided the burgeoning English woollen cloth industry. Higher per capita incomes increased the demand for luxury goods. Agricultural producers began increasingly to focus production on ingredients for beer, liquor and wine. The medieval economy was forced to diversify, and the seeds of Western Europe's economic and technological leap forward in the subsequent centuries were sown.

The Black Plague certainly brought about drastic and rapid change. But it raises more questions than it answers about how societies respond to change. Why did the peasant revolts in England, Italy and France not occur in other European countries, despite conditions that were equally ripe for them to do so? Why were some farming regions quick to adopt or invent new technologies, but others not, when all faced the same labour shortages? Why were political controls strengthened rather than weakened in the plague-ravaged Middle East, and why did commerce, industry, and agricultural production decline so much more rapidly in this region compared with Europe?[9] The questions are endless; the answers fill bookshelves and in turn inevitably raise further layers of questions and contradictions.

The questions remain because much of the change we see in society – fourteenth-century Europe or twenty-first-century New Zealand – cannot be traced to a single cause. Factors such as strong leadership, economic dislocation or a natural catastrophe like a pandemic, seem to be the cause of change, but are themselves impossible to isolate from the other forces that prompt social upheaval. When the Black Plague turned up on Europe's doorstep in 1348, it was entering societies already being shaped by a multitude of different forces: demographic, political, environmental, technological . . . the list goes on. The disease exacerbated some of these factors and negated others. It had entered an elaborate, highly complex system where cause and effect were rarely as apparent as my simple description of the plague suggests. The what, the where, the who and the when are discernible, but the why is rarely so clear.

Outcomes don't just happen, there are *dynamics* at work. Highly complicated dynamics. It is inevitable that societies will change, yet, paradoxically, it depends on the will and the actions of ordinary individuals. We embrace change, but something in our nature fiercely resists it, too. We structure social movements, political campaigns and business strategies around the need for change, yet we barely understand how it works.

That's why the starting point in our quest to understand why adaptation is critical for New Zealand is to understand what drives change in the world. We'll begin this brief portrait of change by looking at the canvas at its most basic . . . the forces at work driving life itself.

Change is endemic in life itself

On 5 February, 1943, the lecture hall at Dublin's Trinity College was jammed with dignitaries, diplomats, leaders of the Irish government and the Catholic Church, artists, socialites and students. They had come to hear Nobel laureate Erwin Schrödinger, the famous quantum physicist. Only five years before, on September 14, 1938, Schrödinger and his wife Anne had fled from Nazi-occupied Austria, taking just three bags and leaving behind his gold Nobel medallions. He now resided in Dublin, Ireland, his newly adopted home, free from persecution and able to continue his work unopposed.

The title of the lecture series was 'What is Life?' and each of the three lectures attracted over four hundred people. (This was a much more interesting topic than the initially planned talk, 'On the Mutation Rate Caused by X-Rays on the Fruit Fly, *Drosophila melanogaster*'.)

The lecture series and a subsequent book of the same name were Schrödinger's attempt to draw together the fundamental processes of biology and the sciences of physics and chemistry. To answer the far from trivial question he was posing, Schrödinger observed that life comprised two fundamental, ongoing processes: one, order from order, and the other, order from disorder. We'll explore each briefly.

First, Schrödinger's 'order from disorder' observation. In essence, Schrödinger saw life amidst the workings of the Second Law of Thermodynamics.[10] Devised in the nineteenth century by Lord Kelvin, the Second Law is the one that states that everything tends to run down.[11] Iron rusts. Logs rot. Clock springs uncoil; wind-up toys unwind. In fact, the law asserts the universe itself is running down.

As Mitchell Waldrop in *Complexity* puts it, it seems as though nature is 'less interested in creating structures than in tearing structures apart and mixing things up into a kind of average'. If you mix hot and cold water, the mixture comes to a uniform temperature. Or when you add milk to coffee, the resulting café au lait will soon lose its initial distinctions in colour and texture, the temperature will fade, and the motion created by the pouring will stop.[12] It won't ever spontaneously unmix itself back into the espresso and milk portions. The coffee has reached what scientists call a state of equilibrium. And that's the fate of our universe under the Second Law: blandness, equilibrium, nothingness.

But the story doesn't end there. Everywhere we look we see evidence that organisms – life itself – are defying the Second Law. Fallen logs rot, sure. But trees also grow. Seeds and embryos grow into fully developed living creatures. Unlike cups of coffee, organisms preserve their distinctions – between feet and hands, between leaves and stems – rather than combining into some uniform organism, as the Second Law demands.[13] In every plant, animal, and human, order and structure appear to abound. It looks as though order is being created from disorder.

The key to the puzzle, Schrödinger discovered, is energy. He realised that an organism stays alive in its highly organised state by taking energy from outside itself and processing it to sustain its structured state. In fact, the very essence of an organism is that it captures and processes energy. It uses this energy to create structured matter: bones, brains, beaks – all the things whose ongoing existence defies the Second Law.[14]

As you might recall from biology class at school, plants take energy from the sun to help them produce glucose. To optimise energy capture, plants of many species arrange themselves specifically into shapes that maximise leaf area exposure to the sun. Plants become highly ordered structures, with the sun helping to bind atoms and molecules found in atmospheric gases and soils.[15] That's why all organisms have some form of barrier, such as a membrane, skin, or shell that keeps their ordered insides distinct from the disordered outside. Without energy to maintain and grow a complex internal order, the odds on molecules randomly arranging themselves into any sort of order are ridiculously low (similar, according to New York University biochemist Robert Shapiro, to those on a tornado in a junkyard creating a Boeing 747).[16]

If your biology is, er, rusty, let's illustrate the point using Waldrop's everyday example of a pot of soup sitting on the stove.[17] If the hot plate is off, nothing happens. Just as the Second Law requires, the soup will sit there at room temperature, in a state of equilibrium with its surroundings. If the element is turned on, heat energy begins rising up through the soup from the bottom of the pot and the system is no longer in equilibrium. Suddenly the molecules begin to rise and fall. The soup has acquired order and structure. In a word, it has begun to simmer. Energy has momentarily defeated the Second Law and life continues.[18] Bravo!

So there you have it in a nutshell: the universe is just like a pot of soup. Forces of entropy trying to dissolve us into nothingness are arrayed against energy working to build the structures of life around which we continue to exist. All organisms, from the gnat to the giraffe, must make a thermodynamic profit to survive and reproduce.

So the kiwi, for example, is a strategy for making thermodynamic profits, and therefore surviving, in the New Zealand bush (but that strategy is not the only one – hence the kakapo, the tui and so on).

But if life is to continue – whether in the New Zealand bush or on the African savannah, or in the concrete jungle of Auckland – another force is required to be at work: order must be created from order. Order from order was the second part of Schödinger's answer to the question, *what is life?* Schödinger argued that the essential part of a living cell – the chromosome – was a strange material that James Watson and Francis Crick would later identify as deoxyribonucleic acid, or DNA. So, by order from order, Schrödinger was referring to the genetic process whereby the child inherited the traits of the parent.

Organisms need to reproduce. When they do, they pass on their thermodynamically profitable strategies to the next generation. The 'order from order' process drives evolution. And evolution, it turns out, is key to a living organism's survival. Biological evolution, then, is a three-billion-year-old quest for thermodynamically profitable strategies in a competitive and ever-changing world.

We're going to return to evolution in the next chapter. First, we need to understand what all this talk of entropy and rust has to do with change in society.

Order in society

We can see remarkable parallels between the work organisms do in their efforts to resist the Second Law, and how societies operate at their most basic level. Just like the organisms within them, societies are by their very nature structures defying disorder. Throughout history, and even today, we see societies coming apart in the absence of a deliberate attempt on the part of the government to impose order, in whatever form.[19] As the seventeenth-century English philosopher Thomas Hobbes said, life in a state of nature is poor, nasty, brutish, and short. And unless forces are arrayed against disorder, life can be even shorter and more brutish.

For a society, as for any living organism, the key to survival is energy. As Robert Wright explains in *Non Zero: the Logic of Human Destiny*, societies convert energy into material structures that preserve order and stave off disorder. 'Even in their most primitive groupings, our hunter-gatherer ancestors used energy derived from the consumption of food to build structures, such as shelters. As societies became more complex, energy technologies change. Farming replaced hunting and gathering as the source of human energy, and human energy gets supplemented by oxen, waterwheels, steam engines. But one thing stays the same: energy keeps getting invested in structure, albeit ever more complex structure: temples, factories, jetliners.'[20]

Similarly, just as an organism's various structures preserve it from entropic forces, social structures protect a society against disintegration.[21] Corporations provide food, clothing and shelter, armies defend a society, and bureaucracies govern it. Most are there to stave off atrophy or disruption (and you thought the IRD just wanted your taxes!). Cut off the supply of energy to an economy – take away the food, oil, gas, and coal – and entropy would rule. Take a look at North Korea, a nation isolated by its leader, or the Democratic Republic of Congo, isolated by the ravages of war – both vulnerable to economic decline as entropy sets in.

Of course, not every human endeavour contributes directly to a more orderly, less chaotic environment. While plants or ants may spend all their working days feverishly maintaining the structure of their environments, humans clearly don't. You'll struggle to find a bunch of ants on their way to the pub on a Friday. And last time we checked, going to a movie or sailing or picking flowers from the garden were not exactly chaos-averting activities, in and of themselves. The point is that these activities are possible because energy has been expended elsewhere (in maintaining law and order, in building a government, in earning a living to buy food, and so on), making this leisure time possible.

If we return to plague-infested Europe, we see this order from disorder struggle vividly. The impact of the Black Plague, as we saw, was dramatic. Centuries-old structures were weakened in a matter of years. The Catholic Church stumbled. The hold of the monarchs and ruling classes on their subjects weakened. The food supply dwindled. Communities and families fell apart. In the words of Boccaccio, who set his *Decameron* during the period, 'Brother abandoned brother . . . Fathers and mothers refused to see and tend their children.'[22] Europe, it seemed during the plague's darkest years, was slipping into chaos.

But life prevailed. Just as the human body built resistance to the disease, so too did human society. Order and structure came fighting back. The rulers returned from their isolated castles and order was restored. People returned to church. The markets were reopened, and trade from village to village, town to town, country to country, was restored. Crops were resown. New universities were constructed. Energy was being invested into rebuilding the very structures of European society. Schrödinger's 'order from disorder' principle was at work.

But there is more to it than that. Schrödinger doesn't take us far enough. The question he posed in Dublin, 'What is life?', can't be answered simply by looking top-down at the physics of matter or the chemistry of organisms. As we saw in the previous chapter, reductionism only provides part of the answer. We need to dig a little deeper.

Open and closed systems

In 1977, chemist Ilya Prigogine stood on the podium of the Stockholm Concert Hall to receive the Nobel Prize in Chemistry. He was being recognised for his exploration of the nature of change in what he calls 'dissipative structures'. To undertand what these are we need a bit more science.

Thermodynamic systems, like those discussed by Schrödinger, fall into two categories: closed and open systems.[23] A *closed* system is one where no energy, matter, or information flows into or out of it. The universe is a closed system because there is no 'outside' to the universe. Closed systems always have a predictable end state: equilibrium. That term means that order decays into disorder and the system eventually comes to rest.

An *open* system, by contrast, has energy and matter flowing into and out of it. Such a system uses the energy and matter flowing through it to fight entropy and create order and structure. Our planet is an open system, capturing the energy from the sun. This energy has created the order and complexity we see all around us. Entropy has not gone away; things on earth decay, and all organisms (you and me included, I'm afraid) eventually die. Because there is this constant tussle between entropy and order, open systems are in a state of *dis*equilibrium.

Prigogine termed a particular set of these open systems 'dissipative structures'. Dissipative structures are open systems in disequilibrium that can produce new structures spontaneously through a process called self-organisation. They include physical processes (e.g., tornadoes), chemical reactions, and biological systems (e.g., cells). Take tornadoes as an example. Molecules of air and water form themselves into a whirling maelstrom spontaneously, without any one molecule being in charge.

Prigogine found that these structures, when far from equilibrium, can transform small-scale irregularities into large-scale patterns. A single fluctuation adding its strength to other fluctuations may become powerful enough to reorganise the whole system into a new pattern. It's the small-change-having-big-effect phenomenon we came across in the last chapter. That's why you get constant fluctuations, sudden shifts that allow for novelty and unpredictable change. It's why weather is so hard to predict, or the course of a tornado impossible to anticipate accurately.

It is only in the last few decades that scientists,helped considerably by powerful computers, have begun figuring out how systems like these, without a central co-ordinating force, manage to work in a remarkably coordinated way. Their field of research has fallen under the title of *complexity science*. As scientists have come to know more about the behaviours of complex systems, there has been a growing interest in systems in which the particles are not simple things with fixed behaviours, like water molecules, but instead have some intelligence and are capable of adapting to their environment. Water molecules cannot adapt their behaviour, but termites, for example, can. That's what makes termites – believe it or not – especially relevant to our quest to understand how adaptation works in complex systems like New Zealand society.

Enter complex adaptive systems

You may not have given termites much thought unless they're eating through the wood in your walls. They're actually pretty impressive creatures. One of the most impressive of the more than 2500 different species is the African termite, responsible for the construction of enormous five-metre-high mounds that are home to millions of inhabitants.

The mound has all the characteristics of an upmarket home: perfect arches, spiral staircases, nurseries, storage facilities, and living quarters that vary according to the status of individual termites. Tunnels radiate out from the mound more than fifty metres in any direction, allowing termites to forage within a twenty-five thousand square-metre area without being exposed to predators. Most amazingly, there is a ventilation system – operated by opening and closing vents – that inhales oxygen into the tower of mud and exhales carbon dioxide. This system keeps the internal temperature constant to within plus or minus a single degree, irrespective of the freezing winter or burning summer temperature outside.

The building of such an impressive structure requires coordination amongst millions of termites. Yet the termites' extraordinary organisational success can't be attributed to strong leadership. That's because, strictly speaking, no one is in charge. The queen termites are no Elizabethan figures issuing orders from the throne and directing the activities of their subjects. The queen's job is simply to lay eggs and be looked after. So without a leader giving orders, how can the termite colony operate? How do worker termites know to switch from nest-building to foraging to raising termite pupae, as external conditions change? How do they ensure they are only collecting enough food for the colony's current size, or building the spiral staircase in the right area?

The answer has to do with something that complexity scientists call self-organisation. In a nutshell, self-organisation is a process in which the internal organisation of a system increases in complexity without being guided or managed by an outside source. If you put millions of termites together, they interact with each other, communicate using signs and coordinate their activities to do things like build elaborate mounds. There is no plan. There is no leader marshalling all the work in a structural way. Because the termite mound is constructed from the unco-ordinated interactions of millions of termites, rather than through those co-ordinated and managed by a leader, it is said to be 'self-organised'.

In describing this self-organisation in bees, Kevin Kelly in his book *Out of Control* describes it as 'the marvel of the hive mind'.[24] He writes that although no one is in control, an invisible hand governs.

> The marvel is that more is different. To generate a colony organism from a bug organism requires only that the bugs be multiplied so that there are many, many more of them, and that they communicate with each other. At some stage the level of complexity reaches a point where new categories like 'colony' can emerge from simple categories like 'bug'. Thus, there is nothing to be found in a beehive that is not submerged in a bee. And yet you can search a bee forever with cyclotron and fluoroscope, and you will never find the hive.[25]

A complex adaptive system like a termite mound is a system of interacting agents that adapt to each other and their environment. These sorts of systems exist everywhere. Immune systems, rainforests, cities, cells, and ant colonies are all examples. We live our lives in the midst of these systems. Our organisations, our economies, and our societies are all examples of complex adaptive systems.

A city is marvellous example of life emerging from self-organisation. Take Auckland as an example. Like any city, it has grown organically, born out of millions of local interactions. Pacific Island immigrants to the city took their cues as to where they should settle from their neighbours. Many ended up in South Auckland. The Chinese did the same, and many of them settled in Howick. No one wills the unique characteristics of neighbourhoods into existence single-handedly; they emerge by a kind of tacit consensus. The artists might congregate in Mt Eden perhaps or Grey Lynn, the professionals in Parnell and Remuera, the environmentalists in

Titirangi or on Waiheke, and so on. Social change like this occurs in every city, bubbling up in an apparently uncoordinated, but oddly ordered, fashion.[26]

But wait: organisations, economies and societies don't self-organise, do they? We have management hierarchies and governments to organise our activities and control our actions. They provide instructions and set laws. In fact, as we saw earlier in the chapter, societies avoid succumbing to the Second Law by building governments and mandating law precisely so they can impose organisation and order upon us.

That's a fair objection. But the control of any government or institution in today's society is less than we might at first think. With a few exceptions, governments in open societies like New Zealand don't dictate who we talk to, where we go, or what we do.[27] Most laws passed are in reality a *reaction* to the changing shape of society, as moulded by the millions of actions and interactions of the individuals within it. While any society needs certain structures in place to preserve order (a stable government, police to enforce laws, an infrastructure to accommodate commerce, and so on – all bulwarks against the Second Law), they operate in a system where the agents – we humans – are free to go about our daily lives: to pursue activities we enjoy, develop ideas we're excited about, congregate with the people we like or need.

New Zealand society continues to evolve in the form that we, as New Zealanders, want. We take our cues from our neighbours and our collective culture emerges. And as our collective culture emerges, so does the society we want. There is a saying that a country gets the government it deserves. Similarly, people get the society they deserve because each plays a part in shaping it. We have self-organised into our current society, and as the environment in which we live changes, we'll self-organise into the next form of society.

As we saw with Europe's reaction to the Black Plague, there are limits to what top-down authorities can change. Most change in society comes from people interacting with each other in complex ways, processing information, learning and adapting their behaviour. The shape of the society (its institutions, laws, buildings, customs, economic activities, leisure activities and so on) emerges from the millions of individual interactions that occur each day.

A different Europe emerged after the plague. The Catholic Church, as we saw, reinvented itself. And the self-organising nature of Europe's complex adaptive system was at play. As the new Catholic Church emerged in the wake of the plague, for example, its new shape was only partially the result of dictates from the top down. There was the papal decree allowing the ordination of younger priests, but the Church was also shaped by the collective action of millions of people questioning the institution itself, stimulating the emergence of new processes, faiths and sects.

Initially it seemed like business as usual for the peasants when they returned to work, but soon the landowners were paying them more, new varieties of crops were being sown and grown, and innovative technologies were reshaping the way they worked. Most of the changes that bubbled up after the plague had passed through, whether as significant as farming practices or as mundane as bathing habits, were driven by the interaction of individuals each taking cues from what the post-plague world looked like and what their neighbours were doing.

Energy was being invested in reconstructing a different society, suited to the changed environment. Adaptation was occurring. The survivors of the plague weren't molecules continuing to act as they always had. They weren't robots blithely following a pre-ordained script. They were adapting to a world populated by fewer people. But exactly what form that adaptation would take would have been impossible to predict at the time. Fourteenth-century Europe was an open system, in disequilibrium, its shape constantly changing and evolving in unpredictable ways.

Let's recap the story so far. We've seen in the first section of the book how disconcerting life is at the moment. It's complicated. It's fast paced. It's barely possible for us to keep up with the world, and impossible to fully understand it. To make matters worse, the future looks equally fast paced and likely to bowl us any number of wrong 'uns. Preparing for that turbulent future is an increasingly tricky affair. Our mechanistic, reductionist understanding of much of the natural world fails to address the behaviour of the many complex systems in the world that appear unpredictable and random.

The thesis of this book suggests that for any society to cope with an uncertain future, it must be great at adapting to the changing environment.

This chapter has been the first step towards understanding why that is the case. At its most basic, life involves a struggle to convert energy into the structures necessary to survive. For an open system like plague-ravaged Europe, that will involve upheaval and change. But often that change is not driven by 'top down' controls from government. Instead it somehow emerges from the interactions of the people. Out of these interactions emerges a sort of 'self-organisation' adequate to drive the adaptation necessary.

What's more it is not just societies, but also ecosystems, our bodies, our organisations, our economies, and a host of other biological and social structures that act in this fashion. Lots of different systems seem to operate amid what appears to be utter confusion. Yet somehow they manage to survive and even prosper in the turmoil.

Lots of people are trying to figure out how these complex systems manage to adapt so effectively to their ever-changing environment. As insights emerge, they're applying them to improve the performance of companies, protect endangered species and build stronger, more sustainable societies. Understanding the way complex adaptive systems work is more than just intellectual curiosity for many. Heinz Pagels, the American physicist, has said: 'I am convinced that the society that masters the new sciences of complexity and can convert that knowledge into new products and forms of social organisation will become the cultural, economic, and military superpower of the next century.'[28]

While New Zealand's ambition may not be one of world domination (except, perhaps, on the sports field), every New Zealander wants to live in a country that not only copes with the turbulent future, but also prospers in it. Understanding and applying the rules that complex adaptive systems, then, should be a part of New Zealand's thinking about the future.

It's to two of these rules that we'll now turn.

5

Two laws and adaptation

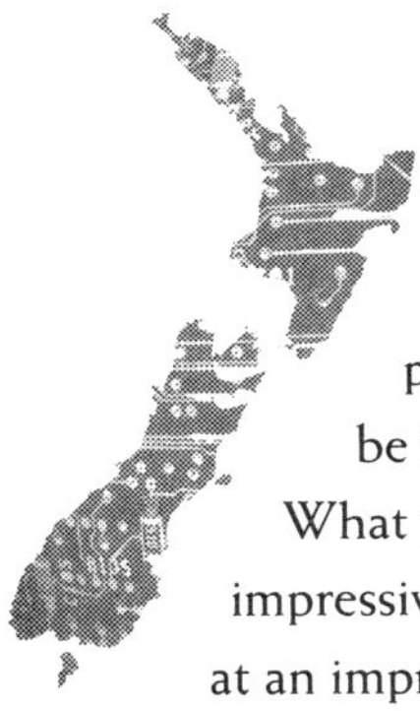

Walk along the coastline the surrounds the Otago Peninsula and you risk tripping over a few varieties of penguin, a seal or two and the odd sea lion. You may even be fortunate enough to be slapped around by an albatross. What you won't encounter, however, is one of Otago's most impressive creatures, the New Zealand giant penguin. Standing at an impressive 1.5 metres tall, this bird pushed the scales north of a hundred kilograms. That made it the second-tallest penguin ever, and most certainly the heaviest. As the American palaeontologist George Gaylord Simpson famously quipped, '[the giant penguins'] height would not suffice for basketball but their weight was about right for American football.'

Unfortunately these sturdy creatures are extinct. They're extinct not, as you might assume, at the hands of Maori or European hunters. They, like most of New Zealand's native species, disappeared well before any humans arrived in the country. New Zealand's giant penguin became another entry on a very, very long list. In fact, it is estimated that about ninety-nine per cent of all species that ever existed are now extinct. The world's many ecosystems are certainly no place for the faint of heart, no matter how heavy a bird you are.

The fate of the New Zealand giant penguin illustrates the core component of complex adaptive systems: the adaptive part. We learnt in the last chapter that all organisms are strategies for generating thermodynamic profits. They stave off entropy by adapting to the changing conditions of their environment. New Zealand's giant penguin was a thermodynamically-profitable strategy for a while, but as conditions in the New Zealand environment changed, it wasn't able to adapt quickly enough to survive. Adaptation is key to complex adaptive systems, and as we'll discover later in this chapter, it's vital to New Zealand's success as well.

Before we get to that, however, we're going to uncover two rules that govern all complex adaptive systems. We'll see them cropping up at various stages during the remainder of the book as we talk in more detail about New Zealand society, so it's necessary that we understand how they work and why they're important.

The two rules of complex adaptive systems most applicable to us are:

Rule One: Many complex adaptive systems are *small worlds* governed by the *power law*.

Rule Two: Equilibrium is bad; change is always necessary.

We'll examine each briefly in turn.

Rule One: Many complex adaptive systems are *small worlds* governed by the *power law*

If you think your job has periods of tedium, be thankful that you were not part of a group of researchers from the University of Michigan studying ecosystems in the 1990s.[1] They were trying to figure out how ecosystems are structured. The researchers divided four fields of grassland in the Cedar Creek Natural History Area in Minnesota into two hundred and seven plots, then studied these plots to determine how diverse (based on the number of species) each was. To do this they measured the area's biomass. In what must have been an unbelievably painful way to spend their time, measuring the biomass basically involved gathering up everything in the plot, drying it out, and then weighing it.[2]

Their persistence paid off. After months of digging, dissecting and weighing, they were able to come to an important conclusion: complex systems are more stable than simple systems. Well, that's the synthesised conclusion. Their actual conclusion was more like this: the greater the complexity and number of species in an ecosystem, the weaker the fluctuation in biomass, suggesting greater stability. To understand what that means, we'll need to take a look at the work a theoretical ecologist from the University of Bern in Switzerland, Peter Yodzis, did back in the 1980s.

Back then Yodzis was tackling the question that had plagued ecologists for many years: what is the likely impact of a single species' extinction on the rest of the ecosystem? To answer that question, he turned to complexity theory to see whether it could shed some light on how complex adaptive systems like ecosystems work. What he discovered not only provides an insight into what happens to an ecosystem when a species within it disappears, but also tells us a lot about the way in which other complex adaptive systems like societies work.

An ecosystem is a system much like a community of humans. Species are linked to one another in a tangled pattern that, to the untrained eye, appears to lack any overall organisation or plan. Take our beloved kiwi for example. It eats earthworms, spiders, fallen fruits and seeds, larvae of beetles and cicadas and a mixture of forest invertebrates. Its droppings are feasted on by various insects, which are, in turn, eaten by tui and other native birds. The kiwi's chicks are prey to stoats, ferrets and wild cats. And so on. Drawn out schematically, the kiwi's ecosystem would look like a tangled spider's web of interactions between species. Extrapolate the web beyond the kiwi, and the ecosystem map for New Zealand's almost 53,000 species becomes even more complicated.[3] Impossibly complicated.

Key to understanding the ecosystem, ecologists are discovering, is to understand the connections of its species to one another. In a social network of humans, not all relationships are created equal. We'll have strong bonds with our good friends and only weak bonds amongst mere acquaintances. What's more, some of us prefer a social circle comprising close bonds with a few people, while others like knowing a larger number of people less well. And so it is with the kiwi, the tiger, the wombat, and every other living organism: a predator may rely solely on one prey as its food, and so interact very strongly and frequently with it. Or it may prey on a hundred different species and have relatively weak and infrequent interactions with all of them. In that case, if one of the hundred species disappears, the predator simply focuses on the ninety-nine other alternatives on the menu.

Yodzis took this insight and concluded that in networks like ecosystems, the more complex they are (the more species they have) the more stable they become. That's the point the University of Michigan researchers confirmed ten years later in their biomass-weighing exercise. As more species are removed from an ecosystem, the stability of that ecosystem would decline. That makes sense, right? No surprises there.

But the ecosystem story doesn't end at that point. While ecosystems might be complex, they're actually very tightly connected. By this I mean that the number of connections you need to make to get from one species to any other is quite low. For example, while the kiwi and the tui may not have any direct interaction in their ecosystem, they both eat the same type of insect. That means that they're connected by two degrees of separation, to use the parlance of network theory.

Studies of various ecosystems around the globe have found that the one hundred and fifty-odd species in each ecosystem studied were linked by no more than two or three degrees of separation from one another. Any system that is closely linked like this is known in complexity science terms as a *small world* system. These small world systems are actually very common. The world's human population is a small world system, with each person linked to any other by no more than six degrees of separation (the implications of which we'll explore in more detail in Chapter Eleven).

The next step was to look at the number of links each species has to others in the ecosystems. You might recall from learning statistics at school that the standard model for plotting variations in any collection of randomly recurring data, including links per species in an ecosystem, is the bell-shaped curve. The shape of this curve suggests that most data clusters around the average, represented by the hump of the bell in the middle. When things vary, they try to stay near an average point and they manage to scatter around the average in a reasonably smooth way. It's called a normal distribution.

But when scientists took all the species in an ecosystem and counted up how many of them were linked to two others, how many to three others, and so on, the graph they got did not look like a bell. Instead it looked like an ice-hockey stick lying on its back, with the head of the stick on the left. The graph exhibits something known in complexity theory as the *power law*. The power law basically states that the number of agents in a network with links to other agents falls off by a constant factor each time you double the number of links. In other words, if a hundred species have two links, then only fifty have four links, only twenty-five have eight links, and so on.

Whenever you see this power law operating in a network, you know that the network is dependent on a few superconnected hubs that possess a disproportionate fraction of all the links in the entire web. So in an ecosystem we find that a few species have a huge number of links to other species. The implications, then, of removing species in an ecosystem become clear. Remove a species that is not connected to many other species, and the impact on the overall ecosystem is minimal. Remove a well-connected species – a superconnector – and suddenly the impact on the ecosystem is dramatic.

Richard Sole and Jose Montoya, two scientists at Imperial College in London, have found that removing even twenty per cent of the most highly connected species fragments the ecosystem into many tiny pieces. As the web falls apart, the disintegration triggers many secondary extinctions as well.[4] In other words, mess with the superconnectors in an ecosystem and you risk decimating it.

Complexity theory, then, becomes useful in identifying the most important targets for preservation. You might assume that large predators would tend to be the keystones in an ecosystem, but this is not necessarily the case. Ecologists have discovered that the superconnectors are often basic plants at the very bottom of the food chain or inconspicuous organisms in the middle. Basically there are no hard or fast rules for determining which species in an ecosystem are keystones. So ecologists must study the ecosystem's network structure and see which species are the superconnectors, the lynchpins of the living fabric.

Ecosystems are not the only small worlds. Despite its size (over eleven billion web pages and counting), the World Wide Web – a dense, complex ecosystem in its own right – remains a small world.[5] University of Notre Dame physicist Albert-Laszlo Barabasi studied the size of the Web in 2002 and found that the degrees of separation amounted to only nineteen.[6] In other words, any document on the entire Web is only nineteen clicks away from any other document. Increase the size of the Web by one thousand per cent and the number of links only jumps to twenty-one.[7] That's a small-world network, governed by the power law. Like the ecosystem, the World Wide Web relies on a series of sites that are superconnectors to many other sites.

Power laws have been discovered in a wide variety of phenomena, from the intensity of solar flares to the ranking of cities by size, traffic jams, cotton prices, the number of fatalities in warfare and even the distribution of sex partners in a social network.[8] Researchers found that earthquakes follow the power law; with each doubling in earthquake energy, the probability of a quake of that size occurring drops by a factor of four. Gross domestic product growth of nations distributes as a power law. The famous economist Vilfredo Pareto even found the power law in income distribution: for every increase of income by one per cent, there was a corresponding decline in the number of households by 1.5 per cent. Number of employees by company? Same again. The amount of time a news story is on the Web? Yes. Stock market movements? Uh huh.

This is why the complexity theory approach is so powerful. It reaches beyond the details of the kiwi, the person or the web page to identify deep and influential principles of organisation at work 'behind the scenes'. Science writer Mark Buchanan reiterates what we stressed in the last chapter: 'In complex systems, it is often not the character of the individual parts of a network that matter most, but the overall order – or lack of order – dwelling within it. Figuring out how a system works is more about focusing on the laws that govern how the agents in the system interact with each other, rather than concentrating on the agents themselves.'[9]

The existence of small worlds, superconnectors and the power law phenomenon provide insights into how complex systems operate. These superconnectors are key to complex adaptive systems acting in small world ways. They are the means by which information is transmitted in a system like a company or a society, greatly enhancing the flow of ideas. We'll come back to these concepts in Chapter Eleven, where we discuss New Zealand's ability to capture the best ideas.

Rule Two: Equilibrium is bad; change is always necessary

The Great Pyramid at Giza is one of the seven wonders of the ancient world. It's easy to see why it made it onto that list. Containing two and a half million blocks of stone, some weighing seventy tons and none weighing less than two, this monument continues to baffle engineers around the world. Those Egyptians could certainly build. Completed in 2589 BC after twenty years of construction, the pyramid rises to a height of one hundred and forty-six metres (which puts it above all but two of New Zealand's buildings, Auckland's Sky Tower and the Vero Centre).[10] While no two sides of the pyramid are identical in length, the distance between the longest and shortest side is only 19.8 centimetres. The four corners form almost perfect right angles. The outside blocks are finished to a tolerance of plus or minus 0.025 of a millimetre.[11] Egyptian society was impressive enough to construct such remarkable structures when most other human settlements at the time consisted of small wooden or clay huts.

Underpinning Egyptian civilisation was an intricate system. At its core was a long thin strip of land along the Nile, never more than a few kilometres wide. This strip accounted for most of the country's food production. The Nile floods annually from June to October, watering the ground and replenishing the soil with a rich fertile layer of silt. To extend the thin strip of fertile land further, extensive irrigation systems were developed in order to cultivate greater tracts of desert land.[12] In fact, Egyptians depended so much on the irrigation and the high level of organisation and authority needed to maintain it that they considered their rulers, the pharaohs, gods. The power and effectiveness of these god-kings corresponded directly to Egypt's prosperity, which itself depended on the regularity of flooding and the effectiveness of the irrigation system.[13]

The people saw the pharaoh as responsible for the floods. As a result, his power and ability to control the local governors and priests in the various city-states would grow, and with it the people's faith in his divine provision. The Pharaoh's increased authority would bring the irrigation system under even tighter and more efficient control, which would further improve Egypt's agriculture, its food surpluses, its taxation revenue, and

. . . its ability to built big stone structures like the pyramids. This cycle would keep repeating itself as long as regular floods continued, and the extraordinary pyramids stand as a testament to the effectiveness of the system.

It was an effective system, yes. But it was also a delicate one. Four hundred years after Cheops built his pyramid, this great civilisation suddenly disintegrated into anarchy and utter chaos. The roots of the collapse were climatic. The onset of a Sahelian climate, a cyclical drought weather pattern particularly severe in East Africa, caused a sudden reduction in the Nile floods during the middle years of the twenty-second century BC.[14] Such was the extent of the drought that the Faiyum, a lake some sixty-five metres deep, dried up.

To a society so dependent on one source of water, the effect was nothing short of catastrophic. Famine gripped the country and paralysed the political institutions. The Old Kingdom collapsed. The last pharaoh of the Old Kingdom, Pepy II (Neferkare), died at the height of the food crisis, and within the span of twenty years after his death no fewer than eighteen kings and possibly one queen ascended the throne with only nominal control over the country.[15] The system collapsed. The Second Law – things breaking down – was winning.

But the underlying reason for the sudden collapse of Egyptian society wasn't the drought. Societies throughout history, even those more primitive than the Egyptians, have struggled with natural disasters and survived. No, the reason for Egypt's social implosion was its inflexibility. The whole system worked well so long as nothing outside the ordinary occurred. Egypt discovered that what the Nile giveth, the Nile taketh away. When the floods stopped, the cycle reversed and Egyptian society unravelled at the seams. The entire society prospered on the back of the Nile's regular flooding, but ultimately became utterly beholden to it.

This idea is captured in the little-known, but important, law of cybernetics called the Law of Requisite Variety. It states that the survival of any system depends on its capacity to *cultivate* (not just tolerate) variety. Failure to do so will result in an inability to cope successfully with variety when is introduced externally.

For example, fish in a bowl can swim, breed, obtain food with minimal effort, and remain safe from predators. But, as goldfish owners know all too well, such fish are excruciatingly sensitive to the slightest perturbations. Fish in the sea, by contrast, have to work much harder to sustain themselves, and they are subject to many threats. But because they cope with more variation, they are more robust when faced with change.[16]

The phenomenon is certainly true in isolated ecosystems. A thousand years ago most native New Zealand birds had no predators. They were completely ill-equipped, then, to handle the arrival of humans a few centuries later. The New Zealand swan, the South Island goose, the North Island goose, the Eyles' harrier, the North Island adzebill, the New Zealand crow, the New Zealand owlet-nightjar, the blue-billed duck, the Stewart Island snipe and of course everyone's favorite, the moa – to name just a few – all threw in the towel in the face of human intervention in their environment. Australia, similarly isolated, lost eighty per cent of its biodiversity in just two hundred years.[17] Hawai'i lost eighty per cent of its native birdlife in similar circumstances. Isolated, blissful equilibrium sounds good in theory, but it can end up proving fatal when things change.

Equilibrium is associated with balance – a good thing, surely. At an individual level, equilibrium occurs when an organism matches the requirements of its environment while meeting its own needs with the available resources. But when an unexpected event abruptly alters the stable environment (the floods dry up), that which had remained latent (the lack of alternative sources of water or food reserves) can suddenly become manifest. Coping mechanisms (the right people and strategies) that have atrophied during the long period of equilibrium usually prove inadequate to the new challenge.

We'll see later that this phenomenon happens in organisations all the time: successful strategies in one environment prove inadequate when the environment changes. David Snowden, director of IBM's Cynefin Centre for Organisational Complexity in Cardiff, Wales, points out that it can lead to 'the entrainment of thinking'. Ideas and practices that have proven effective in the past become akin to accepted norms; they acquire inertia, and often for a very good reason.

We naturally cling to ideas that have worked before. 'We do this in order to survive,' says Snowden. 'But this pattern of behaviour also leads to serious maladaptation in times of rapid change and crisis; it is most dangerous precisely during those moments of discontinuity that define the critical episodes of change in most complex systems. We need to dip people into chaos on a regular basis.'[18] Such frequent disruption-by-design of behavioural patterns keeps individuals and organisations alert and responsive to a changing environment.

Equilibrium can be hazardous. Why? Because the environment in which complex adaptive systems exist (be it an organism, an ecosystem, an organisation, or a society) is always changing. At times, the environment is turbulent. Prolonged equilibrium dulls senses and saps the ability of an adaptive system to rouse itself in the face of danger.

So innovations rarely emerge from systems with high degrees of order and stability. Systems in equilibrium lose diversity and give rise to the sorts of problems one encounters in homogenous communities and centrally planned economies. On the other hand, completely chaotic systems – riots, stock market crashes, revolutions – are not that great either. The key is to find that spot where disequilibrium breeds vitality and creativity, but doesn't do so at the expense of all order and structure. We'll focus on how New Zealand can achieve that in Part Four of the book.

This spot is the 'edge of chaos', a term coined by the physicist Norman Packard.[19] He uses it to describe a state of untidy creativity, between rigidity and chaos. In this zone, the system is best able to function, adjusting constantly to a turbulent world, but without traumatic upheaval. Systems operating at the edge of chaos are excellent information processors and are highly creative. They are sensitive to slight changes in external conditions and internal events, generating innovative responses to these which adapt or evolve to suit the current environment. 'The ghost in nature's machine,' he writes, 'almost seems to be purposefully piloting the system to the edge of chaos.'[20]

Think of the dynamic that occurs when you approach an intersection. The orange traffic light plays a similar role, triggering a motorist's response: apply the brakes, or accelerate through the intersection. The yellow light is analogous to the edge of chaos. It stimulates heightened awareness and generates a burst of adrenaline and mental activity. The same reaction occurs as we get closer to a deadline. Most of us find ourselves significantly more productive (and panic-stricken) as the deadline looms, having cruised along in equilibrium doing nada for too long. A slightly messy office is a productive one; rollicking families are happy; economies flourish under scant regulation. The edge of chaos, but not quite chaos itself.

It's where productive agitation runs high, innovation thrives and breakthroughs occur. It's the place this book argues New Zealand should be. A dynamic, innovative, creative society that is comfortable changing.

Of course, theories about superconnectors, power laws and the edge of chaos are all well and good. But how do they help us build a better New Zealand? To answer that question, let's now take these fairly abstract ideas and put them into the broader context of how societies prosper.

It all comes down to adaptation

Robert Fitzroy was New Zealand's second governor. His was not a happy governorship. He had the impossible task of protecting Maori rights while trying to satisfy the new settlers' thirst for land. Given negligible resources, his governorship came to a sorry end when he was dismissed from his post in 1847 after four tough years in the job, and he was sent back to Britain. This encounter with New Zealand would be his last. But it had not been his first. He had first visited New Zealand in 1836, and enjoyed Christmas in Paihia. At that time he was captain of a vessel called the *Beagle*, and on board was his official dining companion, Charles Darwin.

It was on this voyage of the *Beagle* that Darwin formulated his theory of evolution – the theoretical key to our understanding of the adaptation that occurs in biology. Yet while Darwin's discovery of what has been called 'the single best idea that anyone has ever had' is well known, he initially seemed reluctant to divulge it. After journeying around the world on HMS *Beagle*, he locked his Galapagos notes away, fathered ten children and devoted almost eight years to writing an extensive thesis on barnacles. Finally, fifteen years after his overseas voyage, he produced the true fruits of his labour: *On the Origin of Species in the Struggle for Natural Selection, or the Preservation of Favoured Races in the Struggle for Life*. Published in 1859, it sold out on its first day, even at the hefty cover price of fifteen shillings.

What Darwin realised while observing the turtles and finches on the Galapagos Islands was the simple notion that life was a perpetual struggle and that natural selection was the means by which some species prospered while others failed. This 'descent with modification' idea, as Darwin liked to refer to his theory (he rarely used the word evolution), is a delightfully simple, if controversial, one.

Darwin's discovery was that all organisms competed for resources, and those that had some innate advantage would prosper and pass on that advantage to their offspring. By such means, Darwin reasoned, species would continuously improve. Evolution, then, was a combination of probabilities. Those that had genetic – that was, inheritable – characteristics that were useful would, on balance, survive and reproduce more successfully than others. The more intense the pressures from the environment and the greater the competition for survival, the more likely it was that rapid evolutionary change would occur.

Consider the bombardier beetle. As Robert Wright points out in *Non Zero*, since there was a time when beetles didn't exist, there must have been a time when no animals were specially adapted to kill and eat them.[21] When beetles came along, various animals did acquire, by natural selection, the means to kill and eat them.

This threat spurred a response in the beetle: the bombardier beetle's chemical weapons technology.[22] In one compartment, the beetle carries a harmless chemical mix. In another resides a catalyst. The beetle adds the catalyst to the mix to create a scalding substance that it can then spray on tormentors. This proved effective against predators until, sure enough, skunks and a species of mice evolved specialised abilities to neutralise the effect of the spray and eat the beetles. It's back to the drawing board for the beetle.

Selection pressures like these constantly enforce an ecological upgrade. It's this ongoing to-and-fro, punch and counterpunch. Evolution is really a highly powerful strategy for finding innovative solutions to complex problems. It's a learning algorithm that adapts to changing environments and accumulates knowledge over time. It is a formula responsible for all the order, complexity and diversity of the natural world.

The question is, then, do the same principles that determine which species survive also govern the prosperity of societies? The short answer is 'yes'. The two processes do have common dynamics. At some basic level, social change and biological evolution share the same machinery.

It is this evolutionary process that is responsible for the diverse cultures we see in the world today. National Geographic Society anthropologist Wade

Davis contrasts diversity of the bio-sphere with that of the ethnosphere, the sum total of all thoughts and dreams, myths, ideas, inspirations, and intuitions brought into being by the human imagination since the dawn of consciousness. Each culture, from the Maori to the Masai, is an innovative solution to the complex problem of surviving in the environment. It's an evolution-guided strategy for making a thermodynamic profit in the frozen foothills of the Himalayas or the sunburnt plains of the Kalahari.

Herbert Simon, the Nobel laureate, also explains the develpment of human society in evolutionary terms. It is, he suggests, analogous to the creation of niches in the biological world:

> If there is such a trend toward variety, then evolution is not to be understood as a series of tournaments for the occupation of a fixed set of environmental niches, each tournament won by the organism that is fittest for that niche. Instead, evolution brings about a proliferation of niches. The environments to which most biological organisms adapt are formed mainly of other organisms, and the environments to which human beings adapt, mainly of other human beings. Each new bird or mammal provides a niche for one or more new kind of flea. Vannevar Bush wrote of science as an 'endless frontier'. It can be endless, as can be the process of design and the evolution of human society, because there is no limit on diversity in the world.[23]

In human society, a similar process creates what the anthropologist Grant McCracken calls plentitude: the 'sheer number and variety of social species', and of their technological, artistic, cultural, institutional and intellectual equivalents. But it's not easy to survive in your niche. The struggle for any culture is as intense as it is for the bombardier beetle. That explains why in the turbulent, fast-changing world of today, many cultures are disappearing as ancestral land and languages disappear. Fifty per cent of the world's six thousand languages are no longer taught to children. In fact, according to Davis, every two weeks an elder dies and carries with them to the grave the last syllables of an ancient tongue.

Under such pressure preserving information about what works and what does not, seems fundamentally important. For organisms, this is the role of the genes – to act as information databases about strategies that work. As we have discussed, genes are encoded in the organism's genetic material (usually DNA), and control the physical development and behaviour of the organism. This information is then passed on to the organism's offspring during reproduction. In effect, the survival strategies of one generation are handed down to the next.

DNA, then, is the blueprint for construction of the organism. But as Robert Wright explains, DNA isn't just data; it is a data *processor*.[24] Long after a human being has been 'built', the DNA in each cell continues to absorb information from its environment – adjusting a child's skin hue to the intensity of sunlight, for example. It is this information processing that governs the direction that grass grows. The grass-stalk heads upwards instead of downwards because its cell surfaces have sensed which direction holds more light and heat, and conveyed data reflecting that fact to the DNA, which then deploys signals that govern growth. At all levels of any organism, information guides energy in ways that build structure.

Information is the key to channelling energy into effective means of building structure in human society as well. Where biological organisms transform energy into order, human societies and individuals transform information into knowledge and new physical, economic, and social structures. Frmom the chief issuing instructions on the construction of a hut to the sophisticated computer models used to build sky-scrapers, to the maintenance of corporations and armies, information processing is at work.

Information is the glue that binds a society together. Our collection of individuals, grouped together into the New Zealand society of individuals, actually has a common gene pool, or 'meme pool' (to use the famous evolutionist Richard Dawkins' term). This meme pool we refer to is not the DNA inside our cells, per se, so much as 'ways of thinking or behaving'. Just as genes pass from generation to generation, ideas – memes – may do the same.

These ideas manifest themselves in a society's culture. What some people think of as high culture – the work produced by the Colin McCahons, Kiri Te Kanawas and Keri Hulmes of the world – is only a small part of the vast spectrum of skills, values, traditions and unarticulated habits of thought and action encompassed within New Zealand's culture. So, as New Zealanders, we have far more points of commonality beyond sharing the same international dialling code.

Our New Zealandness is also more than something we get pumped up about at the odd sporting fixture. It's more than that to which we have a sentimental attachment, or on which we base our identity. Our New Zealand culture is our particular way of accomplishing the things that make life possible. It's our way of adapting to the world around us. It's our method of prospering. So at every stage of a society's history, a certain view of the world, a collective mentality, dominates. This mentality dictates a society's attitudes, guides its choices, confirms its prejudices and directs its actions. As historian Fernand Braudel notes, a society's reactions to the events of the day, to the pressure upon it, to the decisions it must face, are less a matter of logic or even self-interest than a response arising from the collective culture.[25]

The Columbia University anthropologist Marvin Harris is famous for his controversial theories on cultural materialism. Harris saw many cultural practices as originating from the physical environment in which a people lived. For example, in *Cows, Pigs, Wars, and Witches: The Riddles of Culture*, Harris looks at the Hindu ban on killing cows.[26] Absolutely necessary as a strategy for human existence, Dr. Harris contended: they are much more valuable for ploughing fields and providing milk than as a one-off steak dinner. 'Westerners think that Indians would rather starve than eat their cows,' he told *Psychology Today* in the 1970s. 'What they don't understand is that they will starve if they do eat their cows.'[27] Harris' point is that a society's culture is constructed out of the requirements of the environment.

Different environments lead to different cultures. Different cultures result in differences in social choices, economic efficiency and political structures.[28] These differences create variations in performance. The result is a world where huge differences in wealth are the rule, not the exception – even though the particular nations and peoples that are rich and those that are poor do not remain the same. Human history, at least as it is conventionally told, is one of the rise and fall of societies. Cities and nations come to the fore, and then yield to newcomers who are bypassed in turn by other newcomers.

Why, for example, had Britain alone produced more than forty per cent of the major inventions, discoveries and innovations in the world at the turn of the nineteenth century? What explained the US ability to produce more than eighty per cent of them by the middle of the twentieth century? In 1994, why did the thirty-six million overseas Chinese scattered around the world produce as much wealth as the one billion people living in China itself? Historian David Landes sums up the point like this: 'This world is roughly divided into three kinds of nations: those that spend lots of money to keep their weight down; those whose people eat to live; and those whose people don't know where their next meal is coming from.'[29]

Of course, while the disparities in wealth around the world are obvious, there is debate over what constitutes a 'successful society'. For the purposes of this book, the simplistic definition of a 'successful society' is one that has sufficient prosperity to meet the physical and material needs of its people in an equitable and sustainable way.

Questions about why one society should be more successful than another have occupied the minds of scholars for generations. The explanations are many and varied. From different perspectives, such eminent scholars as Max Weber, Arnold Toynbee, Samuel Huntington, Francis Fukuyama, Robert Kaplan and Thomas Sowell have seen culture as a major (but of course not the only) influence on a society's social, political and economic behaviour – and on its prosperity.

The power of this 'cultural capital' is never more evident than in those situations when it is removed. Stanford University's Thomas Sowell points to the destruction of the Roman Empire by invading barbarians as producing one of the most catastrophic retrogressions of peoples ever seen.[30] The physical deterioration of buildings, roads, drainage systems, and other physical infrastructure was accompanied by a breakdown in law and order, a political collapse in many countries, and a decline in education. Physical structures left perfectly intact by the Romans when they withdrew voluntarily from Britain in the fifth century AD began to deteriorate over time and were not repaired or replaced for centuries.

Why? Because the Britons, Sowell argues, lacked the cultural capital required for the maintenance, repair and replacement of those structures. Even after the Britons eventually could afford to use bricks again, centuries later, they had to import them bricks from Flanders bricks had not been produced in Britain since Roman times. As late as the nineteenth century, there was said to be no city in Europe whose water supply was as dependable as it had been in Roman times. To Sowell, 'this tragic retrogression is a sobering reminder of the enormous importance of a society's cultural capital as compared to the isolated "ability" of individuals or even the efforts and talents of a whole generation'. What post-Roman Europe lacked was an ability to tap into the great store of know-how that Roman society had accumulated.[31]

The high-tech collection of companies that exists around Silicon Valley in California today has nothing to do with big deposits of silicon. It has to do with the famous Palo Alto Research Center, the location of Stanford University nearby, and the entrepreneurism of a young man named Hewlett and another called Packard. Silicon Valley could sprout up almost anywhere. What allowed Silicon Valley to spring up and produce enormous wealth, when there were no natural advantages to doing so? Cultural capital.

It's at work everywhere. Singapore sits on only seven hundred square kilometres of earth (0.3 per cent the size of New Zealand), and lacks just about every natural resource conceivable – it even has to import water from Malaysia, something New Zealand will never have to worry about doing. Yet its 4.5 million citizens are on the right trajectory to become amongst the wealthiest in the world.

This prosperity isn't derived from plugging the ground for oil, nor from providing a tax haven for multinational corporations. Instead it comes from harnessing its strategically positioned port and building world-beating industries, from electronics to chemicals, to mechanical engineering, and biomedical sciences manufacturing. The beating heart of this little tiger is the cultural capital of its people – their attitude to work, to growth, to innovation and to creativity, and so on. If the Singapore model doesn't appeal, try the Irish or the Finnish version.

A society's culture is the engine that drives its adaptability. The ideas, norms, values, interactions, and the host of other components that can be considered part of a society's cultural capital play a huge role in determining its prosperity. So what New Zealanders are like as a people – how innovative we are, how hard we work, whether we applaud success or belittle it, whether we confront tough choices or avoid them – feeds directly into our country's fate.

Irrespective of which political party is in power, or how isolated we are, or how small we are, or what our climate is like, or what our relationship with Australia or America has become, or any of the other reasons that are trotted out to explain our current performance, one thing is clear: it's New Zealand's culture that is ultimately our greatest strength or our heaviest burden. What we are like as a people is the ultimate determinant of our country's success in the longer term.

Let me restate the argument of this chapter in a nutshell. Complex adaptive systems like New Zealand society are governed by a series of rules like the Power Law, self-organisation, and ongoing creativity at the 'edge of chaos'. These rules help determine the system's ability to adapt. Adaptation is key for organisms and societies for neither exist in static, unchanging environments. They must continually change and respond.

New Zealand's prosperity in the future – amidst all the complexity and turmoil it faces – depends a lot on how adaptable its society is. Just how well New Zealand adapts in turn depends upon its cultural capital – the *sort* of society it is. Boil it all down and New Zealand's culture – our New Zealandness – is a huge part of the country's future success, or failure.

The remainder of this book will address the question: what should New Zealand be like? In answering this question, the book will focus on the extent to which New Zealand's culture exhibits three characteristics that are vital to a society's success:

- **Ingredient One**:
  An ability to generate lots of useful ideas – 'creativity'
- **Ingredient Two**:
  An ability to capture the useful ideas of others – 'connectivity'
- **Ingredient Three**:
  A willingness to absorb new ideas – 'flexibility'

The enxt chapter provides an introduction to each ingredient. As we'll see, while some societies throughout history have applied them well, others haven't. We can glean lessons from the results of each. It is to these examples from history that we now turn.

6

What Peter the Great learnt from the Dutch

If you wander into the marketplace of Zaandam, a northern Dutch town, you'll find a rather strange statue. It's not that of a famous Zaandamite, or even of a renowned Dutchman. The stone figure is, strangely enough, Peter the Great of Russia. Just why Peter warrants a monument in an otherwise unremarkable Dutch town requires some explanation.

Peter the Great was Russia's tsar for forty-three years, from the later seventeenth to the early eighteenth century. One of Russia's most famous rulers, Peter introduced a series of sweeping reforms aimed at modernising Russia. He reorganised the army. He founded the navy. He restructured the taxation system and reformed the Orthodox Church. Of course, Peter also did what all monarchs of the time tended to do: he built himself an enormous palace (the Peterhof, a grand palace near St Petersburg). In 1696, however, he did something other monarchs would have considered rather strange. He left Russia incognito for a two-year overseas experience in Europe.

Rather than spending his time serving drinks at the local pub, Peter used his OE to study various Western European countries. Russia was something of a laggard at the time, so Peter decided to investigate what more economically advanced countries were doing. This tsar-sabbatical took him to Austria, France, England and Holland, and only came to an end in 1698 when he had to sprint home to crush a rebellion.

It was while Peter was in Holland that he visited Zaandam where, remarkably, he spent four months working as a carpenter in the town's famous shipbuilding yards. He did this not to earn some extra cash, but because Zaandam's shipyards were at the forefront of Holland's shipbuilding industry. And Holland's shipbuilding industry was considered the finest in the world. Peter thought that if you wanted to learn about constructing a world-class navy, there could be no better place to start than Zaandam.

This raises an interesting question: how did one of Europe's smallest countries end up producing an industry of such renown that a world leader was prepared to spend four months hammering nails just to learn about it? It's a good question, and one to which I don't profess to know the entire answer. But the thesis of this book, and the focus of this chapter, is that a big chunk of Holland's success can be put down to three critical attributes of Dutch society. We'll discuss each briefly in this chapter, and then in Part Four of the book we'll look at how New Zealand can build these attributes in its own society. But before we get to any of that, let's get a taste of what seventeenth-century Dutch success looked like. Because back then, the land of tulips and windmills was humming.

The dynamic Dutch

The seventeenth century is considered to have been Holland's golden age, and with good reason: the Dutch Republic was then among the most important countries in Europe. An economic superpower, it built a far-flung colonial empire and achieved unmatched prosperity. As historian David Landes explains, 'they became the most important trading centre of Northern Europe; they hunted whales near Svalbard, traded spices with India and Indonesia (via the Dutch East India Company, the first company to issue shares) and started colonies in Brazil, New Amsterdam (now New York), South Africa and the West Indies'.[1] Holland's ports linked an enormous European hinterland to the Atlantic and beyond to become the ultimate destination of cargoes from new worlds overseas. The ships might call first at Lisbon and Seville, but they completed their voyages in the Netherlands. There the cargoes were absorbed, processed, and redistributed throughout the world. The Dutch had created what historian Simon Schama has called an 'embarrassment of riches'.[2]

The Dutch also achieved some remarkable military victories against significantly larger nations. When William of Orange entered England in 1688 the Dutch fleet assembled that September was four times the size of the Spanish Armada. According to one historian, 'when all dimensions are considered – military, naval, financial, logistical, diplomatic, domestic . . . it was arguably one of the most impressive feats of organisation any early modern regime achieved'.[3] Remarkable.

Remarkable, yes. Unexpected? Well . . . sort of. Unexpected certainly if you look at Holland's size. In 1500, the Dutch numbered about one million people; when Peter arrived, just over twice that.[4] By contrast England boasted a population of four million, and France sixteen million.[5] Nor could Holland muster any significant natural resources – no great forests, no great gold deposits. So on paper the odds were against Dutch greatness. But, as we've seen with Singapore, physical constraints don't need to condemn any society to insignificance if they're good at doing something else: adapting. As we saw in the last chapter, societies win when they out-adapt the competition. The Dutch did that in spades.

Nowhere was this dominance more evident than in ship building, the heart of Holland's commercial and military dominance. By 1636 there were at least 2500 seagoing ships in service. It has been said that the Dutch had more ships than England, France, Portugal, and Spain combined. So prolific were Dutch shipyards that in 1628–29 all the warships obtained for the French, Swedish and Danish navies were purchased from Holland. The Dutch could sell a ship at half the price a French shipyard could, and at an even greater discount than the domestic shipbuilders in Spain. And all this at a time when Dutch wages were higher than those of their competitors.

The key to Dutch shipbuilding expertise was a series of innovations. The invention of the camshaft and the crankshaft made it possible to use wind energy for a wide range of industrial purposes. The wind-driven sawmill was introduced in 1591. Wind power was also used to make other parts of the shipbuilding process less time-consuming, like the production of rigging, ropes, and canvas sails. The shipyards were also equipped with large cranes, which reduced the need for manpower and gave Holland a further advantage over its competitors.

Driving much of this innovation were leading Dutch scientists and engineers. Christiaan Huygens (1629–1695) was a prominent Dutch mathematician, physicist and astronomer who invented the pendulum clock, a major step towards exact timekeeping and measurement. Dutch hydraulic engineer Jan Leeghwater (1575–1650) – whose name, appropriately enough, translates as 'void of water' – added to Holland's land mass by using windmills to pump water out of various lakes.

Then there was Holland's dynamic culture. Holland may have been a small country, but it was also a potent one. In the seventeenth century, half the people lived in cities, a higher percentage than anywhere else in Europe. This fuelled the rapid exchange of ideas. The country buzzed with activity: an observer of early-seventeenth-century Holland noted that Dutch roads and waterways were as crowded as those of Rome.[6] Holland became the first bourgeois society, dominated by merchants, not the nobility. It was the land of Rembrandt, Vermeer, Hals, and scores of other renowned painters.

All of this was accomplished without some heavy-handed centralised authority conducting the show from above. Like the dynamic 'bottom up' systems we discovered earlier, Holland was a highly decentralised society. Each province handled the levying of taxes in its own way, and there was no central currency. There was also no uniformity in laws, no common judiciary and no supreme court of appeal. The army was united under the command of a Captain-General, but each province tended to regard the regiments that it paid as its own. The navy was divided into regional components without any central authority. Like all successful complex adaptive systems, Holland's dynamism and success was bubbling up from below without a lot of central control stifling the people's willingness to change.

Furthermore, because the Dutch were such dab hands at international commerce, they became very internationally oriented. This led to a renowned tolerance towards minority views and interests. It was easy for foreigners to travel or even emigrate (often as refugees) to Holland. Dutch cities became melting pots. Jews from Portugal and Belgium fled the zealots of the Spanish Inquisition and became successful entrepreneurs and scientists in their adopted homeland. Philosophers like Baruch Spinoza and René Descartes first published their most famous works in Holland. Many of Holland's most creative and innovative people were those rejected by other nations.

In this context, then, Peter's four months of manual labour in Zaamdam's shipyards begins to make sense. What Peter would have seen was that Holland's defeat of the English, its centrality to international trade, its far-flung empire, and its predominance in shipbuilding were no flukes. No country Holland's size and with as few natural resources could accomplish such feats by chance. Rather, the Dutch had created a society uniquely positioned to adapt.

In seventeenth-century Holland we can see what a great adapting society looks like. It gained much of its competitive advantage in shipbuilding by creatively developing some of the latest technologies in ship construction. It was hungry for new ideas and skills, and therefore encouraging of diversity and creativity. The Dutch were willing to discard ideas and ways of doing things that no longer made sense as the world around them changed. Holland's accomplishments illustrate just what a small, under-resourced country can achieve if it gets the elements of adaptation right.

We can identify three primary ingredients in a society honed for adaptation:

- **Creativity in its veins**: great at generating new ideas
- **A thirst for new ideas**: great at seeking out the ideas of others
- **A willingness to change**: great at absorbing new ideas

This chapter will explore each of these ingredients in turn, primarily by looking throughout history at examples of the good, the bad and the ugly.

Ingredient One: Creativity in its veins

In the spring of 1453, Mehmed II, the twenty-one-year-old Sultan of the Ottoman Empire, gazed at the great city of Constantinople, the capital of the Byzantine Empire. To Mehmed, Constantinople (present-day Istanbul) represented a singular threat to his empire, strategically placed as it was between the Black and Aegean seas. He had mustered an enormous army of 150,000 soldiers, who were now arrayed on the plains surrounding the city. And yet despite his sizeable army, Turkish chronicles tell of the nights in his tent when Mehmed, obsessed and incapable of rest, kept drawing plans and inventing schemes to destroy the besieged city.[7]

The cause of his angst was Constantinople's walls, the most formidable system of defence in Europe. Over the centuries, these walls had thwarted attempts by the Arabs, Avars, Bulgars, Russians, Pechenegs and Persians to take the city. Even the formidable Attila the Hun had attempted, and failed, to breach the city's walls. Now the head of the Byzantine empire, Emperor Constantine XI, was ensconced behind the walls of Constantinople along with his small army of just 7000 soldiers.

Constantinople's stone defences consisted of an inner wall eleven metres high with towers at intervals of about seventy-five metres; a lower outer wall also furnished with towers; and a moat. About sixty-five kilometres west of Constantinople stood the Long Wall, designed to defend the city from attack from that direction. Over forty-five kilometres long, extending from Selymbria to the Black Sea, the wall was 3.3 metres thick and stood at over five metres. The sea front of the city was also defended by a large sea wall that, while not as sizeable as the other walls, was enough to seriously hinder a seaborne invasion. Across the harbour itself was strung a massive iron chain to prevent enemy ships from entering.

Faced with such formidable obstacles, Mehmed realised that the walls couldn't be stormed. The defeat of countless attacking armies in previous centuries had shown that. The only solution was to knock them down. And unlike previous assailants, Mehmed had a new technology – heavy artillery – that would allow him to do it. At about the time this realisation was dawning on him, a skilled Hungarian gun-founder named Orban, was to Mehmed's great good fortune, scouting around looking for someone prepared to pay more for his skills than his current employer, Emperor Constantine. Dissatisfied with the pay he received from the Byzantines, he had strolled over to the Turkish camp to offer his skills.

Recognising the value of what this wandering mercenary offered, Mehmed welcomed the renegade most generously, commissioning him to produce a gun of great size. Orban obliged.[8] The gun that rolled onto the battlefield in May of 1453 was eight metres long and weighed five hundred kilograms. It required a hundred and forty oxen just to move it, more than a hundred men to manoeuvre it, and two hours to reload. When it was finally ready for action, it could send a cannon ball of nearly half a tonne over 1.6 kilometres. The noise it made when fired, chroniclers tell us, caused pregnant women to miscarry. It would remain, by far, the biggest gun to be built for many years. It was also probably the biggest failure. It cracked on the second day of the siege and went permanently out of order on the fourth or fifth day when it exploded, killing Orban and many of the crew.

Fortunately Mehmed's army had smaller-calibre artillery, and for weeks they continued relentlessly to batter the walls. In the words of a witness, Nicolo Barbaro, the Ottomans fired their cannon again and again, 'with so many other guns and arrows without number . . . that the air seemed to split apart'.[9] The high masonry walls made an easy target for long-range enemy guns. The Byzantine defenders fought off Ottoman attempts to assault the inner defences by day, and crept forward to fill in the widening holes with rubble and palisades by night.

Eventually, through some ingenious work by Mehmed's engineers, the seaward defence was breached. Unable to force a passage through the chain and past the Byzantine warships guarding the harbour, Mehmed ordered his engineers to bypass the chain by hauling the ships overland and into the harbour. Using greased windlasses and buffalo teams, the first ships made the trip on the night of April 22, 1453. The next morning the defenders awoke to find a squadron of Ottoman vessels in their harbour. Constantinople's fate was sealed.

As Ottoman soldiers appeared behind those defending the inner wall, the defence swiftly collapsed. Word spread that the defences had been breached and panic ensued. Legend has it that Constantine led a final mounted charge against the enemy. He cast off the imperial cloak and insignia that identified him as Emperor, for he wished to die a common soldier's death. With his demise the final curtain fell on the Roman Empire. Constantine was the last, but certainly not the least, of the sons of Romulus.

Constantinople's fall to Mehmed's forces marked, for many historians, the end of the Middle Ages. It certainly marked the end of the castle. What had once been the ultimate defence against an attacking enemy – the product of a thousand years of evolution in warfare – was rendered impotent by this new technology, the cannon. At about the same time that Mehmed was blowing Constantinople's walls apart, the French were using similar technology to reclaim Normandy from the English. In 1450, following the cannon's French debut at the Battle of Formigny, the home team captured some sixty castles, cities and fortresses in the space of a year, the average siege lasting only six days – a sizeable improvement over the months and years of earlier sieges.[10] So effective were the new cannon that many places politely asked for the terms of surrender as soon as the French rolled their guns onto the field. By 1453 the English were completely driven out of France, never to return.

Put in evolutionary terms, the castle species was out-adapted. While attempts were made to design castles in the fifteenth and sixteenth centuries with artillery in mind, the castle as a defensive structure was finished.

As their defensive value plummeted, many castles were abandoned and fell into ruin through simple neglect. From that point on, every monarch holed up in a castle must have realised that new strategies would be required to counter the threat posed by the cannon. The Byzantines had been out-adapted by the Ottomans, and the hide-in-the-castle strategy of the past wasn't going to cut it any more.

The ability to out-innovate is as innate to survival for organisms as it is for societies. Whether it is the chemical-weapon capability of the bombardier beetle, which we met in the previous chapter, or the helmet that makes the water flea indigestible to a predator, nature has used the development of new technologies as the cornerstone for success in the evolutionary arms race. Indeed, some of our most common technologies have already been developed by other species to aid in the evolutionary struggle. The elephant-snout fish is only one species of fish that can create electric fields to sense disturbances, rather like a burglar alarm. Rattlesnakes invented infrared sensors for night vision. Bats and dolphins were using sonar well before Robert Rines developed it for human use.[11] Why are all these innovations so powerful and so prone to ongoing invention? For the simple reason that they provide those who possess them with greatly improved chances of survival.

But let's be clear. This adaptive edge isn't restricted to technologies. It encompasses the entire set of ideas upon which the progress of human society depends. From the invention of new technologies to improvements in our understanding of nature or philosophy, to the increase in the efficiency of a production process, they're all new ideas. It's this generation of new ideas that we'll call creativity.

Economic historians and economists, such as Joel Mokyr and Paul Romer, argue that creativity underlies *all* economic advancement. The rise of agriculture 10,000 years ago, the advent of trade and specialisation millennia later, the rise of industrialisation in the 1700s, and the formation of modern organisation in the late 1800s and early 1900s, are all examples of new ideas harnessed for progress.[12] As creativity expert Richard Florida from Carnegie Mellon University says, economic history could be interpreted as a succession of new and better ways to harness creativity – a calling forth of new ideas, putting them into action and rewarding them.[13] Creativity, then, is essential to the way we live and work, and it always has been. It manifests itself in story-telling, in art, in humour, in religion-building, in theory-construction, in problem-solving, in technological innovation, and in a myriad other ways.

We see new ideas reflected in lots of places. One of the most common is in the legal protections afforded new ideas through patents, trademarks and copyrights. Florida drew out the implications of patent applications in an *Atlantic Quarterly* article 'The World is Spiky'. The World Intellectual Property Organization recorded about 370,000 patents from resident inventors in more than a hundred countries in 2004. Over half of them went to American and Japanese inventors. Seventy-four per cent went to the residents of Japan, the US, South Korea, the European Union, and China.[14]

Where the patents come from, Florida notes, says less about the creativity of the people, and more about the creativity of the environment. In 2005 India had three hundred and eighty-four patents registered at the US Patent Office and China had four hundred and two. The University of California alone generated more than either country. IBM accounted for four times as many as the two combined. This is not to say that Indians and Chinese are not innovative. Au contraire, says Florida. He cites research by AnnaLee Saxenian, of the University of California at Berkeley, that has shown that Indian and Chinese entrepreneurs founded or co-founded roughly thirty per cent of all Silicon Valley start-ups in the late 1990s.[15]

But, Florida points out, these creative people had to travel to Silicon Valley and be absorbed into its innovative environment before their ideas gained traction. Such environments matter, and there aren't many of them. Tokyo, Seoul, New York and San Francisco remain the front-runners in the patenting competition. Boston, Seattle, Austin, Toronto, Vancouver,

Berlin, Stockholm, Helsinki, London, Osaka, Taipei and Sydney are right up there too. The question is, can we add Wellington, Christchurch or Greymouth to that list?

It's important that we try to. For it is the creative capacity of human beings that is at the heart of a society's prosperity. According to Harvard University's John Harrison, what makes prosperity happen is 'our ability to imagine, theorise, conceptualise, experiment, invent, articulate, organise, manage, solve problems, and do a hundred other things with our minds and hands that contribute to the progress of the individual and of humankind. Natural resources, climate, geography, history, market size, government policies and many other factors influence the direction and pace of progress, he argues. 'But the engine is human creative capacity.'[16] It's that which turns the sand on the beach into semiconductors.

The fifteenth-century Ottomans and the seventeenth-century Dutch were able to win, whether in trade or in war, because they were at the forefront of the latest innovations. The innovations gave them the edge over their competitors. Out-creating was key to their successful adaptation as a society in the changing, volatile, complex world in which they lived. But the story doesn't end at that point. There are a couple of nuances to the creativity message that are worth exploring further.

Applying creativity

Having the idea is one thing. Applying it effectively is quite another. At Constantinople there wasn't a mismatch in technologies. The Byzantines also had cannon. They would fire them from their walls at the attacking Ottomans. But their effect was limited, for they could only take pot-shots at the Ottoman army sprawled near and far outside the gates of their city. In fact, the damage to the walls caused by the recoil of his guns made Constantine's artillery only marginally helpful at best. By contrast, as we've seen, the cannon proved a devastating weapon for the Ottomans. It was the same technology, but the potency of the cannon varied greatly in how each side used it. The Ottomans adapted it best to their use. They out-innovated.

This is a lesson repeated throughout history. On 14 October 1066, the Anglo-Saxons, led by King Harold, fought the invading Norman army under the command of Duke William of Normandy, near Hastings in

England. On the face of it the defending Anglo-Saxon army should have won. They had just ridden from an impressive victory against the invading Norwegians, and now held the advantage of the elevated position, with steep cliffs protecting their flanks. They outnumbered the Normans,[17] and had the psychological home-ground advantage, fighting to repel invaders of their homeland.

Yet the outcome was never really in question: this was a battle, as historian Lynn White describes it, between the military methods of the seventh century and the technologically advanced military methods of the eleventh century. While Harold and his army fought valiantly, William held the initiative with his bowmen and cavalry – two technologies the Anglo-Saxons didn't use. The English could do nothing but stand and resist a mobile striking power that eventually proved irresistible. Once again, technology had triumphed over an enemy with significant battlefield advantages.[18]

But the story doesn't end there. As with the battle for Constantinople, the Anglo-Saxons had access to the same technology as the Normans. But unlike Constantine, who used the technology but ineffectively, the Anglo-Saxons simply chose not to use the technology at all. They even had it available to them on the battlefield, but they didn't think of deploying it as part of their military strategy. It was an extraordinary blunder that ended up costing them control of Britain.

One key technology in the battle was the stirrup, a ninth-century innovation that was revolutionising warfare throughout Europe. Before the introduction of the stirrup, the life of the warrior horseman was somewhat precarious in battle. Swordplay was very limited because, without stirrups, if you missed your intended victim, you usually found yourself falling at his feet. As for the spear, it was thrown or thrust with the strength of the arm.[19] Not completely useless, but not that effective either.

The stirrup changed all that as it effectively welded horse and rider into a single fighting unit capable of violence without precedent. The fighter's arm no longer delivered the blow, for now he could lay his lance at rest, held between the upper arm and the body, and deliver the blow with the combined weight of himself and his charging steed. The stirrup thus replaced human energy with animal power. Mounted shock combat was now possible, and it was used with devastating effect by those who chose to deploy it.[20]

The Anglo-Saxons did not have the excuse of never having seen coordinated cavalry attacks before. In fact, when they first invaded Britain in the mid-sixth century, the local British population used cavalry effectively against them. Then for the last two hundred years, they'd put up with the incessant raids of the Vikings, who also used cavalry extensively in their military campaigns throughout Britain. All of which raises the question: why did the Anglo-Saxons not learn from the enemy they encountered and establish a cavalry competency of their own (especially after the introduction of the stirrup made the horseman such a powerful fighting unit)? They had horses and they had stirrups. But they didn't use either in battle.

The Anglo-Saxons decided not to learn from their observation of other technologies, and it cost them. They all rode to the battle on their stirrup-equipped horses. But then they dismounted and went into battle on foot. They used bow and arrows to hunt, but decided to leave most of them at home when it came to fighting the Normans. Anglo-Saxon use of cavalry and archers could easily have been enough to turn the tide of battle in their favour. The Normans adopted the technologies successfully. The Anglo-Saxons refused to. They were out-innovated. They doomed themselves to innovation purgatory.

When opportunity knocks . . .

As the Anglo-Saxon experience shows us, creativity merely opens a door, it does not compel one to enter. Accepting or rejecting an invention, or the extent to which it is realised if it is accepted, depends as much on the condition of a society and the imagination of its leaders, as on the nature of the idea itself. How an idea is used, rather than the technology itself, is key to out-innovation.

But there is one innovation sin even worse than that committed by the Anglo-Saxons. A society can choose to actually wind the clock back on its development and lose the creativity advantage completely.

Andy Kessler tells the story of the British role in the birth of the computer.[21] During World War II, important Nazi communications were encoded with a secret cipher called Enigma. Central to the Allied effort in cracking the Nazi code was a chap called Alan Turing, a mathematician from Cambridge and then Princeton universities. From the famous Hut 8 at Bletchley Park, he figured out a way to speed up the manual decoding process. In March 1940, Turing constructed the Bombe, a machine that helped speed up the daily cracking of Enigma codes.

But Hitler and his high command weren't done. As early as 1940, they insisted on a tougher code, named Lorenz (which the British decided for some reason to call Tunny). Once this code was cracked the Hut 8 scientists constructed a new device called a Robinson to assist with the daily code-cracking. The Robinson could read 2000 characters a second – a significant jump on human reading speeds. But the British weren't finished either. Two Post Office engineers innovated again with a new machine that worked at more than double the speed of the Robinson. Called Colossus, this mighty machine was the most sophisticated computer of its time.

So by 1945, as the war came to a close, the British dominated the fledgling computer industry. With the German high-tech industry flattened under the rubble of its cities, and the US's first computer, the Electronic Numerical Integrator and Calculator, (a machine designed to run calculations for ballistic firing tables)still being assembled, the British owned the computer business. Britain had an opportunity to usher in the digital age, just as it had ushered in the industrial age two hundred years earlier with the likes of the cotton press and the steam engine.

As Andy Kessler points out, the British essentially had two options at this point.[22] The first was to take the Colossus architecture to every university and industrial company in Britain. Perhaps each might have built its own version. Over time, all the parts needed for the Colossus-class computers would have been made in Britain and her empire. The digital revolution might have happened in Britain. As Kessler says, the sun wouldn't have set on the British Empire – it would have remained encoded in the software of the world's computers.

But this didn't happen. Instead, the British took the second option. When the war ended, they destroyed the technology. That's right, they destroyed the technology. Worried that Russian spies would infiltrate Bletchley Park and steal the design of the Colossus for their own secret intelligence, they took a sledgehammer to all ten Colossus machines and burned the plans. The very existence of the Colossus was classified until the 1970s.

Destroying the Colossus was a costly mistake. Some paranoid bureaucrat cost Britain its shot at leading the coming computer and communications revolutions. It was as if Team New Zealand's innovative hull and rigging designs had been destroyed after we won the America's Cup in 1995 – in case Dennis Conner should get hold of them. It is no surprise, then, that there are few British names or inventions in subsequent stories about the computer. Technological leadership is hard-won, and easily lost.

Unfortunately New Zealand has dropped the ball on more than a few technologies. Take Colin Murdoch from Timaru. He'll be unfamiliar to many New Zealanders, but he shouldn't be. He is the man who designed and invented the disposable syringe, a device that has saved millions of human lives. Sufferers of diabetes depend on Murdoch's invention every day to administer their dose of insulin safely. He also conceived and developed the tranquilliser dart gun, which, in addition to saving the lives of millions of animals, was used to great comedic effect by Will Farrell in *Old School*.

Murdoch had first taken the disposable syringe idea to officials at the New Zealand Health Department and other government organisations. All said the syringes were too futuristic, the need for them too remote. The disposable automatic syringes were eventually patented worldwide and marketed through an Australian company, Tasman Vaccine Ltd.

That wasn't the only example of New Zealand government officials kicking Murdoch's great ideas offshore. In May 1966 he filed three patents at Wellington Patent Office for a silent burglar alarm, a new electrical wiring system and heat detection cells for fire. The three inventions combined to form a revolutionary silent burglar and fire alarm. The alarm worked by triggering off an automatic phone call to either or both the local police station and fire station, depending on what was necessary. Patents were approved and arrangements for manufacture in Japan were made. The alarms were designed to operate without any audible or visible activity unless the external telephone leads were cut, in which case an audible alarm was triggered. Alarms from Murdoch's design never went into production after authorities informed him that such a device would alter the balance of the electrical phone system. Now an alarm based on the same principle is the most popular burglar alarm system produced by global security firm Chubb Securities.

Out-innovating other societies doesn't need to mean out-inventing them. That is a subtle, but significant, difference. The Ottomans didn't invent gunpowder. The Chinese did. The Ottomans didn't invent the use of artillery in battle. The Europeans did. But it was the Ottomans who had the most formidable artillery. They had taken the inventions and innovations of others and moulded them to suit their purposes.

Invention is only half the battle. The fruits of any invention are only determined by how effective the technology becomes when applied. That's why lots of people in white coats doing fancy experiments is fine, but it's not enough in itself. How society uses them is equally, if not more, important. The Soviet Union had very strong science in some fields, but it wasn't coupled with strong institutions in the market. The upshot was that the benefits of discovery were very limited for the people living there.

The economist Joseph Schumpeter was among the first to distinguish between inventions and innovations. Schumpeter pointed out that entrepreneurs innovate, not just by figuring out how to use inventions, but also by introducing new means of production, new products, and new forms of organisation. These innovations, he argued, take just as much skill and daring as does the process of invention.

The ability to generate, then incorporate new ideas is the first ingredient for a society best able to adapt. Successful societies are not only good at generating new ideas, however; they're also able to soak up the ideas of others. To really get innovation humming societies also need to be great at adopting ideas and technologies from elsewhere.

Ingredient Two: A thirst for new ideas

If you had been standing on the hillside overlooking the harbour of Bombay in 1435 and then stood in the same spot again seventy-odd years later in 1498, you would have seen on both occasions the arrival of ships from the far corners of the earth. In 1435, you would have witnessed the extraordinary spectacle of over 300 Chinese ships rounding the headland. When the Portuguese arrived in 1498, their armada was considerably less noteworthy. Only two small ships glided in. The contrast couldn't have been more significant.

Equally different was the goal of the two voyages. The purpose of the visitors from the East was to provide an early version of shock and awe – and they certainly achieved that. The aim of the visitors from the West was to learn. The implications couldn't be more profound. Let's find out why.

Historians have long speculated why it was Europe, and not Asia, that launched the industrial revolution in the eighteenth century. How could China, India and the Near East – all homelands of great ancient empires – be so outclassed, technologically and economically, during the second half of the last millennium? Many possible explanations are put forward. One that is particularly compelling (to me at least) is that China was hamstrung by a series of decisions in the mid-fourteenth century that effectively slowed or stopped its rate of adaptation.

China's rate of adaptation to this point has been nothing short of remarkable. For centuries Europe lagged behind China's level of sophistication. The Chinese developed the modern horse collar in about 250 BC, an invention that took six hundred years to find its way to Europe. The idea of attaching a wheel to a stretcher and dispensing with the second bearer (that's right, a wheelbarrow) does not seem to have occurred to anyone in Europe before the twelfth century, whereas it was first used in China in AD 232. The Chinese used kites for manned flights well before Europeans thought of doing so (perhaps wisely). In military matters, the crossbow and the trebuchet were standard equipment in China centuries before their adoption in the West.

As we may again witness in the twenty-first century, the Chinese were also leaders in commercial innovation. As Robert Wright explains, by as early as the ninth century, tea merchants were using 'flying money' – a bit like traveller's cheques – to spare them the hassle of lugging copper coins around.[23] When the merchants who issued the cheques decided to invest some of the deposited money, banking began in China way before it came to Europe. By the early 1300s, the Chinese had built a water-powered spinning machine capable of producing a hundred and thirty pounds of thread a day. According to Wright, it was as advanced as any such machine that Europe would see for more than three hundred years.[24]

It was at the height of this prosperity that, in 1405, Admiral Zheng of the Chinese navy persuaded the Chinese emperor, Zhu Di, to finance the most extraordinary expedition the world had ever seen. He dispatched a fleet of three hundred and seventeen vessels, carrying 28,000 men – nearly twice the size of the Spanish Armada – to explore trade routes in southern Eurasia.

The largest of his ships, at about a hundred and sixty metres long (compare that with Captain Cook's *Endeavour* at a mere thirty-three metres), had nine staggered masts and twelve square sails of red silk. At four or five times the size of any ship in Europe, it was the largest vessel the world had seen. The fleet even included water tankers, to ensure a fresh supply for a month or more. In a three-year period, from 1404 to 1407, the Chinese built or refitted some 1680 ships – an armada beyond the comprehension of medieval Europe.[25] The voyage (manned, one historian notes, by a 'can-do group of eunuchs') was the first of seven expeditions. Over the next three decades Admiral Zheng's expeditions would reach India, Africa and the Persian Gulf.

As Zheng and his eunuchs were exploring distant lands, mutual awareness between China and Europe continued to grow. By the end of the thirteenth century, the Mongols had brought China into direct contact with Europe. It was no global village, for sure, but mutual awareness was now higher than in ancient times when, according to Wright, the Chinese thought cotton coming from the West was fleece from 'water sheep', and Romans thought their imported silk grew on silk trees.[26] The transmission of the Black Plague was the final sign that the world was slowly becoming global. When the Ming vanquished the dreaded Mongols in the late fourteenth century it should have been a glorious period for China, renewing local control after a century of barbarian rule. It presented an opportunity to import and export goods, technologies and ideas from elsewhere. The sea expedition boded well for the future.

But just as China was beginning to connect with the rest of the world, it made a startling decision. In 1433, the Ming suddenly retreated from big-time sailing. There was a new emperor, and a group of Confucian nobles who scorned commerce and detested the eunuchs who had carried out the maritime voyages. By 1500, it was a capital offence to go to sea in a two-masted ship without permission. Then in 1525, as a precursor to the Colossus decrypting machine debacle in Britain, coastal authorities were ordered to destroy all oceangoing ships and to arrest their owners. Finally, in 1551, it became a crime to go to sea at all on a multimasted ship, even for trade.[27]

The timing couldn't have been worse. For centuries, China exported good ideas, while Europe imported them. Now, just as Europe was kicking into gear with its Renaissance-inspired resurgence, China barred its gates. Just as China was putting its ships in dock, European boats were setting sail for the New World. China's decision cut it off from the lessons and novelties that European travellers would soon be bringing.

Through its exploration of the Americas, Africa, Europe and Australasia, Europe found a trove of precious resources and vast farmlands. The ensuing enrichment helped finance a burst of progress that pushed Europe into the lead during a crucial period of technological change.[28] By contrast, isolationism became China. It purred along for hundreds of years, impervious to the world passing it by. This unwillingness to acknowledge the value of other societies was evident in the attitude the Chinese showed on their voyages. They went to show themselves, not to see and learn. They were what they were.

The attitude of the Portuguese travellers who entered Bombay's harbour sixty-three years after the Chinese couldn't have been more different. For the Europeans the voyages were an opportunity to learn. Take these instructions given to Portugese explorer Diogo Lopes de Sequeira as he set off to explore Madagascar in 1508:[29]

- Enter and study every port, reconnoitre means of entry and exit, explore the possibilities of anchorage with reference winds, currents, and the nature of the bottom, and write all of this down
- First contact the natives: show them a range of articles and metals to see if these things are known to them
- Does the island have its own vessels, and if so, where do they go and what do they seek?
- What does the island produce, and what will the natives take for it?
- Political structure: How do the rulers live? How do they administer justice? What kind of state and dignity, and how do they maintain it? What military force and arms: elephants or horses, weapons, firearms, artillery of any kind?
- What are the customs? How is the land inhabited?

The contrast with the Chinese is striking. The Europeans didn't go to show and tell as the Chinese did. Their explorations were an opportunity to absorb the ideas of others. Good innovators and good imitators are both produced by a society in which practical values are held in high esteem. If something works, it does not matter where it came from. Typical of the European approach in this regard was the great explorer Leibniz, who implored a Jesuit travelling to China 'not to worry so much about getting things European to the Chinese, but rather about getting remarkable Chinese inventions to us; otherwise little profit will be derived from the Chinese mission.'[30]

It's of little surprise, then, that the number of inventions Europe is said to have borrowed from other cultures, in particular China, is large. Europeans appreciated useful knowledge regardless of the source. In the early Middle Ages, Europe borrowed techniques from other cultures the way an underdeveloped country today emulates the industrialised world. After 1500, iron suspension bridges, seed drills and porcelain were examples of Oriental ideas taken up by Europeans.

Innovation flows from openness to new ideas. We tend to think of the stirrup or the cannon as technological breakthroughs that occurred overnight. The reality is, however, that the vast majority of innovation is a gradual, incremental process. Isaac Newton once famously remarked that he stood on the shoulders of giants. A humble man, that Newton. But what he was saying, in essence, was true. Despite his genius, he was heavily reliant on others. Perhaps it's truer to say that most innovators are midgets standing atop a vast pyramid of other midgets. Innovations – the development of languages, technologies, artifacts and institutions – can be divided into many small steps, and during each step the changes are relatively modest. No single innovator, not even a Da Vinci, an Edison or a Newton, contributes more than a small part of the total.

New Zealand's most famous invention, the aeroplane, illustrates this point superbly. Nobody doubts the genius of the aeroplane's inventor, Richard Pearce (or Bamboo Dick as he was known). But when Pearce flew his self-built monoplane a hundred and forty metres into a gorse hedge on his Waitohi property (a full nine months ahead of the Wright brothers), he was simply the next in a long line of flight-fixated dabblers and experimenters.

Humans, after all, have dreamed of flying since at least the days when the myth of Daedalus was first told in ancient Greece three thousand years ago. But it would take many generations and many more ideas to turn flight from myth into reality. In the late fifteenth century, Leonardo da Vinci studied the motions of birds in flight and designed aeronautical-looking machines. In 1783 two Frenchmen designed a hot-air balloon and generously sent two friends drifting over Paris in the first manned long-distance flight.

In 1849 an Englishman called Sir George Cayley built a glider. Then a German, Otto Lillienthal – jumping from an enormous mound outside Berlin – made two thousand glider flights over a twenty-four hour period, carefully recording the result of each except the last, which killed him.

How much of that previous experimentation flowed into Richard Pearce's aircraft is anyone's guess. He was a reclusive man living in a small town in the world's most geographically isolated country. But reports suggest he was an avid subscriber to *American Scientist*, and was often seen reading it intently as he operated his plough. The idea that 'Bamboo Dick', genius that he was, could create from scratch that which had eluded countless others, seems improbable. His ingenuity was enough to push the collective efforts of thousands of others into the air, into the record books and into a hedge.

Typically, its many people spread over a wide area and prolonged period that contribute to human innovation. Individuals are smart, but most of the technologies we use, the languages that we speak and so on, are far too complex for even the smartest innovator to design from nothing. A complex item such as a plane or a watch does have an individual designer, but their creativity sits atop a mountain of previous attempts.

That's why isolation from other designers and formulators is a problem. Shut yourself away from others as the Chinese did, and you miss out on the small incremental steps necessary in the development of an innovation. It's tough on any society if it is solely reliant on its own ideas, no matter how good that society is at generating them.

So when Orban wandered into the Ottoman camp to offer his gun-founding services, Mehmed could easily have dismissed him as an infidel traitor and catapulted him back over Constantinople's walls. But he didn't. Instead, recognising Orban's unique talents, Mehmed immediately welcomed him into the forefront of his military operation. What's more, Mehmed paid him generously and put at his disposal all the people and resources required to construct the cannon. It was a small, but significant, indication of Mehmed's openness to new ideas and skills, irrespective of where, or who, they came from.

In short, while the ability of a society to generate ideas itself is import-ant, it is not in itself enough. The receptivity of a given culture to the ideas and innovations of others, and the ability of that culture to take these advances and carry them further, has always been crucial. Successful adapting societies absorb the ideas of others. Societies too enamoured of themselves shun the ideas and innovations of others to their detriment. Any culture that becomes too self-satisfied or too tied to old ideas will fail to produce the new ideas necessary to prosper.

Ingredient Three: A willingness to change

We've located two out of three attributes of societies that adapt successfully: the ability to generate new ideas (creativity), and the ability to absorb the ideas of others.

But neither really works unless you have the third, and final, attribute of societies that adapt well: a willingness to allow change to happen. A society can have the first two attributes in place, but still be a poor adapter if it can't do the hardest thing of all: allow itself to change. This sounds easy, but it isn't. As humans we resist change. And as a society we resist change. Overcoming this resistance is critical if successful adaptation is to occur.

Some societies have made it look easy, especially if their surroundings are difficult. Athens gifted to the world Plato, Socrates, Archimedes, the Parthenon and the Acropolis. But this rich society was not located in some lush continental hinterland. Instead it sat on the rocky, unproductive lands in a region called Attica, which was frequently subject to drought. Its soil yielded little, and tested the mettle of those who sought to live on it. But as historian Arnold Toynbee explains, when the pastures of Attica dried up and wasted away, Athenian society didn't unravel.

Instead the Athenians adapted. They turned from stock-breeding and grain-growing – the staple pursuits of Greece in that age – to olive cultivation and the exploitation of the subsoil. To make a living from their olive groves, the Athenians needed to export olives in exchange for other crops, primarily grain from Scythia. To place their oil on the Scythian market the Athenians needed to develop tools to package the oil (hence the creation of Attic potteries) and ships to transport it (so arose Athens' mighty merchant navy).

Trade also required currency, so they were forced to develop silver mines. Then the extinction of the Attic forests, Toynbee points out, compelled the Athenian architects to abandon timber in favour of stone and this in turn led to the creation of the Parthenon. In other words, the harsh physical environment forced the Athenians to build an economy that sprang from adaptation to these testing conditions.[31]

India's first prime minister, Jawaharlal Nehru, once wrote a book called *The Discovery of India.* Written in only five months, while Nehru was confined by the British to Ahmadnagar Fort prison in 1942, the book offers an interesting perspective on why the mighty Indian civilisation was conquered so easily by the Europeans. The primary reason, according to Nehru, is that India during this period was 'drying up and losing her creative genius and vitality'; it was the 'afternoon of a civilization'.[32] Nehru attributed the decay to 'the static nature of Indian society which refused to change in a changing world, for every civilization which resists change declines.' In short, India, one of the most ancient and impressive civilisations, had stopped adapting. When it did, it began slipping behind.

Much the same story could be told of Venice, the greatest naval power in the Mediterranean world in the fourteenth century. Its ships were well suited to the relative calm of the Mediterranean, and to the prevailing tactics of ramming and boarding enemy vessels. As soon as it ventured into the Atlantic, however, its vessels proved wholly inadequate against larger ocean-faring vessels built for the rougher waters.

That wasn't a problem for the Venetians when most European trade was Mediterranean-based. But as the reach of Europe extended to the Americas, Africa and beyond, the ship-building competency of other nations evolved. For example, the trials of Atlantic sailing forced the Portuguese to develop a high level of skill in the handling of ships with sails.[33] Exchanging oarsmen for sails meant essentially the exchange of human energy for inanimate power. The Venetians were soon out-sailed and out-gunned, unable to compete against the superior vessels of other nations. They were outdone because they settled for a technology that was superior in one environment, but not in another. They weren't willing to change. The bombardier beetle would be disgusted.

As the Red Queen says in Lewis Carroll's *Through the Looking Glass*, 'It takes all the running you can do, to keep in the same place.' Societies are under the same pressure to keep moving forward. Stop running, and you slip behind. Stop changing, and you'll quickly find yourself out of date.

Nineteenth-century English political economist Walter Bagehot sought to explain the challenges of change in his book *Physics and Politics*. He suggests that societies need two phases of evolution. The first is the establishment of laws and rules to govern men's innate desire to act purely in their own self-interest. The second phase is the need to provide sufficient flexibility in that system to encourage new ideas to prosper. Without the second, Bagehot argues, you never move beyond the first, which greatly inhibits the evolution of a society. Adaptable societies must have cultures and institutions that facilitate freedoms, especially freedom to experiment on a small (or large) scale.

What was acceptable for one period can becomes a hindrance thereafter. Take the ancient Egyptians. They developed a wonderful set of institutions and cultural practices that allowed them to build those magnificent pyramids. But these very same assets became an enormous liability when the society faced a crisis – a disruption in the ordinary course of life. A new variable – severe drought – was introduced into the system that was Egyptian society, and the system didn't adapt. As Bagehot points out, societies need to be continually reinventing themselves – whether they are building great pyramids or not.

Changing from the present course is never easy. Adaptation can never be taken for granted. There are forces of resistance within any society. Economic historian Joel Mokyr describes why 'technological creativity has proved rare and ephemeral':

> Sooner or later the forces of conservatism, the 'if-it-ain't-broke-don't-fix-it,' the 'if-God-had-wanted-us-to-fly-He-would-have-given-us-wings,' and the 'not-invented-here-so-it-can't-possibly-work' people take over and manage through a variety of legal and institutional channels to slow down and if possible stop technological creativity altogether.

> Technological leaders like seventeenth-century Holland or early nineteenth-century Britain lost their edge and eventually became followers . . . It is as if technological creativity is like youthful vitality: as time passes, the creative juices gradually dry up, and sclerosis sets in. Societies become increasingly risk-averse and conservative, and creative innovators are regarded as deviants.[34]

Mokyr points out a few examples of vested interests standing in the way of change.[35] In 1561 the city council of Nuremberg, influenced by the Guild of Red-Metal Turners, launched an attack on the investment of an improved slide rest lathe, a local coppersmith by the name of Hans Spaichl. The council began to harass him and made him promise not to sell his lathe. They then offered to buy it from him if he suppressed it. Finally they threatened to imprison anyone who sold the lathe. In perhaps the most shocking example, the inventor of the ribbon loom was reportedly secretly drowned by orders of the Danzig city council.

Every act of change then, is, in effect, an act of rebellion (and courage, if you live under the jurisdiction of the Danzig city council) against conventional wisdom and vested interests. This will normally lead to some kind of resistance. Good adapting societies, therefore, are those that protect the individuals who challenge the status quo. In Bagehot's view, a free society is defined, in part, by the absence of punishment (cultural, legal, social, or political) for going against the grain. The challenge for any society is to avoid cementing itself in what Bagehot describes as a 'cake of custom'. Effective societies are able to break through this cake and reach for something better.[36] That's an ongoing challenge for any society, at any time.

Let's recap. No society is immune from the judgment of evolution. Each exists in a highly complex, dynamic world. It is a world that is constantly changing – sometimes slowly, sometimes quickly – and invariably unpredictably. Some societies are responsive to the changes, and adapt. Others don't, and struggle.

History seems to tell us that adaptive societies are good at utilising innovations – either new technologies or better ways of doing things – to gain a competitive edge. Not every innovation can be home grown, no matter how big or creative the society is. So great adaptation also requires a willingness to embrace the ideas of others, regardless of their source. And finally, adaptive societies are great at changing. They discard ways of doing things that worked well once but aren't effective in a new environment. They manage to get over the inertia that afflicts both individuals and societies. Embrace innovation, suck up the ideas of others, and become comfortable changing. It sounds like a very simple formula, and yet, as we've seen, every society, from the dawn of human civilisation until today, has struggled with it.

All of which naturally leads a New Zealand reader to wonder how our country fares in this respect. Are we a society that exhibits the hallmarks of great adaptability? Do we embrace innovation? Do we seek out the ideas of others? Do we consistently manage to overcome our natural resistance to change? Well, we'll get to modern-day New Zealand shortly, but first we'll take a look at Maori society. When the Europeans arrived in New Zealand they encountered a highly adaptive indigenous society. Honed by centuries of struggling against New Zealand's environment and each other, the Maori were certainly ready to confront the challenges and opportunities presented by the arrival of Europeans.

The first European to arrive was a Dutchman, Abel Tasman. He stumbled across New Zealand at the height of Holland's Golden Age, in 1642. His travels to the far corners of the earth, and the vessel he travelled on, were the products of a highly adaptive society. When he and his crew entered Murderer's Bay they encountered another society that was completely different, but which exhibited many of the same traits that had made Holland so successful in Europe. As we'll see in the next chapter, it was a society that could adapt with the best of them. Had Peter the Great known about New Zealand, and the adaptiveness of its indigenous inhabitants, perhaps he would have learnt as much from a visit to Paihia as he did to Zaandam.

Part 3

New Zealand's DNA

7

Maori I – a crash course in survival[1]

Early on the morning of July 1, 1845, five hundred and twenty British regulars under the command of Colonel Henry Despard quietly approached the heavily fortified Ohaeawai pa, inland from Kerikeri in the Bay of Islands. On the hill overlooking the pa, British artillery stood at the ready.[2] Thirty crack British marines led by Commander Johnson and a militia of eighty volunteers from Auckland stood waiting in reserve. The sun was just beginning to rise, and as Despard's soldiers crept forward they could make out the contours of the pa against the night sky.

As James Belich notes in *The New Zealand Wars*, if the soldiers had been able to examine the pa walls more closely, they would have seen ruptures in it. Over the previous six days the British had submitted the pa to a heavy artillery bombardment. More than four hundred cannon balls were fired at the pa. Despard was confident the pa had been severely weakened and that the Maori garrison was suffering heavy casualties. He calculated that the time was right to inflict a significant defeat on them.

The garrison of a hundred warriors inside the pa was led by the brilliant Ngapuhi strategist, Kawiti. For the last six months, Kawiti and his ally Hone Heke had become sizeable thorns in the side of the British, leading skirmishes throughout the Bay of Islands region. With approximately three hundred warriors under his command, Kawiti had built a small army of experienced troops, seasoned practitioners of modern warfare. His reputation had grown to the point where he had become the prime target of British attempts to crush Maori resistance.

For the last six days Kawiti and his men had been safe in their bunkers inside the pa, sheltering from the bombardment above. They were sheltering inside the first so-called modern pa, constructed specifically to withstand extensive artillery bombardment. Far from being destroyed by the bombing, the pa was only partially weakened and the Maori garrison inside had suffered few casualties.

Even so, the odds remained stacked against the Maori. For approaching the pa walls were some of the best troops of the most powerful country on earth. Britain was the superpower of its time. It had the world's most advanced economy and arguably the world's strongest army. In the course of Queen Victoria's reign (1837–1901), the British engaged in no fewer than seventy-two separate military campaigns – more than one for every year of the so-called Pax Britannica.[3] In the two decades prior to Ohaeawai the British had defeated a dozen nations, from the Sudan in Africa to Austria in Europe. Often the redcoats had been outnumbered significantly. In 1879, at Rorke's Drift in South Africa during the Anglo-Zulu War, a hundred and thirty-nine British marines withstood an attack by over four thousand Zulu warriors. Any society that can defeat another that has a thirty to one manpower advantage knows what it is doing on the battlefield.

Yet at Ohaeawai, it was the British who had the superiority in numbers. Against each Maori warrior stood five professional British soldiers. The Maori were also considerably outgunned. Not only did they not possess any artillery, they also lacked adequate numbers of muskets. In fact, there was only one musket for every five soldiers. Most Maori soldiers prepared to face the heavily armed British forces with no more than clubs or spears.

Colonel Despard wasn't prepared to take any chances. He had selected his best troops to lead the storming of the pa. Two-thirds of the storming party were drawn from the flank companies of the 58th and 99th – grenadier and light companies, the best men of the regiment. Despard chose the north-west corner of the pa as his main point of attack, partly because the storming party could advance under cover to within seventy-five metres of the palisade, the outer wall of the pa. Despard's men crept forward in silence. Closing in on the outer wall of the pa, the British began their charge and, from a distance of within fifty paces of the stockade, went in at speed.

Kawiti's men were ready and waiting inside the pa as the British soldiers rushed forward. The Maori had time for only one volley before the British reached the palisades, so they needed to make it count. When the British were within a mere twenty metres of the wall the defenders fired a simultaneous volley, cutting cut down a line of British soldiers. The effectiveness of the volley instantly threw the remaining British soldiers into confusion, disoriented temporarily by the effectiveness of the initial Maori response.

Nonetheless, the British were not easily disheartened. They were well trained and highly committed. As Major Bridge said later, 'all went to work supposing the pa must be taken or die in the attempt'.[4] With a well-deserved reputation for having a 'high breaking strain', a large proportion of the attackers would have to be shot down before the attack would stop. There would be few 'pulled hamstrings' or 'twinge in my back' excuses made amongst this lot.

The soldiers pressed on to the palisade and spread out, looking for weak points in the fence. A young officer, Lieutenant Philpotts, leading the small naval component of the storming party, burst through an opening in the outer fence and was promptly brought down by intense fire. Other soldiers threw ropes over the fences in an attempt to pull them down. As they struggled with the outer fence, the British were subjected to a terrible raking fire from the flanks and to equally deadly fire from the main trench to their front. Dazed and pinned down, the British searched desperately for the source of the musket barrage. They didn't stand a chance. Safely hidden in trenches and pits, poking the muzzles of their guns under the foot of the outer palisade, Maori could fire at will without fear of reprisal.

Sustaining heavy fire for between five and ten minutes, the British suffered terrible losses. Two British soldiers in every five were killed or wounded before Colonel Despard sounded the retreat. The British limped back to their camp about half a kilometre away, badly beaten. More than a hundred soldiers lay dead or wounded. The Maori did not lose a single man in the British infantry attack. Belich notes that Maori victory celebrations later that night were so loud and terrifying that some British sentries left their posts and sought the comfort of the campfires – a capital offence.[5]

Kawiti abandoned the pa a few days later, and it was destroyed by the British. Its legacy, however, would long live on in the minds of British and Maori alike. The British had been routed.

To make matters worse, the mighty British army had been humiliated by an enemy barely acknowledged as a worthy battlefield adversary. It was a bitter pill for the British establishment to swallow. Tea was no doubt spilt on more than a few laps when the news reached London. It was the first time since Britain began its quest for empire in the eighteenth century that its troops had been so overwhelmingly defeated by an indigenous population.

But they shouldn't have been surprised. Look closely at Maori society and you'll see that the British faced no ordinary adversary. As we'll discover in this chapter, the previous eight hundred years of habitation of New Zealand had proven time and again that Maori knew how to adapt . . . really well. What happened at Ohaeawai demonstrated the flexibility of a people capable of embracing new ideas and technologies, and skilled enough to apply them appropriately in their environment. In scouring the globe for examples of societies that have caught the adaptation bug better than most, we need look no further than this country's tangata whenua. Adaptability, it would seem, is in New Zealand's DNA.

In this brief tour of Maori history we're going to witness time and again the hallmarks of great adaptation. We'll see that Maori were eager to innovate, utilising homegrown or adapting imported technologies to improve food production, effectiveness in warfare, and building construction. We may be surprised at how hungry they were for new ideas from elsewhere, either from other tribes, initially, or from international sources when the arrival of Europeans brought the rest of the world to New Zealand's shores. We'll certainly applaud the way Maori embraced change, and did so quickly, being prepared to discard traditions or practices that no longer suited their changing environment. Maori didn't just survive in New Zealand. They thrived. It's a legacy every New Zealander should be proud of.

An isolated paradise

New Zealand is a land like no other. While we could attribute this to divine blessing – Godzone indeed – the reality is that New Zealand's uniqueness stems mostly from its isolation. An offshoot of the massive southern continent, Gondwana, New Zealand sat alone for some eighty million years. So long, in fact, that the country has the fourth most diverse biota in the world. *Time* magazine once described New Zealand as the 'ultimate storehouse for discontinued zoological models'.[6] Set adrift from Gondwana before mammals had evolved, New Zealand's vegetation and animal life evolved in the absence of such predators. Birds and insects occupied the places in the ecosystem that mammals filled elsewhere in the world.

So while other countries grew giant mammals, New Zealand grew giant birds and insects. The weta, for example, grew into the largest insect on earth. The moa, the tallest bird that ever lived, would dwarf the ostrich in terms of both size and weight. Even their eggs were the size of rugby balls.

New Zealand was also home to the largest raptor ever known. Haast's eagle, which weighed up to thirteen kilograms, had a wingspan of up to three metres. Those wings allowed it to swoop down on prey at speeds of up to eighty kilometres an hour. New Zealand's largest predator, it preyed on giant moa ten times its weight, their necks and skulls punctured by the eagle's tiger claw-sized talons. Birds ranged from tiny native quail to fifteen-kilogram albatross fledglings. As historian Michael King notes, birds, without any doubt, were the kings of this largely forested land.[7]

Perhaps most significantly, New Zealand was the last place on earth to be inhabited by the most destructive predator of all – humans. Ten thousand years ago, humankind had spread over every habitable continent on Earth. But New Zealand was spared humanity longer than elsewhere. In fact, it was spared contact with anything. New Zealand sat alone in the South Pacific for millions of years, blissfully unaware of the changing world beyond the horizon.

Why eat your greens . . .

Blissfully unaware, that is, until those aboard seven – or nine, or four – ocean-going waka peered over that very horizon some eight hundred years ago. Those Polynesian seafarers could scarcely have known what to expect as the lookout on their large ocean-going vessels first spotted the distant land that was to become their home.

When they set foot on New Zealand's shoreline, they encountered a land that was much bigger and cooler than the islands from which they came. It also contained a range of plants and animals they had never seen before. Sure, New Zealand would have looked like a luscious land, but it was quite different from what the travellers were used to. They would have hoped initially that the plants from their home islands (kumara, yam, taro, ti, gourd) might provide a good chunk of their food supply. However, it must have come as quite a disappointment to the new arrivals that of the twenty root and tree crops cultivated in tropical Polynesia, only six would grow in New Zealand.

But think again if you envisage these people wandering into the bush plucking and eating natural, organic produce. Exploiting nature's bounty took real work. The ratio of calories expended in gathering or capturing and processing the food was very high relative to the calories received as a result of that endeavour. For example, an adult surviving on cabbage-tree pith alone would need to eat 18.8 kilograms daily – and remove their taste buds.[8] An all-year-round living could be wrested from New Zealand nature, but it took immense effort and organisation.

. . . when you can eat meat?

But when the Maori – I'll call them that for the sake of convenience although the name didn't emerge until the nineteenth century – first arrived in New Zealand, eating eighteen kilograms of cabbage tree wasn't necessary when the land abounded with a great variety of far more nutritious, and tasty, animal specimens. New Zealand was richer in big game, most notably moa and seals, than the islands from which the new arrivals had come. So in the early centuries of settlement, the main sources of food were the larger creatures: moa, geese, penguins, seals, and so on. But tapping in to these particular sources of food required the development of a number of new technologies and techniques.

Take moa as an example. They weren't exactly an easy catch for people who were not accustomed to hunting two-hundred-kilogram birds that could comfortably outrun humans through the dense forest. While no one is certain how moa were caught, the most common theory is that it was by the judicious use of dogs. Man's best friend became moa's worst enemy as the Polynesian dogs that accompanied the people journeying to New Zealand became effective moa herders, intrepid forerunners of today's sheep-herding collies.

Giant moa made for plentiful eating. The huge legs carried thirty to forty kilograms of meat, requiring two people per drumstick to carry them across New Zealand's rugged terrain. Even the smaller bush moa could front it with a turkey when it came to body mass. This amount of meat was, of course, a large helping of protein. Anthropologists estimate that the protein intake in the average 'moa-hunter' diet was three times that of the typical Polynesian diet of the day. Not only did this create bigger muscles, it also meant more babies. Fertility rates skyrocketed, and so did population levels – a ten-fold increase, in fact.

At the same time as the population boom was occurring, moa-hunting patterns were changing, driving further innovation. As the more accessible coastal moa were killed off, parties had to trek further for food beyond the range of the very young and very old. For the first time, moa meat would have to be transported back to the whanau. And because doing this one bird at a time wasn't going to cut it, a strategy for hunting, processing and transporting of multiple birds had to be invented. Vast moa-butchering sites, up to a hundred and twenty hectares in size, were established. These sites were invariably located at the mouth of a river. The hunters designed and built river-suitable reed boats that could transport up to a tonne of moa meat along the fast ocean-bound currents.

Once the meat arrived at the base, it was cooked in large earth ovens, in a manner not dissimilar to the modern-day hangi. At the largest such moa-processing site, located at the mouth of the Waitaki River, the concentration of ovens is still apparent from aerial photographs. These sites became highly efficient meat-processing facilities – food production on a mass scale. Estimates of the number killed at the Waitaki River site, for example, range from 29,000 to 90,000 – that's over 2.2 million kilograms of meat, the equivalent of over forty million McDonald's meat patties. The existence of such mass meat-processing facilities is virtually unknown in any other indigenous society around the world.

But all good things must come to an end eventually, and big game in New Zealand proved to be no exception. After millennia of existence without predators, thirty-two New Zealand bird species (and another nine after the Europeans arrived) proved to be no match for the first human inhabitants, who harried with them rats and dogs, and the ability to hunt and to make fire. The flightless goose, for example, would have had no chance and was dismissed early in the innings. The moa and other large, easily accessible game were all driven to extinction by the fourteenth century. According to anthropologist Anne Salmond, 'By the fifteenth century, fewer birds of fewer species were being caught in most North Island communities, while all species of moa were virtually extinct in the North Island and had become rare in the South'.[9]

Time to get creative on the food front

This sudden emptying of the big bird larder would naturally have come as a rather unpleasant turn of events. A dramatic shift would be required to cope with the extinction of major sources of food. The environment was changing, so Maori did what all successful societies do: they adapted.

According to Belich, when Maori were faced with this situation they 'transformed their economy, their politics, including warfare, and their social organisation.'[10] The hunting techniques and tools developed to assist in the capture and processing of moa would need to be applied in the hunt for different prey. As large-scale sources of protein disappeared, a greater volume and more diversified selection of foods would be required to sustain the population. In short, the changes that occurred in Maori society were to be both significant and rapid.

New forms of food production were developed. With the bush not providing the bounty of food it once had, the pluck, process and eat days were drawing to a close. Food would need to be produced at home. So gardening took off. Gardens were to become productive enough to produce about half the total food required by the inhabitants. Wild plants were cultivated. Fernroot grew well on newly cleared land, and good fernland was regularly burned off to promote its regrowth. Cabbage trees were eaten in the south, while yam and taro were cultivated in the warmer north.

And, of course, we mustn't forget every young child's dinner-plate favourite, the kumara. A virtual perennial in the warmth of the tropics, the kumara was less enthusiastic about growing in the temperate New Zealand climate. So, in order to cultivate kumara at latitudes well south of its normal growing range, Maori would plant the tubers in mounds of earth and stones that stored heat and maximised the sun's warmth in the growing season. In the winter months, they stored the kumara in low-roofed storage pits where the soil maintained an even temperature. Prior to use, the storage pits were disinfected using fire and then lined with decaying wood and ferns to absorb moisture and aid insulation. When the Europeans arrived they were struck by these advanced storage and cultivation techniques. 'No people can be more provident or industrious than the New Zealanders in supplying themselves with stores of provisions', noted a voyager to New Zealand in the early nineteenth century.[11]

Preserving kumara tubers in storage pits changed the social dynamic too. Communities had to remain with the pits to ward off would-be kumara thieves. Competition for resources meant that less-well-provisioned neighbours were tempted to raid your pantry, so vigilance was necessary. This competition for food, and the threat it gave rise to, resulted in the development everywhere of the fortified hilltops known as pa.

Maori also began looking for food in new areas, notably in the sea. Huge nets, up to two kilometres long, would be suspended across a bay between two poles. Their construction involved a massive amount of labour, while set-up and harvest required large-scale coordination.[12] At Maketu in 1886, such a net trapped about 40,000 fish in one day. The net took a whole community an entire winter to make, and was carried out into the water on a platform lashed between two canoes crewed by up to forty people.[13] Move over, the Japanese driftnet fishermen of today.

In the south, something akin to 'fishing stations' emerged. These innovations took harvesting the sea to new heights, a bit like the moa meat works. At Purakanui, a fourteenth-century site on the Otago coast, 230,000 fish were caught in three visits within a few years – four hundred tonnes by one estimate. In the Far North in 1855, fifty canoes carrying 1000 workers caught 7000 small sharks in two days. The canoes co-operated, fishing the place at the same time under joint leadership and making joint preparations for preservation on shore. But they also competed with each other – for the first fish and the largest catch.

Complexity grows and grows

Kumara protection was just one incentive to stick around the same spot for longer. Greater numbers of people were required to make this economy work. The highly mobile, far-flung colonies would need to concentrate, settle and cease roaming over large areas of the country. The added complexity of this new economy required a different set of skills. Gone were the days of the hunter/carver/warrior generalist. Roles were assigned and specialist skills developed – weaving, carving, farming. Activities were scheduled and co-ordinated as never before. Routines emerged. Calendars were co-ordinated, appointments made, meeting rooms booked.

As Maori society grew in complexity, trade became more and more important. People were prepared to travel long distances for both minerals and food. Food that was readily available in some districts but not in others, such as pigeon or titi (muttonbird), would be preserved in fat in gourds or kelp bags and bartered with neighbouring tribes. As they are today, imports were necessary to keep the menu as varied as possible.

By the fifteenth century, South Island Maori were exporting pounamu (greenstone) to other parts of the country. They also allowed emissaries of North Island tribes access to it. Bay of Plenty Maori developed a trade in fine-grained obsidian from Mayor Island, off Waihi. Waka were the container ships of this time, traversing river, lake, and coastal highways.[14] Over time the larger ocean-voyaging and double-hull canoes were gradually replaced by smaller ones suitable for coastal or river voyages and weekend fishing trips.

As the complexity of Maori society increased, an encyclopaedic knowledge of the environment emerged. Whether it was the habits of animals, the source of minerals, or the variety and properties of plants, Maori quickly accumulated a deep store of learning. The wealth of vocabulary they used in dealing with trees, birds, shrubs, plants, stones, fish, clouds, winds, and stars has surprised many. Ethnographer Elsdon Best did significant research with the Tuhoe people at the turn of the twentieth century.[15] He established that they had at least one hundred bird names representing some fifty species, two hundred and eighty plant names, and some sixty names for insects. His notes on this forest lore run to a hundred and seventy pages, representing 'only the fragments' of the knowledge of the Urewera, a single tribal district.[16] For a people without written records, that takes a lot of memory.

All this knowledge formed the basis of an extensive economic planning system. Utilising a twelve-month lunar calendar, Maori had a strict schedule to follow with specific economic activities occurring each month. For example, certain fungi and orchids were collected in June, ferns were burned in August, while dry felled trees and scrub were burnt on new cultivation grounds, crops weeded and fenced and the kaka parrot speared in January.[17]

It is misguided to think Maori were either oblivious or indifferent to the constraints of their environment. Their very survival required them to be *extra* diligent in how they treated the environment. Timber suitable for canoes would be marked for felling years in advance. Bark would be cut away on one side of a growing tree so that its natural decay over time would facilitate its carving into a canoe at a later date. Fish would be smoked and wood stored for months as a provision against scarcity. Regulations connected with the preservation of game were designed to ensure stocks of young birds were not depleted (clearly a post-moa initiative).[18]

Maori adaptation to the changing availability of different food sources, their creation of new food production and storage methods, and the knowledge of new plants and animals gleaned from exposure and usage, were prerequisites for scratching a living from the land. These innovations occurred quickly, remarkably quickly in fact, relative to the evolution of food production processes in other, much older cultures. They didn't live in a static environment. It was a complex system that required constant adaptation to changing conditions. Not easy by any means, but Maori society managed to pull it off.

Turning flax into slacks

It would be easy to assume at this point that Maori adaptation was purely driven by the need for survival. It wasn't. The beauty of ceremonial cloaks, the intricacy of greenstone neck ornaments, the dazzling ornamentation of meeting houses, and the size of war canoes, weren't necessary for survival. Maori society's desire to extend its boundaries of resourcefulness and achievement was fuelled by the nature of Maori society itself. As we'll see, Maori society was highly competitive, and it was this competition that helped craft a society so well-equipped to confront and exploit the British colonisers in the nineteenth century.

This competitiveness in inter-tribal relations created a virtual arms race within the isolated world of New Zealand. We've talked about Maori society up to this point as if it was a unified kingdom like China. The reality couldn't have been more different. Maori society was a hotbed of inter-tribal competition. In that respect it was not unlike the Europe we discovered in the previous section – lots of small states competing like mad against one another. And when that happens, it creates a hotbed of innovation and progress.

It was competition, for example, that drove a lot of Maori clothing design. Initially clothing design was more functional. It had to be. When the new arrivals from balmy Polynesia encountered New Zealand's cool climate, their attention turned quickly to ways to warm up. It wouldn't have taken too many nights to realise that their barkcloth attire (the Polynesian cloth manufactured from the inner bark of the aute – the paper mulberry) wasn't going to cut it during New Zealand's winter. Not only did the clothing manufactured from the aute tree provide insufficient warmth, but also the aute tree itself didn't grow in New Zealand.

This quandary had been to some extent foreseen; aute plants were brought along on the voyage. While efforts were made to acclimatise the shrub to its new home, one gust of a mid-winter Wellington gale would have been enough to dispel any hope that the aute was going to accept this climate. A rapid search ensued for an alternative, with most effort concentrated on the inner bark of the whauwhi or lacebark, prepared by the same technique of whacking it into shape with a mallet. But the lacebark, despite its name, failed to offer quite the texture and durability of the aute, and it too was rejected.

So the new arrivals had to cast about for different material and most critically, develop a new way of preparing it. Adaptation was required again. Their solution was found in the harakeke, also known as New Zealand flax, with its two-metre sword-like blades and strong longitudinal fibres. But fashioning the harakeke into clothes required a substantially different technique from that used to prepare tapa cloth. A new technique had to be invented.

Actually, a new technique was not invented; it was adapted from an existing one. For amongst the many smart decisions the Polynesians made as they prepared to journey to New Zealand was the decision to bring along someone who knew how to make baskets. This knowledge was applied to the flax plant and became the centrepiece of the new harakeke-based clothing industry. A whole series of garments came into use. Adoption and adaptation of technologies and ideas was in full force.

But more than purely environmental considerations were responsible for later Maori innovation in clothing. Competition between tribes fuelled many new clothing designs. For one thing the incessant battles between tribes led to innovations in protective clothing. Some tribes developed a thick cloak, woven with a close two-strand weft. This created a strong canvas-like fabric that was virtually impervious to the thrust of spears.

Competition also manifested itself in Maori emphasis on *mana* (status). Enhancing the mana of a chief or a tribe was an equally important manifestation of competition. Befitting this need to impress, dress cloaks were designed and worn at social gatherings to enhance the wearer's status. The kahu kuri, a cloak to which long narrow strips of dogskin were attached, was a highly valued garment worn as a mantle only by persons of chiefly rank.[19] Clearly, when you have the time to put ornamental dogskins on garments, you're at the point where more than the climate is driving wardrobe development.

Competition also prompted the development of tools and buildings, another vast and impressive field of Maori innovation. As the food economy became more complex, and the range of materials and buildings increased, the complexity of tools became more sophisticated. In parallel with the need for better equipment was this culture-driven ambition for greatness in building design.

New Zealand's first construction industry

In the whole field of Maori material endeavour there is perhaps no greater example of excellence than the carved meeting house. These houses also serve as an extraordinary example of how rich and complex a society Maori had developed – far beyond what was required for mere survival.

Some of these houses were of great size. A meeting house erected at Waiapu was twenty-six metres long, nine metres wide, and six metres high, and could hold 1500 people. The house Matatua, carved at Whakatane, was twenty-three metres long and ten metres wide. Hotunui, built to replace it, is twenty-four metres long. In the house Rangitihi, near Rotorua, the carvings alone took over four years to complete.

Constructing buildings of this size involved more than a few Saturday afternoon working-bees. For one thing, you needed an architect of some skill, then plenty of workers to do his bidding. Even the unskilled labour needed for the hauling and setting-up of the mighty timbers for ridgepole and central pillars demanded careful organisation and supervision. Experts in timber dressing, thatching, reed-work panelling and carving were recruited to play their part, often brought in from other tribes.

Feeding the one hundred-plus workers involved in construction was a logistical exercise in itself. Forethought was essential to ensure adequate food supplies had been caught and prepared. All this had to occur over the many months (or years) it took to complete the project. A meeting house at Te Oriori was called Nga Tau e Waru (The Eight Years) because that was how long it took to complete it.

Preserving and enhancing their mana became the lifelong quest for Maori. Tohunga (or specialists) could achieve mana as carvers, for example, as the skill of their work in wood increased the mana of the entire community. Driven by this cultural phenomenon, artistic expression reached heights of intricacy and delicacy seldom seen elsewhere in the Pacific. Maori culture not only created the means to develop a highly productive, complex society, it also created the need for it.

Involved in the building of these magnificent structures was a raft of technological innovations. The fire-plough, for example, was utilised for centuries by Maori to start fires and has more recently been adopted by frustrated groups of scouts. While they did not use metals, stone was used to construct a range of tools. Maori used stone to develop an ingenious cord-drill. They used a wedge for splitting timber and a skid for facilitating the transport of heavy logs and canoes on land, easing this labour with soft mud, or choosing green branches of a tree with a slimy under-bark. For tree-felling they employed a large chisel-hafted adze, resting on guides, and swung by several men. Imagine, if you will, the technique adopted in handling a battering ram and you'll get the idea.

One tribe took this technology a step further. In the Bay of Islands, an ingenious bow-propelled modification of this device was developed. The invention consisted of a springy branch, secured in a horizontal position at one side of the tree near its base. A strong cord secured to either end of the branch served as a bowstring. To this bowstring was attached a stout shaft with a heavy chisel-like stone tool lashed to it. Several men hauled on it as an archer pulls a bowstring, and when the shaft had been pulled as far back from the tree as possible it was released. The heavy stone tool crashed against the trunk of the tree, punching two parallel horizontal grooves.

The world shows up

The existence of this remarkable innovation raises an interesting question: why was it never modified into a weapon of war? One can imagine any tool that could send a projectile at sufficient force to make a dent in a totara trunk could certainly be utilised to make a dent in a human. Yet the link was never made.

It's here that we see the downside of Maori isolation. For over two thousand years prior to settlement in New Zealand, the Polynesian islands had been isolated from other races and their ideas. Then after landing in New Zealand, Maori sat apart from the rest of humanity for perhaps another six hundred years. No one came to visit. No sailing vessels appeared over the horizon. No mail or telegrams arrived with news of the outside world. No one had sailed over the horizon in either direction for a long, long time. As far as Maori were concerned, New Zealand *was* the world. In the language of complexity science, Maori society was a *closed system*.

This isolation from the rest of humanity meant that Maori avoided the conflicts and plagues that other humans inevitably brought with them. But it meant that they missed out on the positives as well. Without access to the ideas and innovations of other cultures, Maori were never exposed to various technologies that had become commonplace in many other parts of the world. While bows and arrows were used for hunting and warfare in regions as close as Papua New Guinea, the application of the technology in this manner never extended this far.

And despite their oral traditions, Maori never developed writing although it was commonplace throughout Europe, Asia, Africa and Latin America by the fifteenth century. To the northwest the Javanese had a written language by the ninth century AD, while the Philippines followed in the fourteenth century. Similarly, Maori never developed the wheel-based technologies that had existed in India and China for millennia. They couldn't avail themselves of new forms of governorship or organisation, different styles of food preparation, innovative construction techniques, alternative clothing styles, or any other ideas and strategies the rest of humanity was grappling with at the time. For as we've seen, no society, not even one as industrious as that of Maori, can possibly develop every good idea or technology on its own.

When Abel Tasman sailed over the horizon in 1642, that isolation from the best and the worst of humanity came to an end. No Maori could possibly anticipate what changes these foreigners would bring, or how soon. While many societies around the world had been confronted with European colonisation, the speed and impact was especially great in New Zealand. The modification of landscapes that had taken place over twenty centuries in Europe and four in North America would occur in New Zealand in a single century.[20] This was to be change on an unprecedented scale.

Maori were again required to adapt to a rapidly altering environment. Only this time the changes were far more dramatic, both in their speed and scope, than had previously been the case. The question was, when the rest of the world eventually came knocking on their door, how would Maori society answer?

Looking back from the twenty-first century, some of you will think you know the answer: a loss of land, followed by a downward slide into over-representation in negative social statistics like crime and unemployment, and under-representation in the positive ones (standard of living, school qualifications and so on). But that commonly held view doesn't really do Maori, or New Zealand, justice. The story is more nuanced than that and, frankly, a lot more positive.

But before we get to that, we're going to step out of Maori society for a bit and take a look at the imported society the new settlers brought with them. We'll check out how the colonisers confronted change when they built the foundations of modern New Zealand. It was a time of bold ideas, bolder actions, and steamships. Let's take a break from the cultural achievements of seventeenth-century Maori to take a look at a Chinese immigrant in 1870 with a penchant for fungus.

8

New Zealand and the crazy 1870s

At thirty-eight years of age, Chew Chong was older than the typical nineteenth-century New Zealand immigrant. Born into poverty in Kaiping, China, he had gone from houseboy in Singapore to shopkeeper in Australia to scrap-metal exporter in Dunedin. Now he found himself in New Plymouth. The year was 1870, and things were about to take off for Chong, and, coincidentally enough, also for his newly adopted homeland.

Woodear, Jew's Ear, Egmont Gold, Taranaki Wool and Black Gold all refer to one thing: fungus. The Chinese also refer to it as 'cloud ear', and 'tree ear', while the Japanese get even more creative and call it 'tree jellyfish'. To give it its scientific name, *Auricularia polytricha*. In 1870 it grew profusely in old logs within New Zealand's dense native forests. Back then it wasn't considered much good for anything. That is, until Chong decided to eat it.

The axiom that rules the food discovery business is: whatever doesn't poison you can be sold to someone. Chong figured he'd chanced upon a new food, so he took his horse and cart from farm to farm in search of the stuff (a valuable, if unanticipated, bonus for cash-strapped farmers). The rest, as they say, is history. Soon fungus depots began sprouting up and before long, Chinese from California to Australia were adding fungus to their meals with great relish.

But Chong didn't stop at fungus! After opening a couple of general stores and butcher shops in the New Plymouth area, he turned his attention to butter. Perhaps sick of receiving complaints about contaminated butter from customers, he set about developing some simple, but ingenious, modifications to how butter was sold. He figured that butter was best sold in one-pound blocks that had been refrigerated and wrapped in grease-proof paper.

Chong's innovative use of refrigeration technologies helped pave the way for butter exports on newly fitted refrigerated ships. He was a founding director of Taranaki Coolstores, and was instrumental in the development of Port Taranaki. The dairy industry, and indeed the country, owe much to Chong and his ingenuity.

Chew Chong lived through a tumultuous period of New Zealand history. It was around this time that the British decided to pull their troops out of the country. Advances in technology, from refrigeration to telegraphs to steam power, were radically changing the economy. What was farmed and where it was sent, the speed with which ideas were communicated, views about who should participate in shaping the direction of the country, even the physical landscape itself, were evolving quickly. People adapted and coped with their changing country, or they left. These were tumultuous times all right. Sounds a bit like today.

Chong's story is about the exploits of an individual. But in his story we again see the lessons that resonate with the theme of this book – success, whether you're an individual or a society, demands an ability to adapt to a changing environment. Whether by chance or good management, Chong's strategy was mirrored by the society he lived in. At times clumsy, but undoubtedly successful, modern-day New Zealand had the adaptability gene right from the start. This chapter explores how this gene manifested itself during one of the most dynamic periods of New Zealand's short history.

Thinking REALLY big, Vogel-style

Eighteen-seventy won't just be remembered as the year we began eating fungus. No, 1870 was a momentous year for New Zealand in a variety of ways. It was the year the first official rugby match was played, a close, hard-fought game between Nelson College and Nelson Football Club, that was interrupted only by a brief argument over the off-side rule. New Zealand's first university (and presumably its first dingy student flat) was established, and the San Francisco to Auckland mail service came into operation. These were indeed exciting times for our young country.

But it was also a time when people looked to the future with some fear and uncertainty. For it was in 1870 that the last imperial British soldiers packed up their red coats and boarded ships destined for Old Blighty. While Te Kooti, Titokowaru and others might have breathed a sigh of relief, the impact of the British troops' departure on the rest of the country's psyche was less positive.[1]

Britain's occupying troops had represented more than just a security blanket for the colonists; they had been the backbone on which much of the fledgling country relied. When roads needed to be built, ports constructed, forest cleared or public buildings hammered together, it was often members of Her Majesty's imperial force who did it. Their departure could only have signalled one thing to the settlers left behind: your country, and its future, is now in your hands.

The young colony responded angrily to Britain's decision to remove its troops. It felt a sense of betrayal. Premier Edward Stafford reminded Britain that 'her colonies have grown great not because of, but in spite of, any care from her'.[2] There was talk of a unilateral declaration of independence and even of becoming the Southern Hemisphere branch of the US. No colonial cringe here. Stafford's successor, William Fox, went so far as to ask Britain to ensure New Zealand's neutrality in any future British war (and avoid occasions for Empire-wide bonding in such arenas as Gallipoli and the Somme). There was no way Britain could misinterpret these signals. Lord Kimberley, the British Secretary of State for the Colonies, wrote in 1870 that 'I would rather enter into no controversy, as it is undesirable to give the New Zealanders opportunities for showing their disregard for us.'[3]

Enter the thirty-five-year-old Colonial Treasurer, Julius Vogel. Perhaps New Zealand's most famous citizen of Jewish extraction, Vogel had a bold plan for the country. He set about kicking New Zealand into a higher gear, initiating a series of major capital works that made Muldoon's Think Big projects a century later look like some minor roadworks. Vogel's plan was to cover the country with a web of modernity: roads, railways and telegraph lines. To succeed, Vogel realised he would need money and people – and lots of both.

To achieve the first, he did what any good treasurer would do: he borrowed – to the tune of a cool ten million pounds, to be exact. When the General Assembly baulked at the proposed cost he coolly replied: 'These proposals will entail on posterity an enormous burden. Granted – but they will give to posterity enormous means out of which to meet it.' It was an enormous amount of money, representing two-thirds of a year's wages for every one of the 250,000 New Zealanders at the time.[4]

The second requirement, people, was solved by an ambitious immigration scheme that led to the arrival of over 100,000 immigrants in the course of the 1870s, including 32,000 in 1873 alone. Thousands of Dutch, Poles, Chinese and Britons jumped at the chance of joining a railway construction gang in the remotest country on earth.

Laying a trail of rail and ice

Rail was Vogel's most famous public works project. Reminiscent of President Kennedy's 1960s call to put a man on the moon by the end of the decade, Vogel announced to a startled nation that a thousand miles of railway track would be laid by 1879. This length of railway track in nine years was an extraordinarily ambitious proposal at a time when New Zealand had few people, fewer roads and was covered head to toe in thick forest. New Zealand's rugged geography offered the engineers no rolling British meadows or flat American savannas. The curves had to be tight and the gradients steep.

And yet they accomplished it. By early 1879, when the initial boom ended and a series of financial depressions began, 1136 miles of railway were in operation – perhaps the first, and only, time in history that a public project over-delivered on budget. Suddenly wheat growers could get their grain to ports for export quickly. Farming took off. From 1874 to 1884 the amount of land on the Canterbury Plains given over to growing wheat increased by a factor of four as technologies opened the way to new markets locally and overseas.

Improvements to railway transportation were quickly followed by the transformation of ocean-going vessels. In 1881 the *Dunedin*, a magnificent sailing ship that had ably transported passengers to England's colonies, had refrigeration machinery installed inside its hull. W.S. Brydone, the local superintendent of the New Zealand and Australia Land Company, built killing sheds at the Totara Estate near Oamaru where freshly killed sheep carcasses were carried by rail to Port Chalmers and frozen aboard the ship.

On 7 December 1881 the loading of frozen sheep carcasses began in earnest. Of the sixty passengers who had booked a journey with their mutton shipmates, only a Mr Coggins and a Mr Berry actually arrived with their suitcases and deck chairs on the day of departure. The remaining passengers were afraid to sail on the *Dunedin* because while in Port Chalmers the driving shaft of the refrigerating machinery on board broke. This raised the trifling concern that a broken crankshaft might bore a hole though the bottom of the ship. Broiled fish for dinner they could tolerate, sea sickness they could endure, but holes in the bottom of the ship mid-ocean were clearly out of the question.[5]

A delay of several days was necessary while a new shaft was made, and in this interval several hundred carcasses of mutton and lamb were removed from the ship and were either sold to locals patient enough to thaw them, or unceremoniously dumped into the sea. The shaft was eventually fixed and on February 15, 1882, New Zealand's first refrigerated ship set sail with a cargo of nearly five thousand sheep carcasses and two slightly nervous humans.

Ninety-eight days later, on May 26, the vessel arrived in London.[6] To the delight of the owners, the cargo of sheep and lamb carcasses was in near-perfect condition. It was snapped up quickly over the following fortnight at the nearby Smithfield market at prices double those it would have fetched in New Zealand. It was a small but significant start to what would become a booming trade for New Zealand, one that today over five million sheep are proud to be a part of each year.

Refrigeration radically changed the nature of farming. Up until then sheep had only been considered useful for their wool and the occasional meal, so the primary way to manage livestock numbers had been through the innovative method of driving them over a cliff. Refrigeration provided farmers with the opportunity to sell sheep meat. Smaller farms became viable. New industries sprung up around the transportation, preparation and freezing of meat, and by the mid-1890s there were twenty-one freezing works; twelve in the North and nine in the South Island. The ports of Bluff, Oamaru, Timaru, Gisborne and Napier were energised as local farmers sought convenient places to access what was literally a world of opportunity.

Refrigeration also allowed for the export of other animal products such as butter and cheese. Land was cleared to make way for dairy cattle. New Zealand's landscape was being transformed.

Dunedin's successful voyage cast the die for New Zealand farming. And the fact that it did points to an important lesson about change we'll discuss in more detail later. Change is critical, but it must be ongoing. Refrigerated shipping provided a means of getting meat, and shortly afterwards, dairy products, to a ready and willing British market. The Brits couldn't produce enough for themselves, liked the flavour of the New Zealand produce and were prepared to pay good money for it. For the New Zealand farmer, and the New Zealand economy, it was a great deal.

For decades the Brits sucked up our refrigerated lamb as if it was going out of fashion. During World War I, New Zealand producers were encouraged to produce as much lamb as possible to feed a hungry, battle-scarred Britain.[7]

New Zealand's love affair with, and dependence on, the British market were strengthened at the 1932 Ottawa Conference when New Zealand and other British dominions obtained preferential access to the UK market relative to foreign suppliers.

But good deals never last forever. And the shipping-of-frozen-meat-and-dairy-to-Britain deal was no exception. It came to an end in the 1970s when New Zealand was unceremoniously dropped as a pre-eminent supplier of meat and dairy products to Britain. Great Britain had entered the European Common Market and would, from now on, source much of what New Zealand had to offer from French and Greek farmers.

Britain's decision in 1972 came as a shock. As a country heavily dependent on agricultural exports, we had been caught with our gumboots off. Although Britain had signalled its intentions to enter the EEC in 1961, eighty-six per cent of New Zealand's lamb exports and ninety per cent of our dairy exports were still finding their way onto British dinner tables a decade later.[8] The subsidies and exports required to keep New Zealand's farming ship afloat proved unsustainable and the inevitable restructuring that occurred in the mid-1980s saw farm closures, mass slaughter (of sheep) and some real pain for New Zealand's most beloved industry.

New Zealand's farmers adapted and now run the world's most efficient, productive farms, with lamb exported to one hundred and ninety different countries. It's a remarkable turnaround in just two decades. But it was a painful lesson in adaptation, or the lack of it, for us all. Refrigerated shipping was a wonderful, country-changing innovation that revolutionised our farming industry. But for much of the twentieth century it also induced a certain stasis. It became too easy. We didn't have to look seriously to other markets or to diversify our products. We didn't adapt voluntarily during most of that time, so when it was forced upon us in the 1970s and 1980s, it hurt. Adaptation has to be ongoing. It can never stop. Like the Red Queen we encountered earlier, New Zealand must continue running just to stay in the same spot.

We'll discuss this more in later chapters. But for now, let's return to nineteenth-century New Zealand, because refrigerated ships were the tip of a large iceberg of change the country was experiencing.

The death of wind power and the shrinking of New Zealand

The inception of a refrigerated meat trade coincided with the introduction of another new technology – steam-powered ships. When these metal monstrosities chugged over the horizon they signalled the end of the slow, unpredictable and labour-intensive sailing ship. The first steamship to visit New Zealand was a six-gun warship, the HMS *Driver*, which reached Auckland in January 1846. Essentially a sailing ship with big side paddles, it must have looked as though maritime design had taken a disturbing turn for the worse. Often used to transport the Governor on various jaunts along the coast, it was also used to carry British troops and Maori prisoners of war.

On one occasion it was used to transfer some Ngati Toa prisoners from Waikanae to Wellington.[9] Included in this group was Te Rauparaha himself (the chief most famously known for writing the haka that was later adopted by the All Blacks). During the night, while it was steaming, a great commotion erupted in the prisoners' room. Hurriedly opening the hatch to ascertain the cause, the sailors found the room full of steam and the prisoners in a dreadful state of alarm. Rather than being a cruel and unusual punishment, the steam bath was the result of a leak in one of the boilers. Very thankful to be relieved of their moist quarters, Te Rauparaha and colleagues opted to sleep on deck for the rest of the night.

The introduction of steamships over this period and their connection with rail links also sped up travel and mail services within the country. The *Rotomahana*, the fifteen-knot 'Greyhound of the Pacific', was the world's first ship built of mild steel, and it sped thousands of Australians and New Zealanders to each other's shores. At 1727 tonnes, this Tasman Sea steamer dwarfed anything running between Britain and New Zealand at the time.

The first full-powered steamship to bring immigrants from Europe, the *Mongol*, arrived in Port Chalmers in February 1874, fifty-one days out of Plymouth, England. As those aboard the *Mongol* puttered out of Plymouth Harbour, they would have observed another ship hoisting its sails. It was the *Scimitar*, also bound for New Zealand, and also carrying a cargo of immigrants. By the time the *Scimitar* arrived in New Zealand – a full nineteen days after the *Mongol* – those aboard must have been ruing their decision to take the environmentally friendly option. Thanks to steam, people were getting to New Zealand faster than ever before.

Keeping in touch

The introduction of the telegraph at this time took communications in New Zealand to a new level, and the country has not been the same since. It was the South Island that first introduced the new technology. Only eighteen years after Morse's first long-distance line had been built between Washington DC and Baltimore, the first electric telegraph line linking Christchurch and Lyttelton was laid in 1862, primarily to inform a shocked Christchurch citizenry that: 'Mr Oakes is coming round in schooner *Colleen Baun* with good dog Pedro poisoned and dead.' Four years later a telegraph cable was laid between the North and South islands, although it was frequently cut by the swirling currents on the seabed of Cook Strait.

In 1876, when the first telephone cable from Sydney came ashore at, coincidentally, Cable Bay, near Nelson, New Zealand's remoteness diminished even further. Messages from England now arrived in four days, rather than seven weeks by one of the steamships. Then, just a year after the telephone was invented by Alexander Bell, a Mrs Sheehy received a call from a Roxburgh farm in 1877 enquiring about the number of eggs in a pavlova, and became the first Kiwi to have a telephone conversation on a private line. (No doubt the next fifty calls recorded were all made by teenage girls.) The first telephone exchanges were opened in 1881 at Christchurch (twenty-seven subscribers) and Auckland (twenty-six subscribers).

While the South Island embraced the new communication technology, progress in Auckland was less encouraging. In 1866 the roll-out of a Wellington to Auckland cable route started in the capital. Though the cable reached Napier through Masterton two years later, it did not reach Auckland for a further four years. A route through the King Country was considered too difficult due to Maori hostility and the ruggedness of the bush-covered terrain. The line was eventually extended from Napier, through Taupo and Rotorua, to Thames.

Ten years after the establishment of the first telegraph line, more than two thousand miles of cable had been erected and four hundred thousand messages a year were tapped out in Morse code. A decade later in 1882, the lines had almost doubled in length and 1.5 million telegrams were being handled annually (about half the number of text messages now sent daily).

Becoming a nation

All these innovations enabled the colony's widely scattered settlements to communicate better with one another, and with the world beyond New Zealand. It made the country smaller. In 1859, the fastest journey possible from Dunedin to Auckland took fifteen days. By 1879 that had been reduced to five and a half days, and by 1898, three days. Of the two hundred and eighty-six mail services operating in 1874, half were carried on horseback along slow bush trails (and a further thirteen services by foot).[10] The total length of these services was more than seven thousand miles with a total annual mileage of 1.4 million miles. It was faster to send a letter to Britain than it was to send it to some of the more remote parts of New Zealand.

That soon changed. In 1878 the first Railway Travelling Post Office, in which mail clerks occupied a van and sorted, closed (and, one suspects, read) mail en route, began between Christchurch and Dunedin. By 1881 the railways were providing fifty mail services at various stretches along their main lines. Letters per Pakeha jumped from 4.6 in 1855 to 30.5 in 1875. Ideas were starting to flow around the country and it was technology that was making it happen.

With this explosion in communications and transportation of people, New Zealand couldn't help but become more unified; the flow of news and ideas was knitting New Zealand into a collective whole. Suddenly people in Dunedin knew what was happening in Auckland (even if they pretended not to care). What had once taken weeks to learn about was now known in hours. In 1851 most of the commercial information a reader of the *Lyttelton Times* absorbed about Auckland was thirty-six days old. By 1878, that had dropped to 1.1 days.[11] Business could now be conducted on a nationwide scale. People at opposing ends of the country became more aware of, and reliant upon, each other. So much so, that in 1868 New Zealand adopted an agreed time zone – New Zealand Standard Time – on a longitude west of Christchurch, destroying, in the process, some well-worn excuses for being late to work.

Trading, gossip and access to frozen meats were not the only benefits these technologies brought. Whenever means of communication are enhanced, new ideas are dispersed and some kind of significant social change invariably occurs. The arrival of the printing press in the fourteenth century led to a tumultuous period in European affairs when radical ideas (like Luther's beef with the Catholic Church) were given a tangible means of broad dissemination. Telephone wires, railway tracks and better roads similarly encouraged a wellspring of social change in New Zealand.

When Kate Sheppard stood on the steps of Parliament on September 19, 1893 and claimed victory in her fight for woman's suffrage, her success had been aided in no small way by the enhanced ability to get her ideas to more people more quickly. A staggering seventy-eight per cent of the eligible women ended up registering to vote. It's always been tough, after all, to start a movement for social change when it's a thirty-day round-trip just to get to the kick-off meeting.[12]

Universal suffrage was just one of the many social reforms of the late nineteenth century. The new communication technologies facilitated the mobilisation of interest groups and raised awareness of abuses in the system. What came to be known as Bradshaw's Act (1873) restricted the employment of women in factories to an eight-hour day and, in 1875, the act was amended to limit child labour to a four-hour day. The 1877 Education Act provided for 'free, secular and compulsory' primary education for all New Zealand children, and the four hours per day of child labour became the unpaid kind: homework. In 1882 the Justices of the Peace Act established that non-homicide indictable offences committed by a child could only be punished by imprisonment, fine or whipping. Progress indeed.

The unifying effect of these technological changes also caused a shift in the political landscape. The centralised administration in Wellington could now send instructions and hear of electorate dissatisfaction quickly. The politicians in Wellington seized the opportunity and federal power grew steadily. In 1876 provincial government was officially terminated, while the important task of land surveying was also centralised. Broader, collective identities gradually replaced local ones. Cantabrians became New Zealanders, Wellingtonians became New Zealanders, and Southlanders . . . well, they too became New Zealanders.

The New Zealand of 1890 ended up looking a lot different from that of 1860. And not only did New Zealand look different, it *behaved* differently – and not only did it behave differently, it *thought* differently. The nation was taking off. As James Belich so eloquently puts it, New Zealand had grown to 'five hundred thousand people from a standing start in fifty years, 1200 miles from anywhere and 12,000 miles from *the* somewhere'.[13] People wanted what New Zealand had.

Despite its size and the lure of a suntan on a Gold Coast beach, immigrants didn't flock to Australia at nearly the same rate as they came to New Zealand during that period.

New Zealand came of age, maturing quickly from a small colonial outpost to a nation with the characteristics we recognise today. As we've seen, fuelling many of the changes in New Zealand society were technological innovations rapidly and enthusiastically adopted by the young nation. The steamship, the telegraph cable, and the railway, amongst others, brought the rest of New Zealand, and the outside world, closer. Ideas flowed. Institutions changed. And most significantly, so did the way we thought. Commerce and trade were transacted in new ways, with new products, and extended to new markets. It was a period of dramatic change, no doubt bewildering and at times alarming for many of the country's citizens. Britain had not only let go of New Zealand, she had let go of her into a rapidly changing world.

So long and thanks for everything, Britain

Yet Britain's unceremonious cutting of the apron springs became a blessing in disguise. By gently nudging New Zealand off to play with the other kids, Britain gave the young colony two great gifts. The first gift was the freedom to make its own decisions, to chart its own course. Gone were the requirements to consult London over policy and procedure. New Zealand was now able to make decisions for the good of its own future, free from the political machinations and budgets of Whitehall and Downing Street. It scarcely seems conceivable that the British Secretary for the Colonies would have signed off on Vogel's ambitious, but ludicrously expensive, railroad plan. It was only a New Zealand free from the purse strings of London that could make the investments (and accept their accompanying risks) necessary to propel the country into the modern era.

The second gift offered by Britain's exit from New Zealand's internal affairs was related to the first: freed from the slow, bureaucratic decision-making process of Britain's political system, New Zealand was able to make, and then act on, rapid decisions about its future. New Zealand was changing quickly, and it needed the ability to alter its laws and structures to keep up. Advances in transportation and communication technology were unifying New Zealand into a functioning whole.

New Zealand could move fast if it needed to. Inconsistent regulations and procedures between provinces began hindering this progress. So laws abolishing provincial governments were drafted, debated, passed, and acted upon within three years – an extraordinarily short amount of time given the scale of change required. New Zealand needed capital, so it went out to the world's financial markets to get it. New Zealand needed people, so it went out to the world and shipped them over. Waiting for Britain to move its political and bureaucratic machinery to the same point could only have hurt New Zealand's ability to take advantage of the new world emerging within and beyond its shores.

New Zealand was not an ancient society with immovable institutions and traditions stretching back thousands of years. New Zealand's youth and small size were tremendous assets. It needed a flexible and adaptive society and set of institutions. The country had to be prepared to discard old ideas that failed to meet the requirements of the new world. New Zealand's youth as a nation ensured that few reactionary vested interests had had time to establish themselves. There was, at the time, no big business or ruling elite with significant investment in the status quo to stand in the way of change. It's easy, after all, to discard one institution in favour of another if few people care for the old one.

Similarly, New Zealand's small size and population aided its ability to change quickly. Ideas flowed faster. Decisions could be made with a speed simply not possible in Britain or even in Australia. New Zealand had the manoeuvrability of an America's Cup yacht, not that of an oil tanker. By being nimble and responsive, New Zealand was able not only to survive the changes of the second half of the nineteenth century, but also to prosper through them.

Let's reiterate the lessons we can take from New Zealand in the 1870s. Technologies and ideas were quickly adopted from overseas, modified for New Zealand's local conditions, and then put to work building a stronger local economy. Vogel's 'top down' investment in public infrastructure produced a flurry of 'bottom up' activity as people responded to the raft of economic and social opportunities that the likes of the steam engine and telegraph service provided. The skills required to build a vibrant economy were, if lacking in New Zealand, aggressively (and shamelessly) sourced from elsewhere in the world. New ideas were actively sought out and adopted. Institutions and laws no longer applicable to New Zealand's changing environment were replaced by those that were. And this was done quickly.In short, New Zealand adapted and changed. It wasn't always pretty, but it sure was effective.

But let's also not get too carried away here. Not everyone participated in the country's take-off. Some found the country's rapid turn towards industrialisation an unwelcome one. Those who thought they had escaped the ravages of an industrialising Britain by coming to New Zealand may have felt an uncomfortable sense of déjà vu. Change rarely occurs without its casualties.

Many would point to the experience of Maori after Pakeha arrived as an example of a group that failed to adjust to the new New Zealand. We're all aware of the struggles they endured during the latter half of the nineteenth century and then throughout much of the twentieth century. But using our theme of adaptation, we see a more nuanced story emerging. The adaptive culture we discovered in the last chapter ensured that Maori survived the challenges of New Zealand's terrain in the centuries before European arrival. Then once Cook and company showed up at the end of the eighteenth century, Maori were confronted with some extraordinary changes. Did New Zealand's adaptation gene, so faithfully developed first by Maori and then by the early settlers, fade away? Could Maori mould their society to the constraints and opportunities of a new world? Just how well they adapted is the topic to which we now turn.

9

Maori II – a new world

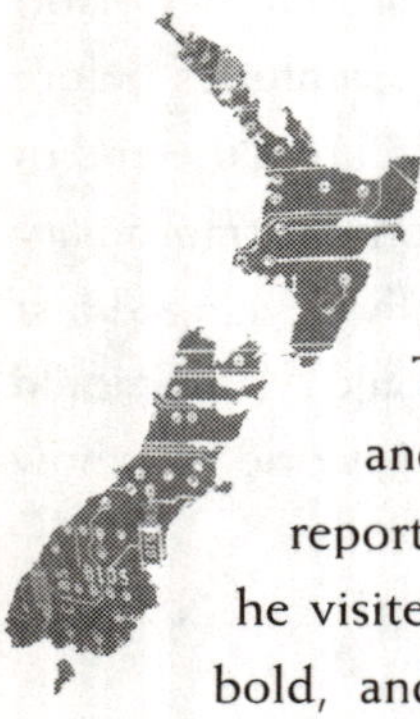

When the rest of the world came to New Zealand, Maori embraced what it offered with enthusiasm. They quickly became vigorous adopters of the ideas and technologies from elsewhere. Robert Jarman, who reported the presence of a great many Maori in Sydney when he visited in 1833, described them as 'industrious, intelligent, bold, and enterprising'. He predicted that the size of their country, the productiveness of its soil, the spirit of its inhabitants, and its convenient situation for trade with Australia, Tahiti, and Hawai'i, would cause it to become 'a place of considerable importance'.[1]

But after such a promising start, things started to go downhill. By the end of the nineteenth century, population decline, land losses, declining health and living standards, and widespread unemployment were all dramatically eroding the foundations of Maori society. Had adaptiveness deserted the Maori? And does it still elude them today? These are the primary questions for this chapter. But before we turn to them, here is the story of New Zealand's first capitalists.

The Maori capitalists

Europe's 'rediscovery' of New Zealand with Captain James Cook's voyage to Australasia was motivated by astronomical interests. The official reason for Cook's first voyage to the South Pacific in 1769 was to observe the

Transit of Venus from Tahiti. It may seem a long way to travel for a bit of stargazing, but these were exciting times of new discoveries and possibilities. It was Europe's Age of Enlightenment, after all.

After Cook's ship sailed away from New Zealand, a new wave of Europeans found their way into this part of the world motivated by something entirely different: profit. Whale oil and seal fur lured Europeans and Americans in the 1790s. As historian Christopher Bayley observes, 'commercial rivalries during the British "continental blockade" of Napoleon's empire intensified the search for whale oil in the southern ocean, releasing whalers and "beachcombers" onto Australia, New Zealand and the Pacific Islands.'[2] Whaling off the New Zealand coasts is first recorded in 1791 and sealing in Dusky Sound in 1792. Timber and flax trading followed shortly afterwards in the Firth of Thames in 1794–95. By the later 1790s, shiploads of timber were being exported to India and China by enterprising traders.

The rest of the world had arrived and it wanted what New Zealand had. New Zealand's love affair with trade had begun, and Maori were in the thick of it from the beginning. The demands of Atlantic capitalism opened up overseas horizons to Maori that had been closed off since the disappearance centuries earlier of the art of, or will to make, long-distance ocean voyaging. Maori trade became so prolific by the 1810s that the Northland zone around Kororareka was ranked among the top three commercial centres in the Australasian 'archipelago', behind Sydney and Hobart.[3]

Maori took to the new markets with vigour. Pigs and potatoes, introduced by Cook and others for the convenience of Western seafarers, proved lucrative trade items, but indigenous products such as flax were also in demand. In 1831, more than a thousand tonnes of flax were exported to Sydney, seven hundred and twenty-five of which had been contracted by the British Navy. Experiments in manufacturing sailcloth and paper from the fibre were carried out in England. But most of the exported fibre was used in rope-making, primarily to rig the ships of Her Majesty's Navy.

According to Bishop Williams, Maori so eagerly threw themselves into the flax business that, for several years, the cultivation of crops and other occupations were neglected. At Te Tumu and Maketu, flax was scraped day and night to fill a thirty-seven-metre shed, prior to shipment to Sydney.

Peter Tapsell, a Danish trader, established a permanent flax-trading station in Maketu for the powerful Arawa group of tribes. Simply feeding the hundreds of mouths involved was a significant undertaking. Tonnes of fish were caught each day; much of this was dried and sent inland in return for potatoes, carried 'by hundreds of women, like a string of pack-horses'.[4] This was no small commercial enterprise.

Time to see the world

When foreigners arrived Maori jumped at the opportunity to explore what the world had to offer. Perhaps they had been incubating a case of cabin fever for six hundred years. Many couldn't wait to explore this wider world. Seventeen-year-old Te Weherua and twelve-year-old Koa, from Queen Charlotte Sound, joined Captain Cook as he left New Zealand for the island of Huahine. They were the first Maori to venture beyond New Zealand's shores for many hundreds of years.

Others soon followed. Maori hopped aboard whaling ships to begin their global exploration almost as soon as those vessels appeared in New Zealand waters. University of Auckland historian Hazel Petrie, whose detailed work in this field I have relied upon heavily in this chapter, notes that by the late eighteenth century, Maori were packing their bags for the Pacific Islands, Australia, North and South America, and Europe.[5] Each voyage introduced Maori to new markets, products, economic systems and ideas.

Maori had a thirst for the ideas, technologies and capital of others. And, critically, they knew who held them. In 1805, Te Pahi became the first influential Maori leader to visit New South Wales. He expressed keen interest in cultural and technological exchange and welcomed Governor King's plan to settle a party of official observers in the Bay of Islands. Sounding like a Mafia boss, he offered settlers his protection. In return Te Pahi suggested that several of his people should visit New South Wales to learn the skills of Australian shepherds. Two years later his son, Matara, on a visit to England, met George III.[6]

Nobody did schmoozing with foreign dignitaries better than Hongi Hika, a Ngapuhi chief. In 1820 Hika travelled to England on board the whaling ship the *New Zealander*. He spent five months in London and

Cambridge, where his mokoed visage attracted considerable attention. When asked by the *Cambridge Chronicler* what his purpose in travelling to England was, he responded that he wished to 'see King George – the multitude of his people – what they are doing – and the goodness of the land'. He also expressed an interest in recruiting settlers, particularly miners to look for iron ore, blacksmiths, carpenters, soldiers to protect the settlers, and an additional number of preachers.[7] Hongi Hika had private interviews with at least six bishops and in Norwich Cathedral sat in the bishop's pew with his family at matins.

Hika's request for an audience with King George IV was finally granted. Wearing Western clothes over his native dress and bowing gracefully, he reportedly greeted the King with 'How do you do, Mr King George'. The King was impressed with his guest from the Antipodes and treated him like royalty, eventually bestowing upon him a suit of chain mail. He also gave Hika a case of gifts in appreciation for the chief's assistance in introducing Christianity to New Zealand. His mission accomplished, Hika set off home. Upon his arrival in Sydney he sold the gifts given for his services to Christianity in order to purchase muskets. (The irony is perfect.) Thus armed, Hika triggered the deadly Musket Wars shortly after his return to New Zealand.

Trade to the four corners

With the likes of Hongi Hika on the job, it isn't surprising that Maori were considered entrepreneurial trading partners. And it was a truly global trading base. The early trade in sealskins, for example, was largely for the Chinese market. The majority of visiting whalers and trading ships were not from Britain, but from America. In 1830 alone, twenty-eight ships averaging a hundred tonnes made fifty-six voyages between Sydney and New Zealand carrying Maori-grown potatoes and milled grain, creating a very healthy trade surplus (remember those?) for New Zealand. Other vessels came from France, Tahiti, Brazil, Portugal, the Netherlands, New South Wales and Tasmania.

Purchases of European ships had gained such momentum that, by 1852, Maori were the major players in New Zealand's coastal shipping.[8]

Establishing the country's trading links with the rest of the world was almost exclusively a Maori affair. Rather than running from the world, it seems as though Maori sought to profit from it.

Opening the doors to the world required journeying up a steep learning curve. For example, a global set of trading relationships quickly introduced Maori to the nuances of international commerce. In 1830, the Hokianga-built ship *Sir George Murray*, with chiefs Patuone and Taonui on board, was seized in Sydney for not flying a national flag. This spurred a number of northern chiefs to petition King William IV for an economic and defence alliance. There was no sentimentality in their petition. It simply cited the volume of sales of timber, flax, pork and potatoes to British traders put at risk by the curtailment of Maori trading. At a meeting of the New South Wales Executive Council on December 22, 1831, Governor Darling and his successor, Major-General Sir Richard Bourke, stressed the importance of Maori trade to the colony of New South Wales and Great Britain.

In March 1834, the newly appointed British Resident in New Zealand, James Busby, convened a meeting of Maori chiefs to deal with the difficulties faced by Maori and European-owned shipping in international waters and problems with Sydney's customs regulations. It was on this occasion that the first New Zealand flag was selected, a key piece of New Zealand's early national identity motivated by purely commercial considerations. In the following year, a Declaration of Independence was signed by the Confederation of United Chiefs for preserving, amongst other things, 'the regulation of trade'. There were to be no more ship seizures for failure to fly a national flag. Maori were thus instrumental in establishing New Zealand's legal standing in international law.

Te Rauparaha led a migration of his tribe south from Kawhia. At Kapiti he traded with the whalers, and established an economic stranglehold on the southern region.[9] Captives from intertribal battles were 'encouraged' to join the labour force and scrape flax, the key product used to trade for the essentials in life: muskets, powder and tobacco. All tribal efforts were folded into supporting these trading enterprises, many of which were managed by women. This included sealing crucial alliances with foreign traders by marrying them. Capitalism had found enthusiastic disciples in Maori.

Introducing foreign tools, crops and ideas

As more settlers poured into the country, Maori turned their commercial focus to the domestic market. Whereas visiting ships had sought pork and potatoes for resupplying their galleys, and flax and whale oil for on-sale, the settlers were more interested in grain and fresh produce. And they needed it badly.

When Europeans showed up in their ships after months of 'portable soup', orange and lemon juice, sauerkraut and few vegetables, they weren't going to wait around while they planted and grew fresh crops. They were eager to gain some instant nourishment through trade with Maori, who all too readily saw the leverage they had in this particular commercial relationship.

The nascent Auckland settlement only survived in the 1840s because inexpensive provisions were made available by local Maori. Soon trading ships were purchased to convey surplus produce directly to centres of European settlement around the country.

According to Petrie, Maori who journeyed overseas brought home a raft of innovations.[10] One was commercial dairy farming, first established in New Zealand by Rawiri Taiwhanga, one of Hongi Hika's warriors. Maori very soon had the production of flour mastered as well. As Petrie notes, 'Prior to European contact, Maori had no grain crops, but the cultivation of wheat spread rapidly so that, only six years after annexation by Britain, Maori had begun commissioning their own water-powered flourmills.'[11] A report from the government inspector of mills compiled in June 1856 listed twenty-nine mills in the Waikato and Rotorua districts alone. At least six operated in Taranaki during the 1850s, as well as others in Wellington, the Eastern Bay of Plenty, Heretaunga and elsewhere. So effective were the millers that at the Great Exhibition at the Crystal Palace in London in 1851, a sample of 'Maori flour' from a watermill belonging to Kingi Hori Te Waru and Hoani Papita Kahawai from the Waikato earned a 'worthy of notice' award.[12]

Then there was the spud. The Maori almost certainly hold the record for the most rapid adoption of the potato as a food staple outside the Americas. European explorers introduced it around 1790 and by 1805 'immense quantities' of potatoes were reportedly produced by Maori in the northern Bay of Islands. By 1813, large Maori potato plantations were reported at Bluff, in the extreme south of the South Island.

What took centuries to introduce into Europe seems to have taken only years in New Zealand. But that shouldn't surprise us. We saw in Chapter Six that from the day they arrived in New Zealand, Maori had been figuring out how to adapt subtropical plants to the colder regions of New Zealand. They quickly appreciated the significance of the potato as a crop, and after years battling the adversity of their environment, they had no problems growing potatoes in it.

Products weren't the only things adopted by Maori. They also entered the service sector pretty quickly. Some Maori were paid to deliver official dispatches from Waimate to the Bay of Islands shortly after the Treaty of Waitangi was signed.[13] The country's first posties were Maori, charging a rate almost double what Hobson had agreed with the settlers.

Maori commercial successes were not lost on the Pakeha. Few could deny that Maori soon constituted a very significant market, not only for millwrights and shipbuilders, but also for British and Australian imports. Governor Robert Fitzroy suggested that those who viewed Maori as 'impediments to the prosperity of British settlers' should consider that they were the settlers' best customers, paying in 'ready money', 'native produce', land or labour, and that settlers consumed surprising quantities of Maori produce at low prices.[14]

In 1848, Governor George Grey suggested to his boss Earl Grey in London that the Maori market for manufactured goods was already of considerable consequence to British merchants. Maori demand for trading vessels formed the basis of the local shipbuilding industry and their custom was eagerly sought. Shipping agents, brokers, shipwrights, and engineers offered their services in Maori-language newspapers as did millers, millwrights and water surveyors. In fact, if anything, Maori were viewed as being too successful. Tizard Brothers, a millcasting company, complained that too much interest was taken in Maori as customers at an 1857 trade exhibition.

Pragmatic and flexible

Driving this commercial acumen was a deep-rooted pragmatism. Ideas or traditions that were no longer practical were discarded. Snake eels, for example, were frowned upon during early periods of Maori settlement. But they were embraced as legitimate sources of food as shortages required a re-evaluation of their merits.

Commerce between Maori and European required a greater degree of adjustment, but even the most fundamental of Maori cultural practices were flexible. Incidents, such as touching the head of a chief – a transgression of the fundamental code of tapu – would likely result in death for another Maori. But they might be excused in the case of non-Maori if commercial advantage could be accomplished from a diplomatic resolution. Even in the sacredness of their art work, practicality trumped tradition. For example, stone tools were quickly replaced with metal chisels as carvers saw the improvements they offered.[15]

As an early missionary to Hawke's Bay, the Reverend T.S. Grace, explained, Maori 'will listen to theories with delight, but that is all. When they see a practical demonstration they get to work at once.'[16] His perspective was borne out by first-hand experience. Upon trying to relocate from Hawke's Bay to Matata, he discovered the hiring of bearers, the chartering of a ship, the purchase of a canoe and the building of a store and a house, could only be achieved by tendering ploughs in return – the most valuable currency to Maori who were in the process of rapidly adopting new agricultural practices and tools. The Bishop of Wellington, Octavius Hadfield, claimed that 'Few people have been known with less prejudice, or . . . less wedded to their customs' than Maori.[17]

As Petrie has observed, Maori social structure was very fluid. For one thing, workers had lots of discretion as to where they punched their card, and it could change from time to time. 'The inherent links between individuals, whanau (family), hapu (sub-tribe), and iwi (tribe) allowed for a variety of regrouping in the face of social, political, or economic stress . . . alliances of hapu were typically shifting affiliations, prone to internal splitting or recombinations.'[18] Individuals could choose to link up with the hapu of any parent or grandparent, or move to another community for a variety of reasons. They participated in kin-based enterprises on a voluntary basis, as it suited them.

Certainly the family ties were strong. But the strength of cohesion and degree of control exercised by leaders was not a given. It depended as much on their personality, powers of persuasion and economic wealth. According to Auckland's first harbourmaster, David Rough, Maori were 'as independent as American citizens . . . Indeed New Zealanders are complete republicans; even the highest chiefs have little direct authority, although they have considerable influence'.[19] John Gorst, a young Englishman who had spent considerable time with the second Maori king in the 1860s, would later observe of Maori leadership that 'Maories are, in their opinions and sentiments, the most independent people in the world, and exhibit an individuality which would delight Mr John Stuart Mill.'[20]

But it did not pay to isolate oneself entirely from those with political clout in the region. Rawiri Taiwhanga, New Zealand's first dairy farmer (who we came across earlier), lost his herd of forty cows when he refused to support his kinsman Hone Heke in the 1845 rebellion.[21]

Thus balance between the communal and the individual was achieved. It meant that the collective needs of the community could be met without eroding the individual's ability to reap the benefits of his work. There was fluidity in social interactions that allowed Maori tribes to ebb and flow across various commercial opportunities as they occurred.

The Maori warrior

This model proved effective in commerce and equally so in warfare. It was for their accomplishments in warfare that Maori of the early colonial period are perhaps best known. Their achievements induced an historian of the British army to claim that the British soldier considered the Maori to be 'on the whole the grandest native enemy that he had ever encountered'.[22]

Early European arrivals to New Zealand could not fail to notice the centrality of war to Maori society. Charles Darwin himself on his visit here observed the warrior tendencies of his Maori host. 'I was surprised to find that almost every hill which I ascended had been at some former time more or less fortified . . . I should think that a more warlike race of inhabitants could not be found in any part of the world than the New Zealanders.'[23]

While warfare was clearly a big part of Maori culture, honed by centuries of inter-tribal warfare over limited land and food resources, there was nothing to suggest that they would make effective adversaries to the more technologically advanced British forces. The British and colonial forces which Maori faced in the 1860s were not just superior in numbers but were also equipped with the results of a mid-century revolution in military technology: breech-loading, repeating rifles; powerful artillery; and steam-powered, armour-plated ships with the capacity to destroy shore defences.

It was a bad miscalculation. By 1864, New Zealand was costing London £500,000 a year. There were more imperial troops in New Zealand than in Britain, and twenty-five times the number of troops stationed in Australia. In New Zealand there was one British soldier for every seven Maori. In India there was one British soldier for every fifteen hundred Indians. Had Maori been prepared to be more like the Indians in their approach to the British, Hobson, Fitzroy, Grey and company would only have needed a mere eighty soldiers in New Zealand. Yes, nineteenth-century Maori constituted the pebble in Britain's imperial shoe.

The Maori blocked the British in two wars, and regularly defeated forces several times their own number – enemy forces that were not trapped or surprised, but who actually chose to engage in battle. In the end, it required eighteen thousand British troops equipped with the latest artillery and rifles, together with careful preparation and logistical organisation, to defeat Maori – and even then their opponents were able to delay and limit the British victory. During the 1870s and 1880s, after the wars were officially over, large sections of the inland North Island were still, in effect, under Maori control. Neither the British troops nor later the colonial forces ever captured a completed and defended pa.

Maori success was grounded in the realisation that some rapid change in their approach to warfare was required. First off, attack and open battle were struck off their list of tactical options. This was no easy decision in itself. Maori, like many indigenous tribespeople, had traditionally adopted an aggressive military strategy, utilising surprise to catch their opponents unaware and unprepared. But that wasn't going to work against an enemy with such superiority in numbers and firepower. So Maori adapted. They avoided open field confrontations. They developed impressive defensive strategies, based on specially modified pa.

Second, they became proficient in the new military technology: guns. Traditional fighting weapons – the pole (taiaha) and club (mere) – would have to be relegated to a supporting role. Initially, use of the musket wasn't exactly second nature for the Maori. But they got in a lot of practice during the Musket Wars, which raged from 1821 to 1830. And rage is the appropriate word: an estimated thirty thousand Maori were killed in these battles.

These brutal conflicts ensured competence with the musket spread far and wide across many tribes. The conflicts also honed their military strategies around this new technology. It wasn't long before new defensive measures were adopted by those holding pa against attackers. For example, they saw how potent firing in volleys, a strategy typically favoured in European warfare, was against an attacking force. As firearms were diffused among the Maori tribes, this tactic became widespread.

But most remarkable of all Maori adaptations in warfare was the creation of the modern pa – the cornerstone of their military strategy against the British. If open-ground battle, surprise attacks and hand-to-hand fighting were no longer options, then the next best alternative was to use pa as defensive bastions combined with guerilla attacks on settlers. Unfortunately, the traditional pa weren't going to be adequate against an enemy with guns. For example, fighting from elevated and highly visible platforms was commonplace with traditional pa. However, when men with rifles arrived, standing on a high, exposed stockade became a precarious occupation for the defender. It wasn't too healthy when artillery shells started landing nearby either. So Maori developed a new pa for a new type of warfare.

But these weren't Constantinople-like structures with big walls of the sort that have artillery officers salivating with anticipation. We saw in Chapter Six that those kinds of defensive structures had long been outdated. No, modern Maori pa were quite different. They were very easily built. They were also completely expendable. The so-called 'L pa' at Waitara was built by eighty men, overnight. Time and again the British would mount an elaborate, often lengthy, expedition to besiege an annoying pa. It would absorb their bombardment and possibly one or two attacks and then the next morning they'd find it had been abandoned.[24] Shortly afterwards a new pa would appear in another inaccessible site. The defenders mass-produced them by the dozen. It was an asset-light, flexible strategy that worked marvellously well.

Built specifically to deal with the weapons introduced by the British, modern pa were essentially disposable systems of earthworks, combining anti-artillery bunkers and complex sets of concealed firing positions reached by concealed communication trenches. They were more sophisticated than the trench systems of the American Civil War or Boer War and were, according to Belich, 'strikingly similar to the pattern on the Western Front in 1914–1918'.[25] Located at strategic positions around the country (often near important water or food sources), pa in New Zealand were estimated by some at close to six thousand, with an overall density of one to every 9.6 square kilometres below the three-hundred-metre contour.[26]

Sustaining this resistance was a series of innovations in resource management. During most battles, Maori were outnumbered between three and five to one. Given that most Maori soldiers were part-time warriors and part-time farmers, sustained Maori resistance required a complex process of rotating call-ups. This 'fight on Monday, plough on Tuesday' policy allowed a maximum fighting force to be deployed without completely disrupting the agricultural base of Maori society.

According to Belich, the New Zealand Wars involved co-operation among Maori throughout both islands. South Island Maori sent ammunition to the King Movement. Ngapuhi protected Kingite prisoners of war, and their warriors marched to distant Waikato to support traditional enemies. Models of Kawiti's Ohaeawai pa were carried all around the country by Maori messengers in 1845. This was done, in the words of an Urewera chief, to 'show sympathy for the island in trouble'.

Maori accomplishments in warfare against the British remain one of the enduring reminders of how strong a society the British encountered when they began settling New Zealand. The Maori were not a numerous race, nor were they exceptionally advanced in their technologies. Their greatest strength, however, was their culture – a culture that proved highly adaptive, and remarkably innovative. The British encountered a people with an uncanny ability to adopt the best technologies and strategies from elsewhere, and then to mould them to the New Zealand context. It was adaptation at its best. Cue applause from the bombardier beetle.

The real test

But the story of Maori adaptability, of course, doesn't end on that high note. As the European presence in the country increased with remarkable speed from the 1850s, Maori society was subjected to extraordinary pressures and challenges. A trickle of foreigners turned into a flood, and soon what had been a bounty of European-introduced blessings (clothing, better shelter, new crops, and trade opportunities), became a plague of European-introduced curses (crippling diseases, land confiscations and restrictions, foreign laws and practices, and alcohol).

To make matters worse, the winds of capitalism began to blow against Maori. The focus on the domestic market left many enterprises vulnerable to the fickle nature of New Zealand's nascent economy. Its gold and kauri-gum booms were met with equally devastating busts. The transient settler population came and went. Investments in new mills and ships faltered. Debts were called in and the best land was sold to pay them. Traditional lifestyles became increasingly unsustainable. Maori workers left for distant lands to find a stable pay cheque. Communities began disintegrating.

But that wasn't all. In the previous chapter we saw the magnitude of changes New Zealand was experiencing during the late nineteenth century. They were exciting times for many, but few Maori were smiling about it. Railways, refrigerated shipping, and all the other technologies that had remoulded New Zealand so dramatically from the 1870s on, left many Maori reeling. It was too much change too fast. Change, always a steady river in this land, had suddenly become a torrent. A new era had begun that required still greater capital in order to compete, but by now few Maori had the economic or political clout to keep up.

The Maori way of life, while always changing, had sustained its intrinsic elements for centuries. It would never exist again. By 1890, a mere twenty-five years after the brilliance of Gate Pa virtually brought the British Army to a standstill, Maori society was in freefall. European-introduced diseases like smallpox and influenza took a heavy toll on the Maori population. By the late 1890s there were only forty-three thousand Maori left, down from perhaps a hundred and ten thousand a century earlier. The huge influx of Europeans meant that Maori dropped to a mere six per cent of New Zealand's total population. They had become a tiny minority in their own land. It was a near-fatal blow for Maori society.

An all-time low

As their population waned, so did their influence on the national consciousness. Despite gaining the right to vote before any other indigenous population in the colonised world, and the tireless work of such notable Maori leaders as Sir Apirana Ngata, Sir Maui Pomare, Meri Mangakahia, Sir Peter Buck and others, Maoridom in the first half of the twentieth century was a mere shadow of its former self.

A painful new beginning

The Maori response was to fall back on tribal roots. By the 1920s, around eighty-five per cent of Maori were living in rural areas, primarily on traditional tribal lands. Ultimately, this wasn't sustainable. There was inadequate work, and diminishing tracts of forest made self-sufficient living impossible for most Maori.

So, making it in the city became an appealing prospect. Before long Maori were packing their bags and journeying to the big smoke in droves. In 1945, only twenty-six per cent of the Maori population lived in the towns and cities. By 1956, a mere eleven years later, thirty-five per cent were city dwellers. By 1966, the urban population had grown to a staggering sixty-two per cent, and it reached nearly eighty per cent by 1986.[27] In the space of a mere forty years, the vast majority of Maori had migrated from the country to the city. Again, Maori society was undergoing some tectonic-sized shifts.

It was a staggering migration of people, and the implications could not have been more significant. Abandoning the world they knew, Maori had to start afresh in a new world. City life required an enormous adjustment. As Maori Party MP Dr Pita Sharples points out, 'The change from the rural to an urban way of life was a huge culture shock . . . They were broke, they had their power and water cut off, they owed rates, and stuff like this.

The discipline of the city was totally different from the discipline of the country.'[28] *Te Ao Hou*, a Maori magazine of the time, warned its readers of the dangers of city living: 'Life in the city is not easy: you have to work regularly, be very careful with money, accommodation often gives trouble, and friends and relations have a habit of getting themselves into difficulties you have to help them out of.'[29]

The warnings were not far off the mark. As you'd expect, the transition from a quiet, rural existence to the bustle of city life was not easy for many. Historian Michael King talks about the difficulties 'with managing salaried incomes for the first time, with budgeting, savings and investments, and with accommodation, hire purchase and door-to-door salesmen.'[30] The majority of the new migrants were males aged between sixteen and thirty, with few elders joining them.[31] Disconnected from traditional tribal support networks, some fell into crime. Others struggled to find work. Many families living in cities ceased to have active links with their iwi and hapu, losing their observance of tikanga Maori. Many grew up in a cultural vacuum, ill-equipped to be Maori, yet made only too aware by the way they were treated that they were not Pakeha.[32] Isolation followed. The social statistics deteriorated.

Many Maori had come to the cities in the 1950s and 1960s to fill jobs in the manufacturing sector. While the pay wasn't great, the work was steady. But it was these parts of the economy that bore the brunt of dramatic, and painful, modernisation in the 1980s. This process wasn't much fun for many New Zealanders, and for Maori it proved a considerable setback. Because many Maori worked at the most vulnerable points of a modernising economy, they were particularly hard hit by the restructuring that occurred. Industries that had received government support in the forms of subsidies and tariffs were suddenly cut from the government's purse strings. Inevitably these were industries in which many Maori worked, and job losses were severe. Maori unemployment spiralled in the decade that followed, reaching a peak of twenty-five per cent in 1996.

With their social structure upended and their economic foundations undermined, the social statistics from the mid-1990s were not surprising. Maori died on average ten years younger than people of Anglo-European descent.[33] Had the avoidable mortality rates for Maori been the same as those for others, Maori would have experienced 970 fewer deaths each year than actually occurred; this represents forty-five per cent of all Maori deaths up to age seventy-four, respectively.[34] Although approximately fourteen per cent of New Zealand's population is Maori, this group accounted in 1999 for fully thirty-eight per cent of prison admissions.[35] Maori experienced rates of theoretically avoidable hospitalisations between sixty and seventy per cent higher than other New Zealanders. Maori were twice as likely to be hospitalised for ambulatory care-sensitive conditions – conditions that are usually amenable to prompt primary care intervention.[36] It's a depressingly familiar story: Maori on the wrong side of so many social indicators.

The changing face of Maoridom

But the story doesn't end at that point either. The good news (for every New Zealander) is that many indicators are beginning to surface that suggest Maori adaptability is as strong as ever. Look beyond the negative social statistics and you see signs that provide even the most cynical with some cause for optimism.

Across the board the very statistics that have condemned Maori for so long are beginning to move in the right direction. Maori life expectancy is up (dramatically), rates of smoking are down.[37] Participation in tertiary and early childhood education is way up, youth suicide is down.[38] Average wages and salaries are up, while Maori fatalities from car accidents are down. More Maori leave school with higher qualifications than ever before.[39] The Maori employment rate fell from 61.2 per cent in 1986 to a low of forty-six per cent in 1992. Since then it has improved, at a faster rate than for Europeans, reaching sixty-four per cent in 2005.[40] The gaps between Maori and the rest of New Zealand society remain, but they are narrowing.

There is a resurgence in Maori culture. The first national Maori language survey in 1973 estimated that the proportion of fluent speakers had fallen to eighteen per cent. Today that number has jumped to twenty-five per cent.[41] Maori are now participating at a higher level than any other ethnic group in tertiary education, an increase of two hundred and fifty per cent over the last ten years. Maori women are the leaders in that increase, making up approximately sixty-four per cent of all Maori students, and twenty-four per cent of all female students in tertiary education. Maori women with postgraduate or 'higher' degrees have the highest median income of all ethnicities. Maori, it seems, are over-represented in universities as well as in prisons.

Patrick Snedden's *Pakeha and the Treaty* lists a series of Maori-run social-service providers that are among the best in the country.

> Ngati Porou Hauora runs all health services on the East Coast, inclusive of secondary hospital services, and is accredited nationwide to the highest standards. Mai FM . . . is this country's highest-rating music station . . . operating in a fiercely competitive radio market that is dominated by two multinationals . . . Likewise Ngai Tahu has shown huge financial acumen in its business activities, making it one of the highest-performing corporates in New Zealand.[42]

A recent study, for example, found that if Maori were defined as their own nation, they would rank as the fourth most entrepreneurial country in the world.[43] Twenty-five per cent of the Maori population is expecting to launch a start-up in the next three years compared to thirteen per cent for non-Maori.[44] Maori also have the highest informal investment rate in the OECD. Footprints Waipoua and Whalewatch Kaikoura are two examples of the many successful businesses in New Zealand owned and operated by Maori. Both Footprints and Whalewatch were started in economically depressed parts of the country. Both have subsequently grown to become award-winning tourism businesses that regularly receive rave reviews from the likes of *Lonely Planet*.

The progress over the last thirty years alone has been remarkable. Major claims regarding the historical dispossession of tribal land have been brought before the Waitangi Tribunal; the management of Maori-owned assets has been rearranged; a Maori-language education system has been established and widely deployed; and Maori have started major industry initiatives from fishing to aquaculture to farming to tourism. Additionally, there is now significant political representation, and an increasing number of individuals are gaining international reputations for their achievements. Maori social models, such as its form of restorative justice, are gaining traction here and elsewhere. Maori academics are finding their way to the top of our academic institutions in many fields.

Perhaps nowhere is the Maori renaissance more apparent than the extent to which Maori culture has infiltrated broader New Zealand society. As Snedden notes, 'We sing our national anthem in English and Maori without hesitation. Our Maori artists, filmmakers, commercial and sporting heroes are now representative of "more of us" than ever before . . . We are discovering ways of being a New Zealander that are not solely Maori or Pakeha, but an amalgam of the two.'[45]

There are clearly many, many contributing factors to this Maori renaissance. It's easy to point to the top-down solutions: the court cases in the 1980s, the ongoing Treaty of Waitangi settlements of land grievances, and the government initiatives to re-establish Maori iwi on a solid, independent economic foundation. They've all been of key significance, obviously.

But perhaps there have also been some bottom-up forces at work as well. Maybe our understanding of complex systems can point to another dynamic at play in the Maori turnaround.

The network effect

It sounds crazy to suggest that the migration of many Maori to the cities was a good thing. After all, weren't many of the negative statistics outlined earlier exacerbated by urbanisation? Didn't the shift to the cities break the traditional support structures of the iwi? Didn't Maori lose their tribal identities when they moved away from their rural homelands?

All of that is true, but there is another side to the urbanisation coin. Maybe the mass migration to the cities was also a blessing in disguise for Maori. Maybe the urbanisation of Maori helped fuel the Maori renaissance. Perhaps it was a move to the cities that reignited Maori adaptation.

As we've seen, cities are often the breeding ground for new ideas. Writing in the early decades of the twentieth century, Robert Park, the pioneering University of Chicago sociologist, noted the vibrancy of city living. Out of the cities, Parks notes, had sprung the new breeds and the newer social types. 'They have multiplied the opportunities for the individual man for contact and association with his fellows, but they have made these contacts and associations more transitory and less stable.'[46] Progress often flows from cities to the rest of society. The close interaction of peoples generates a quick flow of information. Networks emerge. The diversity of a city creates an explosion of new thinking.

Perhaps that very same dynamic was occurring in Maori society as more and more Maori left their relatively isolated rural iwi and began congregating in the cities. Take the innovations in social structures that occurred amongst urban Maori. Cities can be lonely places, especially when you come from a close-knit community. For some Maori the disconnection from the established social networks of their hapu or iwi meant falling into crime, or establishing replacement social networks like gangs, or both. But many other Maori responded by establishing new ties and social networks that compensated for the loss of traditional iwi networks. New associations were formed where Maori could meet and share activities, concerns and interests. For the first time, most of these voluntary groups were not kin-based but were pan-Maori. Maori society was changing again.

Maori wardens were introduced into urban areas. Urban, pan-tribal marae, such as the Hoani Waititi marae in West Auckland, te Unga Waka at Epsom, and Maraeroa in Porirua East, were built. The Waikumete cemetery in West Auckland has an area known as the Urupa, where anyone who can trace their Maori ancestry can be buried. It was the start of a multi-tribalism that helped foster a different style of leadership. The hereditary basis for hapu and iwi was diminished in rural settings in favour of merit-based authority.[47]

Maoridom redefined

As Michael King notes, 'urbanisation required Maori to redefine aspects of Maoridom: the nature of the extended family; how to hold hui in the city; what to do with tupapuku (corpses);' how, and whether, to keep alive links with rural tribal bases; the tribal status of people who were removed from live iwi contact.[48] Maori cultural practices were modified to confront the opportunities and constraints of urban living.[49] But as historian Joan Metge points out in her study of Maori urbanisation, traditional Maori practices were not replaced by Pakeha practices – rather their cultural traditions were modernised.[50]

Perhaps the most significant initial response to the challenges of urban living was the Maori Women's Welfare League. Founded in 1951 under the leadership of Northland kuia Dame Whina Cooper, it was the first pan-Maori nationwide organisation. Established to care for the young, the elderly and the sick, it became a central force in the mobilisation of resources across Maoridom to address the challenges facing an urbanising society. It was, for many years, the most effective voice of Maori hopes and aspirations.[51]

Urbanisation has enhanced the prominent role of women in Maori society. They have been instrumental in setting up, and running, a host of social programmes including tu tangata, kohanga reo, kura kaupapa and matua whangai. They have played a vital role in iwi authorities, Maori trust boards, and urban Maori authorities. And they have been the driving force behind the success of many health and social services by Maori, for Maori.

The cities encouraged diversity. For the first time, large numbers of Maori and Pakeha came into close contact with each other. Both Maori and Pakeha were exposed to new ideas and contacts. No longer isolated in the country, Maori suddenly had opportunities to re-absorb a world full of ideas, just as their forebears had when non-Maori first showed up two hundred years earlier. Non-Maori were exposed to Maoridom – it was now on their doorstep. For example, the 1960s witnessed the widespread beginnings of urban marae projects. These were to serve as traditional marae but were built within an urban environment.

Awareness of Maori culture, and its people, gradually increased amongst non-Maori. By the 1960s te reo Maori (the Maori language) was widely considered under threat of extinction. But pre-school kohanga reo (language nests) appeared in the early 1980s. These were followed by kura kaupapa (total Maori-language immersion) schools. Then under the Maori Language Act of 1987, te reo Maori was declared an official language of New Zealand and Te Taura Whiri i te Reo Maori (the Maori Language Commission) was established to foster and encourage the use of Maori.

Perhaps urbanisation, painful as it has been for Maori, was a necessary step in adapting to the new world. Forced to break from a traditional tribal structure, Maori coalesced into a more unified pan-Maori structure that was strong enough to push for the reforms of the 1980s and 1990s. The smaller, more isolated iwi versions of the Maori network turned into a more powerful, more adaptive nationwide version. The ability of Maori society to continue its ongoing adaptation to a fast-changing world is the stronger for it.

How well it does in fact work in the future will depend on Maori willingness to continue nurturing the seeds of adaptation. Despite the extraordinary progress, few would dispute the myriad challenges that continue to confront Maori society. And not just Maori. The challenges confronting New Zealand as a whole are equally onerous, and adaptation never more necessary. It won't be easy, but if the old bugger Koro – to quote Nanny Flowers – can do it in *Whalerider*, then there is hope for us all.

It is easy to forget how far Maori society has come, and how quickly, since Cook first showed up just over two hundred years ago. Even over the last fifty years, as Maori have migrated to the cities, the changes have been dramatic. Consider the changes they've had to confront in just a couple of generations: new ways of earning a living have been learnt; new areas to live have had to be found; new social structures have had to be developed; a new identity has had to be built. And all of this had to happen in a society that itself was undergoing major changes over that period. To top it all off, these changes had to occur amidst a foreign culture that, for most of those years, demanded conformity to its way of doing things. It's a big ask for a single family to succeed when facing all of that, let alone an entire people.

But as we've seen over the last few chapters, it is a demand not unfamiliar to Maori. The Maori story in Aotearoa New Zealand is a tale of adaptation to, and shaping of, a new land. What necessitated this adaptation were changes in the environment in which Maori lived. Whether it was fewer moa, the competition over land, the arrival of Europeans, the impact of firearms, or the lack of work in rural areas in the twentieth century, Maori society was continually buffeted by change. The environment was complex and unpredictable. While it wasn't always pleasant, adaptation was always necessary. It's a timeless lesson, but a lesson that has particular currency today for all New Zealanders – Maori and non-Maori alike.

This wander through a few slices of New Zealand's history suggests we're a country that has adapted well at times in the past. But we can't afford to become complacent. Especially not now. The magnitude of the changes New Zealand is facing, and the pace at which they'll arrive, places a premium on good adaptation as never before.

To take advantage of what these changes bring, New Zealand must continue to improve its ability to adapt and grow. That requires enhancing those three attributes of effective societies we came across in Chapter Six. Let's repeat what they are. First, New Zealand must be great at generating new ideas and applying them in a way that gives our companies, schools, hospitals, government, and society broader advantages. Second, because it can't generate all the good ideas it needs itself, New Zealand must be really good at absorbing ideas from elsewhere. Third, and finally, New Zealand must be willing to change, overcoming the innate love of the status quo and fear of change we all feel.

The fourth and final section of this book will look at each of these attributes in turn. I'll dive into a bit more detail on why each attribute is important, then throw out some very broad-brush ideas for how New Zealand can become better at them. While these chapters are not highly prescriptive, nor the ideas contained in them particularly original, they represent some initial thinking about what New Zealand can do to prepare better for its future.

Part 4

A few ideas for a more adaptable New Zealand

10

Unstoppable creativity

George Bernard Shaw, the British Nobel Prize-winning playwright and music critic, visited New Zealand in 1934 to great fanfare. Adoring crowds flocked to his every public appearance. He was the first major celebrity to visit New Zealand, and his celebrity attitude didn't disappoint. For instance, when his ship pulled into port he wandered down to the waiting crowd and greeted them with: 'Oh, good morning, ladies and gentlemen. I suppose you have seen at least fifty million pictures of me. You want to see the animal walk about and you want to hear the animal talk.'[1]

He toured the country for a month, and people everywhere swooned in his presence. At his only official reception, in Christchurch, a Professor James Shelly said that Christchurch had become the intellectual capital of the world due simply to the fact that it contained Mr Shaw. He doled out advice to an eager nation. One reporter asked him his impression of the country and, after a pause, Shaw replied: 'Altogether too many sheep.' He observed that New Zealand was a communist country without really knowing it, and denounced tourism as an unsatisfactory industry. Perhaps most tellingly, the cover to a booklet published at the end of his trip, *What I Said in NZ: The Newspaper Utterances of Mr George Bernard Shaw*, was adorned with a picture of Shaw holding his head in his hands.[2]

But beyond the patronising, he also said various things that might strike a New Zealander today as rather important. For example, he recommended the creation of a local film industry. Otherwise, he said, New Zealand would lose its soul without even getting an American one. But it was during a public address at the Chateau Tongariro that he made his most interesting observation. He urged New Zealand to start producing things other than butter. When asked by a member of the audience what he had in mind, Shaw replied: 'Start producing brains, perhaps.'

What Mr Shaw failed to realise is that New Zealand *has* always been good at producing brains. It's just that they've belonged to ruminant quadrapeds known as sheep and domesticated ungulates known as cows. Not that there's anything wrong with those brains. They're brains that do a great job at producing milk for drinking, wool for wearing, and meat for barbequing. Unfortunately these brains haven't quite figured out how to use a TV remote, send a text message or do any of the other things required of twenty-first-century humans. They certainly haven't figured out how to produce more highly valued things like world-class fashion or world-beating yachts or world-entrancing films or world-engrossing novels.

Thankfully, since Mr Shaw's visit, New Zealand has been producing brains that *can* do those things, and much more. From Witi Ihimaera in literature, to Niki Caro in movies, to Alan MacDiarmid in science, to Bruce Farr in yacht design, to Graeme Hart in business, to Angus Tait in electronics, New Zealand's brain production has shown far greater output than Mr Shaw might have anticipated.

Brain production . . . let's stop using that term . . . *idea generation* is critical for any society. As we saw in Chapter Six, idea generation is the energy behind any society's adaptation. It's the key to any society's strategy to avoid slipping behind. Societies need new ideas to sustain their activities. They fuel new ways to earn a living, entertain ourselves, and navigate the complexities of life. In short, they provide an evolutionary edge.

But creativity does not enact or sustain itself; it needs to be continually cultivated. Unlike land or capital, creativity cannot be passed down from generation to generation. So even if New Zealand was an idea-generating nation in the past, that does not necessarily mean it is today, or will be in the future. The capacity for new ideas needs to be constantly fermented and reproduced by society.

With that in mind, this chapter seeks to understand what creativity is; to understand how New Zealand measures up on the idea-generation front; and to propose a few ways in which New Zealand can ensure its creativity furnace is stoked as powerfully as ever.

What is creativity?

In the mid-1950s, a father in an industrial city in England spent almost a fortnight's wages buying his son a guitar. The boy showed an interest in music, so his father decided to encourage it. When the kid tried to join the school choir, however, the teacher said that he really wasn't very musical – he failed his audition. Fortunately he persisted with the guitar, became pretty good at it, worked at his singing and started his own band. The boy's name was Paul McCartney and his band became The Beatles.

As a society, we're shockingly bad at recognising creativity and talent. We're even worse at developing it. Sir Ken Robinson knows this better than most. An expert on creativity and innovation, he has in fact advised the Liverpool Institute for Performing Arts, whose leading patron is Sir Paul McCartney. In 1998, he led a national commission on creativity, education and the economy for the UK government. His report, *All Our Futures: Creativity, Culture and Education* (also known as the Robinson Report) was published to huge acclaim. In its review *The Times* said: 'This report raises some of the most important issues facing business in the twenty-first century. It should have every CEO and human resources director thumping the table and demanding action.'

Today, Robinson is senior advisor to the J. Paul Getty Trust in Los Angeles. He spends a lot of his time on the speaking circuit, preaching a message many seem willing to hear. He was one of four international advisors to the Singapore government for its strategy to become the creative hub of South East Asia. He has also advised Hong Kong and the European Union on their creativity strategies.

Robinson's primary focus is on the creative challenges facing business and education in the new global economy. His core message is that the key to the future, for organisations and societies, lies in new approaches to developing the creative talents of all their people.

To begin with, he challenges a major misconception about creativity that we pick up at school and have reinforced at work. That misconception is that only special people are creative. Companies everywhere reinforce this myth by dividing their employees into the creatives and the suits. The creatives, according to Robinson, are the people who wear jeans and don't wear ties and come in late because they've been struggling with an idea.

The other stereotype about creativity is its association with almost divinely inspired talent. Much of the psychological literature dealing with creativity has concentrated on 'successful creativity' or 'influential creativity'.[3] This is where creativity is studied by examining the lives and circumstances of famous innovators in the arts, science and business worlds.

While studying the lives of the highly creative is helpful, it can leave one with the impression that a person either is or is not creative. On top of that, there's not much anyone can do about it. We're left with the assumption that real creativity is an exceptional capacity that's limited to people of rare ability like the Rutherfords, the Goldies and *Shortland Street* stars. Again, according to Robinson, that's simply not the case.

Robinson argues for a completely different approach to the way we think about creativity. The truth is, he says, we all have profound creative capacities. Societies (and organisations) that are serious about churning out great ideas and innovations must work hard to develop the creative capacities of *all* their people.

Creativity here, there and everywhere

In 2003, Professor Richard Florida was a keynote speaker at the Knowledge Wave Conference in Auckland. Citing research material from his bestseller, *The Rise of the Creative Class*, he explained how important creativity is becoming to the modern economy. Creativity, he maintained, is to the twenty-first century what the ability to pull a plough was to the eighteenth century. Creative occupations are growing and firms now orient themselves to attract the creative. Employers prod their employees on to greater bursts of inspiration. The lesson to be taken from Florida's message is that cities that want to succeed must aim at attracting the creative types who are, he argued, the wave of the future.

He called this wave of the future the creative class. This segment of society, Florida says, is comprised of members 'engaged in work whose function is to create meaningful new forms'. Florida's creative class consists of two components. First, a super-creative core that includes 'scientists and engineers, university professors, poets and novelists, artists, entertainers, actors, designers and architects, as well as the thought leadership of modern society: nonfiction writers, editors, cultural figures, think-tank researchers, analysts and other opinion makers.'[4]

This group is supported by the second component of the creative class, the creative core. The creative core comprises creative professionals who work in a wide range of knowledge-intensive industries such as high-tech sectors, financial services, the legal and health-care professions, and business management. It is their job to support the super creative core in the work they do. His basic argument is that cities must do all they can to attract this creative class (in other words, turn themselves into cauldrons of culture and coolness).

Florida returned to the topic in 2005 with *The Flight of the Creative Class: The New Global Competition for Talent*, a sequel that extends his argument internationally.[5] Florida's basic point is that the entire global economy increasingly revolves around innovations that flow from the creative classes. He points to the small creative empire constructed in Wellington around Weta Workshop as an example of global talent magnets that are sucking the most creative people from places like the US.

He used International Labour Organisation data and job classifications to develop an index of the creative class in countries around the world. Since 1991, Florida says, New Zealand's creative class has jumped from nineteen to twenty-seven per cent of its workforce. That places New Zealand fifth in the world (behind the likes of Ireland and Australia, but ahead of thirty-five other countries including Finland, Singapore, the UK, and the US). Those are the kinds of statistics that get our politicians excited.

While Florida's notion of a creative class may be compelling, the dichotomy between the creative person and the non-creative or average person seems a little artificial or, to use one critic's term, 'formulaic'.[6] Certainly artists and designers and film makers and architects are creative generators of new ideas, forms and representations. These creative activities

– music, literature, visual arts, design, architecture and performing arts – are central to New Zealand's identity, economy and social tapestry. They are what we often think of as the creative part of our society.

But in thinking about how New Zealand can build its adaptability, our use of the term creative has to be broader than that. After all, New Zealand society consists of thousands of separate fields of expertise from farming to cooking to to music to mathematics to computer programming to religion to art. Each of these fields comprises a set of instructions for behaviour. There is a commonly accepted way of starting a company or writing a will or being a tow-truck driver or publishing a book or managing a shop or treating a fractured wrist or fixing a bike. The instructions for operating in each field are passed from one person to the next through learning. In most fields, they don't change that often.

However, there are individuals who are always trying out to farming techniques, new methods to compute quantities, new ways to think about cells or economies or educational techniques, and so on. If these are deemed to be better than the old ways, the new idea will be called creative and be absorbed into the set of instructions or knowledge in that field. New ideas fuel improvements. It's how societies learn, adapt and grow. It's how they prosper. That's why a leading expert on economic development, Harvard University's Laurence Harrison, suggests that the societies that progress the fastest are simply those that help *all* their people realise their creative potential.[7]

That's why even if progress is narrowly defined in economic terms, it's not just the entrepreneur who creates progress. As Harrison explains:

> The inventor of the machine employed by the entrepreneur; the scientist who conceived the theory that the inventor turned to practical use; the engineer who designed the system to mass-produce the machine; the farmer who uses special care in producing a uniform raw material to be processed by the machine; the machine operator who suggests some helpful modifications to the machine on the basis of long experience in operating it – all are contributing to growth. So is the salesman who expands demand for the product by conceiving a new use for it. So, too, are the teachers who got the scientist, the inventor, and the engineer interested in their professions and who taught the farmer agronomy.[8]

And so on. The point is that everybody contributes to a society's march forward. Each person adds their creativity in their field of work. To Harrison, development is as much a process of millions of small breakthroughs as it is of a few monumental innovations, the work of geniuses. A society that smooths the way for these breakthroughs and encourages them is a society that will progress far. For that reason, New Zealand shouldn't take Florida's idea too far and become overly picky about who it turns to for new ideas.

Looking for creativity

Teresa Amabile, head of the Entrepreneurial Management Unit at Harvard Business School, has been grappling with the question of where creativity is found for three decades. She has collected nearly 12,000 daily journal entries from two hundred and thirty-eight people working on creative projects in the consumer products, high-tech and chemical industries. Without telling the study participants that she was focusing on creativity, she asked them, in a daily email, about their work that day. She then went through their emails looking for moments when people struggled with a problem or came up with a new idea – in other words, when creativity surfaced in their work.

One of the things she found was that creativity can be found anywhere in an organisation. 'The fact is,' she says, 'almost all of the research in this field shows that anyone with normal intelligence is capable of doing some degree of creative work. Creativity depends on a number of things: experience, including knowledge and technical skills; talent; an ability to think in new ways; and the capacity to push through uncreative dry spells.'[9]

If we define creativity then as *the generation of new ideas,* we can see the traces of creativity everywhere. A parent becomes creative when he devises novel ways of making the everyday life of his children stimulating and comfortable given a limited budget. A farmer is creative when she comes up with a more efficient way of distributing feed to her livestock. The entrepreneur is creative in developing a new product or service, then thinking up new ideas about how to differentiate his goods or services from those of others. So under that broader definition of creativity, some of New Zealand's most prolific idea generators are located in our country's homes, hospitals, schools and companies.

This creative economy, then, is one where people don't do just a nine to five routine, repetitive job. It's where people, at any stage – talking to their spouse, sharing a bottle of wine with friends, watching the rugby or swinging a golf club – think they may have an idea that will actually work. Not just an idea that gives some sort of esoteric pleasure, but an idea that will make a difference in their life and in their work. It's why Robinson defines creativity simply as 'individuals having ideas'.

The point is that New Zealand needs to ensure it is spreading its idea-generation net as widely as possible. That means avoiding the tendency to only look for new ideas in certain areas or from particular people. The young, the old, the conservative, the alternative, the uneducated and the overeducated: all have a creative capacity, like anyone else. While their ideas will invariably differ, the stock of ideas open to an organisation or a society is enhanced when different ideas are brought to the fore, tested, modified and integrated. New Zealand is too small to afford exclusivity when it comes to idea generation.

So the message is: creativity exists everywhere and in everyone. Let's make this more tangible by understanding why creativity is important and how New Zealand stacks up.

Why creativity counts

We hear a lot of talk these days about what New Zealand needs to do to sustain its economic growth. It's talked about a great deal because it's very important for the country's future. It funds, after all, the standard of living we hope to enjoy in the future. If we don't grow our economy, our schools, hospitals, public areas, and so on all deteriorate. Without a minimum level of economic growth, we'll struggle to provide for our children the bright future other societies are able to give theirs. It's easy to forget, however, amid all the economic jargon we constantly hear, just how simple the basic laws of economic growth are and the central role creativity plays.

At its most fundamental, economic growth occurs when people take resources and rearrange them in ways that are more valuable. Stanford

University economist Paul Romer uses a kitchen metaphor.[10] To create valuable final products, we mix inexpensive ingredients together according to a recipe. But the cooking we can do is limited by the supply of ingredients. Human history teaches us, however, that economic growth springs from better recipes, not just from more cooking. New recipes generally generate more economic value per unit of raw material.

Romer likes to provide a very innocuous example. You may not have noticed, but in many cafés you can now use the same size lid for small, medium and large cups of coffee. That wasn't the case for a long time. That small change in the geometry of the cups means that a coffee shop can serve customers at lower cost because they only need to carry one type of lid. Employees can replenish supplies more quickly throughout the day. Customers can get their coffee just a bit faster. Romer points out that while big inventions like the Walkman or antibiotics or the cellphone grab the headlines, it's the millions of little discoveries like coffee lid designs that are equally important in driving up a nation's income.

The good news is that while the world is filled with finite resources, there is an almost unlimited number of ways in which these resources can be combined. Romer explains the concept of *combinations* this way. There are 10^{88} particles in the known universe.[11] That is a very, very large number. But it is nothing compared to the number of ways things (or ideas) can be combined. To illustrate, take a deck of cards. It can be rearranged in many, many ways. In fact, there are 10^{68} possible card decks, which means that the order of the last deck you shuffled has probably never appeared before.

What this means, according to Romer, is that we are limited only by our imagination. There are lots of new recipes to be invented. By coming up with new ideas on how to increase, say, the power of a microprocessor, humans can increase productivity, open up new opportunities for profit, and ultimately power economic growth.

The problem for developed countries like New Zealand is that there are lots of countries in the world, as we saw in Chapter Two, who are churning out lots of workers able to work to existing recipes – very cheaply. They can follow a recipe, take the ingredients, and put it all together for a fraction of the cost New Zealand can. That's why New Zealand needs to focus on generating new recipes. That's what we do well, and that'll fuel our economic growth far more powerfully than trying to compete on old recipes.

That's why creativity is so important for New Zealand's future. Many other developed (and developing) nations are quickly coming to the same conclusion about their economic futures. Many countries recognise that the future of national economies depends upon a steady flow of innovative ideas. So, for example, Singapore aims to be the creative hub of South East Asia and they have in place the Creative Singapore Strategy. Even China, the manufacturing powerhouse with an abundance of cheap labour good at following old recipes, is desperately trying to figure out how to educate its people to be creative.

The US is certainly very worried about how equipped its workforce is to generate the ideas necessary to grow its twenty-first-century economy. A report on the future of the American workforce entitled *Tough Choices or Tough Times* was released at the end of 2006.[12] The New Commission on the Skills of the American Workforce – a high-powered bipartisan panel that includes senior government officials, business and civic leaders – issued the recommendations in an effort to light a fire under the country. Fostering creativity lies at the heart of the commission's recommendations.

> Those countries that produce the most important new products and services can capture a premium in world markets that will enable them to pay high wages to their citizens. In many industries, producing the most important new products and services depends on maintaining the worldwide technological lead year in and year out, in that industry and in the new industries that new technologies generate.
>
> But that kind of leadership does not depend on technology alone. It depends on a deep vein of creativity that is constantly renewing itself, and on a myriad of people who can imagine how to use things that have never been available before, create ingenious marketing and sales campaigns, write books, build furniture, make movies, and imagine new kinds of software that will capture people's imagination and become indispensable to millions.

If the world's largest economy is that concerned about the need for creativity for its future growth, then tiny New Zealand certainly can't afford to ignore the vital role creativity will need to play in our future.

So how does New Zealand measure up?

The notion that New Zealand is a society of innovators has become part of New Zealand's folklore. From the ingenuity of the Maori to the making-do of the early, isolated European pioneers to the tinkering of twentieth-century heroes like motorcycle speed-hound Burt Munro, it's easy to gain the impression that creativity's in our drinking water. But how creative a people are we really?

There's no absolute way of knowing, of course. So I'm going to use a metric, albeit an imperfect one, for establishing our collective creativeness: patents. A patent is the legal protection anyone receives who invents or discovers any new and useful process or item. What's more, it's not just new products that are patented. The US Patent and Trademark Office has given Dell Computers a patent not for the computers it sells but for the *way* it sells them. The British Patent Office has also headed off into new territory by awarding a patent for the technique of cloning Dolly the sheep, which covers the 'possible use of the technology in cloning human cells'.

As of 2004, there was a total of around 5.4 million 'live' patents registered with the World Intellectual Property Organisation. That year almost 1.6 million patent applications were filed.[13] New Zealand filed sixteen hundred and thirty-one of those, which means New Zealand filed about four hundred patents per million people. That puts us in sixth place in the world behind Japan, Korea, the US, Germany and Australia. New Zealand is in fourth place when patents are measured against gross domestic product, ahead of both Australia and the US. We're also in fourth place when our patents filed are compared to our research and expenditure budget. So it seems as though our creative juices are flowing strongly.

But simply looking at worldwide patent statistics can be somewhat misleading, since different countries follow different standards for granting patents. That's why I'll look at patents granted in the US. It receives patent applications for nearly all major innovations worldwide, and holds them to the same strict standards.[14] Looked at from that angle, a slightly different light is shed on New Zealand creativity.

In 2005, around seventy-five thousand of the hundred and forty-three thousand patents granted in the US went, not surprisingly, to Americans.[15] Some thirty thousand went to Japanese inventors, and nine thousand to

Germans. The next ten most innovative countries – including the usual suspects in Europe plus Taiwan, South Korea, Israel, and Canada – produced around twenty-five thousand more. The rest of the world accounted for just five per cent of all innovations patented in the United States.

New Zealand chipped in with a hundred and forty-three of them. 'Drug, Bio-Affecting and Body Treating Compositions' was New Zealand's most popular category, with eight patents, but there was also a patent granted in the 'Buckles, Buttons, Clasps, Etc.' category, and another under the 'Bed' category. There were even four patents for 'Chairs and Seats'.

Spend a bit of time snooping around the statistics and a telling story emerges. The first thing we find is that while we scored highly on the world patents index, we didn't seem to do so well at the US patent office. In fact, we're quite a bit off the pace relative to some other players. There are about as many New Zealanders as there are Singaporeans, and yet for the last five years they have managed to register well over twice as many patents as New Zealand. There are only half a million more Norwegians, yet they have registered almost twice as many patents in the US as New Zealand. There are only a million extra Finns, yet their patent generation in the US is over five times New Zealand's. Put another way, it took about five thousand New Zealanders to generate one US patent in 2005. That's a lot more than the twenty-one-hundred-odd Singaporeans, the twelve-hundred-odd Fins, and the eleven-hundred-odd Swedes.[16]

A couple more pieces of New Zealand's innovation puzzle emerge. First of all, a very high proportion (eighteen per cent) of New Zealand's patent applications were from individuals. In other words, they were individually owned. That eighteen per cent is a lot higher than the figure for many other small countries. Only five per cent of Singapore's patents were from individuals, four per cent of Finland's and six per cent of Denmark's. Some countries had nearer fifteen per cent of their patents filed by individuals, but they tended to have significantly larger populations (like Australia).

Some may say that the high number of individually owned patents is another example of New Zealand's Number-Eight fencing wire genius at work. Perhaps it is. But what it also suggests is that many of the new ideas generated in New Zealand do not have the support (money, expertise, infrastructure) of an organisation helping them realise their innovation.

That's a problem, as we'll see in a second.

The other piece of New Zealand's innovation puzzle is that very few of New Zealand's patents originate with a single organisation. In fact, New Zealand's largest US patent-getter over the last five years, Fisher & Paykel, managed a haul of around sixty-five US patents – about eight per cent of New Zealand's total. For Singapore, Chartered Semiconductor, the big manufacturer of microchips for computers, generated four hundred and forty-two patents alone over the last five years. That constituted twenty-two per cent of the country's total. A big chunk of Sweden's eleven hundred and eighty-nine patent applications came from the telecommunications giant, Ericsson, which alone contributed two hundred and nine. And Nokia, the other communications giant, contributed a whopping thirty-nine per cent to Finland's four thousand two hundred and twenty-four patents over the last five years.

What this suggests is that New Zealand is a little hamstrung without a couple of big exporters in highly innovative industries like semiconductor or cellphone manufacturing. It turns out that there is something about large organisations that drives greater innovation than is the case with the equivalent number of smaller companies.

Innovation in big organisations

To understand why big organisations can out-innovate smaller ones, let's return (oddly enough) to genomics (the study of an organism's hereditary information). In 1996 the scientific community was shocked to discover that the yeast genome contained as many as six thousand three hundred genes. That was more than many had expected. On that basis, biologists estimated the human genome, considering our place at the top of the evolutionary food chain, would come in around the hundred thousand genes mark. But they were in for another surprise. When the human genome was decoded five years later, it turned out we humans had only about twenty-two thousand five hundred genes. To make matters worse, that was only ten thousand more genes than the humble roundworm – a dent to *Homo sapiens'* pride for sure.

But before you invite a family of roundworms around for dinner, consider this: a small increase in the number of nodes (genes, cells, people) in a complex system can radically affect the system's level of complexity. It is no different for organisms like humans or roundworms. It works like this. If any one gene in a cell can be either 'on' or 'off', independently of one another, a cell with, say, a hundred genes could display 2^{100} distinct states. If the potential number of distinct states a cell could be in is a measure of complexity, the difference between the worm and humans is staggering. Humans, by this measure, end up being10^{3000} times more complex than our wormy friends. Hope you feel reassured now.

Add more genes to a cell and complexity increases exponentially. Add more people to an organisation and the same thing happens. Think of the difference between your local coffee shop and Telecom.[17] Your local café employs, say, seven people, whereas Telecom has around six thousand people clocking in each day for work. The jump from ten employees to six thousand is only three orders of magnitude (10^3) but the jump in complexity from making lattes to keeping New Zealand's telecommunication system running is many, many orders of magnitude greater.

That means an organisation the size of Telecom has inherently more capacity for innovation in the future – the larger number of states in the Telecom network means there are more *potential* ways for Telecom to make a profit than for the local coffee shop.[18] As organisations grow in size, the space for possible innovation unfolds exponentially. It's the same with societies as well.

Of course *what* the company does is also important. A very big company producing say, apples, many not have the same capacity for innovation as a smaller company making microchips. Unfortunately for New Zealand, the majority of our products are grown, and mountains of butter or carcasses of lamb lack the complexity of some other products. Hence the range of potential innovations is smaller.[19]

The other issue for New Zealand is that it is a nation of small companies. New Zealand is a world leader at starting companies, but not great at growing them. The Total Early-Stage Activity (TEA) index is a measure of the prevalence of individuals engaged in the start-up or gestation phase or in managing a young business, less than forty-two months old. New Zealand ranks top of the OECD, clocking in at around fourteen per cent of the working age population.[20]

In 2006, New Zealand had over 345,000 enterprises, employing around

1.76 million people. Ninety-six per cent of New Zealand enterprises employ fewer than ten people.[21] Close to sixty per cent of New Zealand entrepreneurs are self-employed, and two-thirds of them are home-based.[22] If you're setting up shop in your garage or spare room, there isn't much room to grow, and typically that's fine for those who elect to work from home. But it means that New Zealand remains in the realm of tiny businesses.

More significantly, most of New Zealand's entrepreneurs (the vast majority of the 281,000 businesses) are involved in what is known as the 'economic core'.[23] They are typified by the corner dairy, the lawn-mowing and house-cleaning franchisees, and shopkeepers in Newmarket and Levin. We need these businesses, and it's difficult to imagine life without them. But they're also characterised by their low rates of innovation (how do you continually innovate in a corner dairy?) and low rates of growth. So a great wad of our entrepreneurs are in businesses that will never be big drivers of new ideas in the economy.

What this all means is that the innovation story for New Zealand is mixed. On the one hand we have the good news that New Zealanders have never been short on creativity and improvisation. We're a creative bunch, for the most part.

The bad news, however, is that as individuals we don't live in a vacuum. Individuals often need institutional support to harness their creativity most effectively. As economic historian Joel Mokyr puts it: what makes individuals implement, improve, and adapt new technologies, or just devise small improvements in the way they carry out their daily work (in other words, what makes them innovate), depends on the attitudes and resources around them.[24] Without the right support, good ideas just stay that way – as ideas. Our ability to build and develop them into money-generating activities is limited. Put another way, we're not coming up with enough new recipes.

Small countries like New Zealand have to work extra hard at generating creativity, and then turning it into innovation. Although we cannot predict creativity, we can foster it by providing environments that encourage it. Necessity is not always the mother of invention. Creativity is a very emergent property, and we'll now turn to a few ideas that might help it bubble up further.

Investing in our idea-generation infrastructure

Any society makes conscious choices about where it invests its resources. Some societies choose to invest more of their resources into activities that generate ideas. They figure in the long run that will help them prosper more successfully.

New Zealand is not one of those societies. Our total investment in research and development (key idea-generation activity) amounts to a paltry 1.2 per cent of our gross domestic product, a fraction of our spending on housing, infrastructure and other physical capital, and way below most other developed countries.[25] In fact, we're in sixteenth place when it comes to our expenditure – as a percentage of GDP – on investment in knowledge.[26] It's not surprising, then, that we top the OECD when it comes to the percentage of our manufacturing exports that are considered 'low technology'. We can come up with all the justifications and excuses we like, but the fact is that as a nation we're not investing in the creation of new ideas in the way other countries are. That hurts our ability to adapt.

Thankfully, that is slowly changing. New Zealand is gradually evolving into an idea-generating economy. But this is a generation-to-generation journey. It will require ongoing 'show us the money' scrutiny of those entrusted with the public's coffers. The fact is the payback in purely economic terms would be far greater if we channelled a fraction of the money we spend on, say, sports stadiums, into supporting new biotechnology or software research.

In 2006 Auckland wrestled with the choice between spending about a quarter of a billion dollars upgrading Eden Park, or up to a billion dollars building a new waterfront stadium, to host the 2011 Rugby World Cup. It appeared a painful process for all involved. The decision was made to go with the Eden Park option. There was fierce debate about which option was the best but little was said about whether investing such vast amounts of money into any stadium was in the country's longer term interests.

We need our sports stadiums, of course. But we also need to be honest about the reasons for them. They're there for our enjoyment of sport and the odd concert. That's a perfectly legitimate reason for any society, especially one as sports-mad as New Zealand. Further, building a new stadium may help Auckland become a 'world-class' city, some claimed.[27]

But when people begin claiming 'long-term economic benefits' as a reason for building a new stadium, we need to pause for a minute.[28] It's important that they articulate how New Zealand's longer-term economic benefit is better served by spending an additional $500 million on a new stadium versus the economic benefit of spending that money in the country's idea-generating infrastructure (scholarships for engineering and science students, funds for university research labs, and so on).

Perhaps we need a higher standard of what 'economic benefit' means. Supporters of a new stadium point to the added benefits: extra profits for nearby restaurants, shops and hotels, and extra tourists. But can't we do better than that? Are a few more meals sold or hotel rooms booked or souvenirs flogged the best New Zealand can expect from its investment in economically productive assets? The longer-term economic benefits of investing that money in idea-generating infrastructure will inevitably be greater – new products for export or licence, the absorption of overseas capital, attracting and retaining smart people, and so on.

Let me reiterate: New Zealand needs its sports stadiums, and economic benefits are certainly not the be-all and end-all of any decision. But as a tiny nation we also need to be clear about what we're gaining, and losing, from our investment of public funds. We need to understand the significant trade-offs we make when we plug money into a sports stadium over a science park, into a racecourse over a research lab. These are not trivial choices. In a country the size of New Zealand, the legacy of $500 million decisions like that will last for generations.

By adding to the stock of what Richard Florida calls creative capital, we'd increase New Zealand's wealth substantially. Such investments generate substantial ongoing returns by attracting top scientific, technical and creative talent. They spin off new companies and attract firms from other countries. That all tends to make things like better hospitals, more schools, and even new sports stadiums a lot more affordable. This is territory that has been well travelled in public discourse over the last few years, but it would be remiss in a book of this sort to ignore how important investing of public funds in idea-generation is to the future of our nation.

Growing creative kids

Here's a remarkable thought: the children who start school today will be retiring around 2065. Does anyone have any idea what the world will look like in 2065? We've seen already that it's hard enough venturing a guess beyond the next ten years. Yet it's the job of today's education system to prepare our children for a future that we cannot predict.

The *Tough Choices or Tough Times* report – from that high-powered US panel – puts the imperatives of twenty-first-century education like this:

> This is a world in which a very high level of preparation in reading, writing, speaking, mathematics, science, literature, history, and the arts, will be an indispensable foundation for everything that comes after for most members of the workforce. It is a world in which comfort with ideas and abstractions is the passport to a good job, in which creativity and innovation are the key to the good life, in which high levels of education – a very different education than most of us have had – are going to be the only security there is.[29]

The report points out that this is a world where mechanics will need to understand the computers embedded in new cars, architects will need familiarity with nanotechnology, where software engineers with a familiarity with music will have an edge over those who do not as the entertainment industry evolves, and small businesspeople who construct custom boats will only survive if they understand the scientific foundation of carbon fibre composites.[30]

As the report alludes to, the current way we educate our children may not be preparing them optimally to face a future no one can anticipate.

A century ago, education's function was to pass on the knowledge, skills, and wisdom of the past to the next generation. As the schoolmaster in Charles Dickens' *Hard Times*, Thomas Gradgrind, said:

> Teach these boys and girls nothing but Facts. Facts alone are wanted in life. Plant nothing else, and root out everything else. You can only form the minds of reasoning animals upon Facts: nothing else will ever be of any service to them . . . Stick to the Facts, sir!

But in the course of the twentieth century that changed. In the paraphrased words of the British science philosopher Alfred Whitehead, for the first time in human history the wisdom of our forebears will be of less practical value to our livelihoods than the knowledge produced during our lifetimes.[31] To reflect this the emphasis in education has slowly shifted from simply learning facts to building sills and driving creativity. And that shift needs to continue in earnest.

That shift in educational methods needs to quicken. For despite the progress in educational methods over the past hundred years, research suggests the challenge to grow creative children into creative adults remains a daunting one. George Land and Beth Jarman, in their book called *Breakpoint and Beyond: Mastering the Future Today*, report on research they did, over a series of years, into divergent thinking.[32] Divergent thinking is the capacity to think non-logically – to think associatively, and it's a good example of creativity. Land and Jarman gave a series of tests to sixteen hundred three- to five-year-olds. Ninety-eight per cent of the children scored at the genius level or higher for divergent thinking.

They gave the same tests to the same children five years later at the ages of eight to ten. At that stage thirty-two per cent scored at the genius level in divergent thinking. By the time the children were fifteen the number of divergent-thinking geniuses had dropped to just ten per cent. When the researchers gave the same test to over two hundred thousand adults only two per cent were in the same category. Something eroded in the capacity of those children to think creatively. It might just have had to do with the way modern educational systems teach children to think.

That's why we need to continue to update the way we're teaching our children. The human brain is intensely interactive. As Ken Robinson points out, the school curriculum tends to kill these interactions by setting up separate subject departments. So we teach maths for an hour and then music for another half an hour. Perhaps there is a way of making these processes more interactive.

New Zealand has been experimenting with various education models that do just that. For example, the Primary Enterprise Program (PrEP) develops the entrepreneurial capabilities of primary-school children through the establishment of micro-businesses.[33] From pizza and smoothie shops to travel agencies to film documentaries, it's a thriving economy that in 2004 involved two hundred and twelve schools and twenty-four thousand students. Job are applied for, CEOs appointed, mayors voted in, and bank managers pleaded with. Laws are passed, and then broken. The total curriculum time is a couple of hours a week. It's a taste of real life that breaks students out of the compartmentalised learning environment, allowing them to use their maths and their English and their art cohesively. It's about engendering creativity, problem-solving, and curiosity.

Mitchel Resnick, a professor of technology and learning at Massachusetts Institute of Technology, is all for that. He explores how new technologies can help children learn new things in new ways. He's inventing technologies that radically change how and what kids learn, fostering 'decentralised thinkers'.

Corporate structures, scientific theories, computer architectures, political and economic models are all becoming more decentralised. And the Internet is accelerating this trend. As we discovered earlier, in a decentralised system lots of simple parts interact with one another in simple ways, with no single part in charge: birds in a flock, cars on a highway, buyers and sellers in a market economy. If today's children want to succeed in tomorrow's world, Resnick believes they need to be comfortable with decentralised approaches.

Part of the challenge is to build an education system comfortable with decentralisation. Whether they end up creating organisations, technologies, communities, or theories, Resnick believes people will need to think this way. To understand decentralised systems, children need opportunities to design, create, play with, and explore decentralised systems.

Some New Zealand schools are experimenting with completely different education models. 'Unlimited Paenga Tawhiti', for example, is a relatively new state secondary school located in the city centre of Christchurch. It was established in 2003 by the Christchurch-based Learning Discovery Trust. It is one of just eleven schools running under the Designated Special Character criteria of the Education Act, and has a roll of just under three hundred students.

What makes Unlimited Paenga Tawhiti school special is its novel approach to learning. Each student is given an individual learning plan based on consultation with parents, teachers and the student. The students have dedicated one-on-one sessions with teachers where progress is evaluated and improvements are worked on. The New Zealand curriculum underpins the learning at the school, but does not drive it. Students are immersed in technology and interactive learning environments both in and out of the classroom. They don't wear uniforms, sit at desks in classrooms or work to set timetables. For some people an education programme that loose is unfathomable. But then perhaps the thought of sitting in a classroom rote-learning facts and figures from a set curriculum as a way of equipping students for the future is pretty unfathomable as well.

PrEP, or unlimited paenga tawhiti, or other novel education methods and models may not be perfect. Inevitably there will be some failures along the way. But at least New Zealand is experimenting with education methods that might equip our children for the twenty-first century. We get upset about text message abbreviations being permitted on examination answer sheets, but perhaps we're getting upset about the wrong things. Maybe we need more national angst about the fundamental question of whether our schools are developing creative, stimulated, confident children.

No one is disputing the need to develop children who get their quadratic equations correct, work their way around a periodic table with ease, and can conjugate their verbs with aplomb. No one is disputing that the education system must instil in children an ethos of discipline and hard work. People are not even disputing that children need guidance and structure in their learning.[34] All these elements must be a hallmark of a twenty-first-century education system. What is disputed is whether all of the above is achieved with education methods that, at their most fundamental, have changed little in a hundred years. We now know so much more today about how the brain works, what stimulus it responds to, and how the learning needs of one child varies from the next. We can't be afraid to use that.

The fact is, no one has all the answers to the question of how to prepare a nation's children for the future they will face. But every nation is struggling to figure it out. New Zealand can't be left behind. It's often said that education is the key to the future. It is. But as Ken Robinson points out, a key can be turned in either direction: locking resources away, or releasing them. We won't survive in the future simply by doing better what we have done in the past. Our future idea-generating capability will require much more than that.

Understanding the value (and limitations) of the incremental

In the 1940s, Genrikh Altshuller began work as a clerk in the Soviet patent office. He became interested in the invention process and set out to establish some generic rules that would explain the creation of new, inventive, patentable ideas. It was a task that would not even be interrupted by imprisonment in a labour camp during one of Stalin's purges, where fellow inmates assisted him with his research.

His study scrutinised over two hundred thousand patents (others have continued his research and that figure has now reached over 1.5 million), to determine how many of them represented truly new knowledge. The result? Only five per cent of them were truly new concepts. The rest were simply improvements on what had already existed.

That's an important nuance to the whole creativity story. Up until this point in the chapter I've used the term creativity in its most general sense. All new ideas fall under this broad rubric. But obviously not all ideas are created equal. Some represent a completely new solution using an entirely different set of principles. Other ideas – the overwhelming majority, in fact – are simply incremental improvements in the way something has been done before.

Conceiving and making the first Post-it notes was a completely new idea. Making them different sizes, shapes and colours was an incremental improvement on the original creative idea. Even though planes had existed before, the 747 design was actually a daring, novel, risky and original one. Much larger than any existing commercial aeroplane at the time, its design, construction and operation meant starting afresh on many aspects of conventional aircraft manufacturing. The widening and lengthening of the cabin, plus the myriad other changes to the wings, cockpit and engines that have occurred in the 747 design since, are incremental improvements on the original idea.

This distinction may seem trivial, but it's actually quite important. It's important to distinguish between novel and incremental ideas because the processes are different, the risks are different, the starting points are different, and the environments needed to achieve them are different. Organisations and society need both. To grow and prosper, most organisations need to constantly improve their existing products and services; but to survive, they also need to create new products and services before existing ones become obsolete and non-competitive.

Generally most businesses are more comfortable with the incremental than with the new. Why? Because the incremental is a lot safer. It's far easier to achieve success improving something that exists than starting with something that doesn't. The incremental requires a much lower level of risk and it can be stopped at any time. The end point is generally known. There is often less of a need for long-term commitment of resources and money.

Completely new ideas, on the other hand, require a different mindset, tolerance of mistakes, an acceptance of risk, and a commitment of time and resources. They require the acceptance of possible failure. Continuity has to be allowed for. Taken together, these requirements affect the culture of any organisation or society that aspires to be creative.

But this is far from easy. Most organisations find it far easier to do the incremental than the extraordinary. In their book, *Creative Destruction*, management consultants Dick Foster and Sarah Kaplan looked at *Forbes* magazine's list of the hundred largest US companies in 1917 and compared it with *Forbes'* list in 1987.[35] What they found is quite astonishing. A mere seventy years after the first list of one hundred was compiled, only eighteen companies were still on the list. A staggering sixty-one of them no longer existed.

These eighteen that did survive weren't exactly champion performers. With the exception of just two companies, General Electric and Kodak, all eighteen underperformed the average growth in stock-market value during that seventy-year period. Then Kodak disappeared off the list in the 1990s, leaving only General Electric. One company, out of a hundred!

One reason leading companies struggle so much to maintain their performance is due to the difficulty they have with continuous change. In his book *The Innovator's Dilemma*, Clayton Christensen, a professor at Harvard Business School, revealed that companies find it very difficult to move from one innovation to the next.[36] If a technological innovation pushes up the performance of a product then the technology tends to preserve the power of existing players. However, when a new, disruptive technology comes along, the entrenched companies that support the older technology often struggle to adjust.

That's because in business organisations there is a constant tension between two critical requirements: to perform in the short term and to invest and innovate for the long run. For this reason, Tom Peters and Bob Waterman, the authors of perhaps the most famous business book, *In Search of Excellence*, argue that organisations must simultaneously be tight in executing and loose in adapting.[37]

While this executing versus adapting challenge crops up regularly throughout business literature, most organisations are much better at the executing part of the equation than the adapting. Better at the small incremental improvements than the larger, more significant changes – like developing entirely new solutions or products as opposed to endlessly tinkering with their existing product line. The corporate record is littered with examples of companies that chose to stick to their knitting, rather than change.

Polaroid, the manufacturer of 35mm film for cameras, grew into a large, successful company in the 1970s and 1980s. As the company prospered during this period, and the longer the industry remained relatively stable, the more convinced the management team would have become that it really understood what was going on and was able to predict where the business was going. The more convinced the management team became, the more precisely and specifically it would have tuned its assets, skills, and people to continue doing the incremental – small improvements to their traditional 35mm product range.

Then in the early 1990s, Phoebe Moses's hand trembled – digital technology was developed. The world started to change. To begin with, the company's leaders would have believed that the problems they were experiencing were just a temporary anomaly. The new digital technology hardly looked likely to set the photography world on fire: it was horribly expensive, bulky, and unreliable.

But while the executive team waited for more evidence, the world kept changing. Digital photography took hold. The company suddenly found itself in a new game and stuck with the wrong strategy, the wrong assets and the wrong skills. Sure enough, fewer than ten years later that executive team was looking for a new job as Polaroid went out of business. The technology improved, as it always does. It became cheaper, smaller, and more reliable. Poor 35mm, and those who made it, didn't stand a chance.

It's hard to be too critical of Polaroid's management for not wanting to erode their existing 35mm product line. Especially when the long-term pay-offs from this new digital technology would have been far from certain. That's a difficult message to sell to your board and shareholders. It highlights the difficulty organisations face. The path of least resistance is invariably that which optimises our short-term gain at the expense of our ability to prepare for the future.

The New Zealand government has been doing some real thinking in this area over the last few years. Its Growth and Innovation Advisory Board has been talking to businesses about their attitudes to growth and innovation. In one study, the Board found that New Zealand businesses are good at making lots of small innovations, with people at all levels working on continuous improvements to the business.[38] But when it came to big innovations, New Zealand businesses struggled. Part of the reason why they struggled to produce industry-changing innovations, the board found, was the absence of structural mechanisms for innovation. As one respondent in the study said, the challenge is getting the ideas from ninety-five per cent to a workable solution.[39] It's that five per cent which requires a disciplined approach to creativity, what another respondent described as 'structured creativity'.[40]

New Zealand's number-eight wire mentality has become a cliché. But if it exists, then it suggests we're at the incremental rather than the completely new end of the creativity spectrum. Sure, we have our 'one out of the box' breakthrough moments, like the carbon fibre America's Cup yacht, but generally we're tinkering, improvising, to make improvements on the new products and services of others. There's nothing wrong with that as such. That's often the best strategy for the small, the resource-constrained and the risk averse.

But it does mean we're less likely to generate the game-changing leaps forward that come with completely novel ideas. To get into the radically new idea game, New Zealand will need to re-evaluate its thinking about the importance of research and development, the types of industries that have the capacity for radically new thinking (biotechnology, rather than hotels, for example), and a broader tolerance for failure.

Collective creativity

In 1497, the French ambassador to the Vatican commissioned a sculpture of Mary holding the body of Jesus after his death. In less than two years, Michelangelo had carved from a single slab of marble one of the most magnificent sculptures ever created. When Michelangelo finished his *Pieta*, he was a mere twenty-four years old. A year later he began tapping out his *David*, and had completed that before he was thirty. It's hard to think of a better word to describe Michelangelo than genius.

Michelangelo's creative contributions to humankind are not disputed. Neither is his talent. But we tend to imagine Michelangelo toiling alone on the scaffolding high above the floor of the Sistine Chapel. In fact, he wasn't alone. Thirteen people helped Michelangelo paint the work. Michelangelo wasn't only an artist; he was, as his biographer William E. Wallace points out, the head of a good-sized entrepreneurial enterprise that collaboratively made art that bore his name (an opinion piece by Wallace in *The New York Times* was aptly headlined 'Michelangelo, CEO').

The Renaissance scholar, in fact, no longer exists. According to Vera John-Steiner, author of *Creative Collaborations*, the power of the unaided, individual mind is highly overrated.[41] Although creative individuals are often thought of as working in isolation, the role of interaction and collaboration with other individuals is critical to creativity. Given our continuing obsession with solitary genius, reflected in everything from the worship of film directors to our fascination with Stephen Tindall, Sam Morgan and other high-profile entrepreneurs, it is no surprise that we tend to underestimate just how much creative work is accomplished by groups.

Ronald Burt, a sociologist at the University of Chicago, has spent most of his career studying how ideas move from place to place.[42] The usual image of creativity is that it's some sort of genetic gift, some heroic act. But according to Burt, creativity is more often an import-export game. As we'll see in the next chapter, when it comes to solving complex problems, getting the right combination of skills on a team is as important, if not more so, than trying to get the smartest team members.

Creativity, whether you're designing a stone axe or a space shuttle, is easier when a group, rather than an individual, is trying to assemble the pieces. As Alexander Graham Bell once said, 'Great discoveries and improvements invariably involve the co-operation of many minds.' Or, to put it another way, none of us is as smart as all of us.

Individual creativity is critical to New Zealand's adaptiveness. But it isn't enough. Our understanding of complex adaptive systems tells us that simply looking at the individual agents in a system, while ignoring the interactions between them, doesn't get us all the way there. We need to understand how individual and social creativity interact with each other. Put another way, in order to meet Mr Shaw's 'produce some brains' challenge, we need to understand how to hook those brains up to each other and the outside world.

11

A sponge for ideas

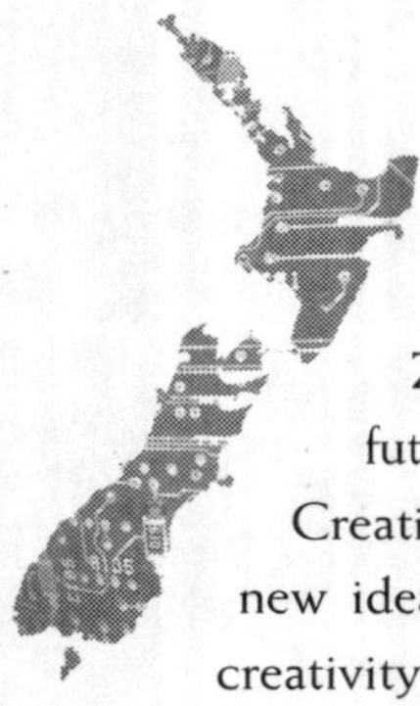

The central argument of this book is that an extraordinary ability to adapt lies at the heart of New Zealand's successful navigation of a turbulent, uncertain future. Adapting successfully requires lots of new ideas. Creativity, as we saw in the previous chapter, provides the new ideas necessary for innovation. We need to nourish the creativity in each of us.

But it's not enough in itself to have individuals generating lots of new ideas, and for two reasons. First, ideas need to be shared. Interaction and collaboration with others is critical to the creativity process. Second, New Zealand can't possibly generate all the good ideas it needs on its own. We need to be an aggressive importer of new ideas, absorbing like a sponge the best ones from around the world.

That's what this chapter is about. It looks at why New Zealand should absorb ideas from elsewhere, and then offers a few ideas on how to do it.

The power of groups

The importance of the group in devising new ideas to solve problems is obvious. At least it's obvious to the intestine-dwelling bacteria known as *E. coli*.

In a series of experiments, scientists took a community of *E. coli* bacteria away from their normal cuisine and offered it only salicin – a pain-reliever squeezed from the bark of willow trees.[1] To any individual *E. coli*, salicin is completely inedible. An individual *E. coli* bacterium can crank nourishment out of this unpalatable medication only if it undergoes a giant step *backwards* in evolutionary development. The odds of pulling this off through random mutation are less than one in – ready for another big number? – ten billion trillion. Yet the *E. coli* in the experiment consistently managed it.

Their secret was that they harnessed the power of groups. These bacteria basically teamed up like a human organisation to beat this challenge. Colony members played distinct roles. Some felt out the new environment; they did the market research. Others studied the genome, like research and development staff. Yet others collected the information passed along by their colleagues and worked like engineers to turn existing genetic parts into something new. The colony became a supermind – to use University of Tel Aviv physicist Eshel Ben-Jacob's term – that even sucks in lessons from other colonies. That's how the genomic leap was made possible – through the collective effort of the *E. coli* network.[2]

The same principles of collective intelligence are at work in any human organisation. Organisations have the ability to process information and solve complex problems that individuals cannot process or solve on their own. Telecom, for example, is like a computer built for solving the problem of facilitating telephone calls between thousands of customers. No one at Telecom can tell you, in full detail, just how that immensely complex problem is solved. As capable as any CEO is, they will be aware of no more than a fraction of the thousands of decisions made at any given moment.

Telecom relies on groups of people. With six thousand employees, it's a marvel of human co-operation. The vast majority of its people have never met and never will meet. Instead they are bound together in a web of social structures, norms, protocols, legal arrangements and incentives that enable them to work together for a common purpose. That web of co-operation also extends well beyond Telecom's immediate employees to include its hundreds of suppliers and thousands of shareholders.[3] It's a massive social network, specifically designed to ensure, amongst other things, that you can get Doris on the line to ask her about that pavlova recipe.[4]

In short, groups of people get things done in a way no individual ever could. They facilitate the flow of information. Whether you are inventing a new gadget or running a phone company, social networks provide the web of connections necessary for information and ideas to flow as they must. Without effective social networks, an organisation or society won't generate the new ideas – the creativity – it needs to change.

So if social networks are so important, how can we get the big social network that is New Zealand society working effectively?

How to build a great social network

Biologist Stuart Kauffman, based at the Santa Fe Institute in Arizona, is one of the world's leading complexity theorists. In his book, *The Origins of Order: Self-Organisation and Selection in Evolution*, he talks about how complex systems like societies 'behave'.[5] His insights are based on some fancy computer modelling of some hypothetical complex systems, called 'cell automata'. Cell automation is a technique used by scientists to model how complex systems work. It basically involves the creation of huge grids of cells that evolve based on rules governing the cell's reaction to its neighbouring cells.

Part of the insight Kauffman gained from the cell automata experiments he ran is that any complex system 'behaves' in one of three ways: they freeze, they're chaotic, or they 'melt'. First, the 'frozen' category of systems. These systems are isolated, and as their name suggests, they don't do much.

Kauffman noted that 'frozen' systems have three characteristics. First, the 'frozen' systems contained relatively few participating nodes. Second, there were few links between the different nodes in the system. The nodes weren't very well connected to one another. They were fragmented. Third, many of the nodes were quite similar. In other words, the system had a high level of homogeneity. Kauffman found that when a population becomes too small, fragmented or homogeneous, it becomes 'stagnant'. When that happens to a society, it's bad news.

At the other end of the continuum are systems that had the opposite problem. These are the 'chaotic' ones. If the nodes are too many, too highly connected and too diverse, the system becomes volatile. Stability in the system begins to collapse. Chaos breaks out, and before you know it, the water molecules or ants or whoever are smashing bottles and throwing chairs at each other. According to Kauffman, the optimal state for any complex system operating in an uncertain, turbulent world – i.e., New Zealand – is in the 'melting zone' on the 'edge of chaos'. We came across the concept of the 'edge of chaos' in Chapter Five.

With that in mind, we could point to three ways for New Zealand to improve its social network and become better at absorbing new ideas from elsewhere.

- **Increase our scale**. New Zealanders are a rare breed. There aren't many of us. In some respects, that hurts our ability to generate lots of good ideas. Unfortunately, there's really not a whole lot New Zealand can do to double or triple its population size any time soon, nor do many of us particularly want that.
- **Build our level of connectivity**. With lots of links to each other and the outside world, we can access the best ideas from here and abroad.
- **Increase our diversity**. With diversity in our society, we're generating the range of ideas we need to choose from. Diversity doesn't just mean our ethnic diversity. It also includes diversity in the ways we think and solve problems.

Given the fact that we can't (and probably don't want to) drastically increase the size of our population, we'll look instead at the second and third characteristics of complex adaptive systems (the level of connectivity, and the amount of diversity in the system). These two provide insights into how best to capture the great ideas that are floating around.

Let's delve into each of these in turn, and then we'll look at a few ideas for improving each.

Building our connectivity

In Chapter Five we looked at the small-world characteristics of some complex adaptive systems. By small world we mean that none of the agents or nodes in the system is ever more than a few links from each other. We examined the level of connectedness of species within an ecosystem, and discovered how any two species – say, the kiwi and the kauri – are rarely more than three degrees of separation apart. The same applies to the other sort of Kiwis – us.

Travel anywhere in the world, and no matter how remote the village or obscure the town, chances are the couple sitting next to you will have a New Zealand accent. The ability of four million New Zealanders to somehow be drawn to each other like magnets in a sea of 6.5 billion other humans is mystifying. And if that coincidence is not enough, we'll be likely to discover that the strangers sitting next to us are the very good friends of someone we're acquainted with. Any New Zealander, it seems, is never more than two or three degrees of separation apart from another.

Three degrees of separation is a lot smaller than the six degrees that separates everyone on the planet. But even six degrees is still pretty small. Essentially that means that you can get from the President of the United States to a native in the Papua New Guinea rainforest through the acquaintances of six people.

Science writer Mark Buchanan tells the story of a German newspaper that accepted the challenge a few years ago of trying to connect a Turkish kebab-shop owner in Frankfurt to his favourite actor, Marlon Brando.[6] After several months, the staff of *Die Zeit* made the connection through six people. They discovered that the kebab-shop owner had a friend who lived in California. This friend happened to work alongside the boyfriend of a woman who was the sorority sister of the daughter of the producer of a film in which Brando starred.

There are two secrets to this small-world phenomenon. The first, as we discussed in Chapter Five, is the existence of superconnectors. Superconnectors are the agents, nodes, species, humans, in a system that are connected to multiple others. They radically reduce the number of links between any two agents. The second secret is the existence of weak links, which we'll focus on in this chapter.

The case for weak links

A popular British TV quiz show called *The Weakest Link* featured a headmistress-like host who sarcastically chastised participants when they answered trivia questions incorrectly. She would put participants down with such zingers as, 'Go home to your mother and learn something', or, 'Your headlights are constantly on dim.' It says a lot for the appeal of a

£10,000 prize that the participants would stand in front of a nationwide television audience and take the verbal beating with little more than an embarrassed grin.

When we talk about weak links in the context of complex adaptive systems, however, we're not referring to capability. Nor are we alluding to the strength of the link – it's not an indication of the depth or quality of our relationship with the person. Instead, a weak link is one where few, if any, other people we know also know this person. It turns out the weak links between people in a system are, paradoxically, the most useful in keeping the system small. They help explain why any two people on earth are only six, rather than sixty, links apart.

To understand why, let's return to this idea of connecting with a celebrity through six degrees of separation. Think for a minute about the steps you'd take if you wanted to have lunch with a current Hollywood celebrity – Tom Cruise, for instance. The nineteenth-century American novelist Herman Melville once said, 'A thousand fibres connect us with our fellow men.' Your first link, then, is through these fibres – your friends, family, work colleagues and other acquaintances. Most of them are people you know through work, people you went to school with, friends at your tennis or golf club, those who belong to your church, and so on.

The problem we have in getting to Tom Cruise is that some of the people in our first line of contacts know each other. Families do, obviously. So do friends. Even our acquaintances often do. That's because as social beings we belong to neighbourhoods, companies, schools, towns and professions. Through work, I know colleagues, and they know not only me but each other as well. We also know other people in our area with similar interests. Many of the dentists in Wellington tend to know each other. So do railway enthusiasts in Dunedin. The effectiveness of your social cluster in linking you to Tom Cruise is somewhat diminished simply because there is a pretty significant overlap in people its members know.

But you'll also have some acquaintances who aren't connected to your clusters of friends. These are people who are not in your normal social circle or just outside it, but who you somehow met and became friendly with. It might be someone you happened to sit next to and chat with at a cricket match, or someone you happened to meet while idling the hours away in your doctor's waiting room. These random relationships we establish with strangers are our weak links. Weak in this context means that we don't know many, or any, other people who also know them.

These people who don't fit into our normal social clusters become bridges out of our social networks. They connect us to other social networks – they're social bridges, if you will. These connections are a key reason why the maximum number of degrees of separation between any two humans is considered to be six, and not ten or fifteen.

Perhaps a simple exercise will help illustrate this idea. First, get a piece of paper and a pen. Next, draw a circle that comprises 6.5 billion dots. Now imagine that each dot represents a person on this planet. Let's assume each person is linked to his or her nearest fifty neighbours. The number of degrees of separation inside this circle is something like sixty-five million – this being the number of steps it takes, even moving fifty at a time, to go halfway round the circle.[7]

But throw in a few random links (our weak links, or social bridges), however, and this number comes crashing down. Even if the fraction of new random links is two in 10,000, the number of degrees of separation drops from 60 million to about eight; if the fraction is three out of 10,000, it falls to five.[8] Weak links are like Auckland's southern motorway, allowing you to jump quickly (in theory at least) from the heart of the city to Papakura, without the tedium of driving along lots and lots of small streets.

The power of weak links is more than a matter of intellectual curiosity. It has practical application as well. Sociologist Mark Granovetter made some important discoveries back in the 1970s in understanding how these random links impact on networks. He illustrated the point about weak ties with an experiment that looked at how people found jobs through their network of contacts.[9] He discovered that only sixteen per cent of the people he interviewed got their jobs through a contact they saw often, whereas eighty-four per cent got their jobs through contacts they saw occasionally or rarely.

Introducing new ideas

In a paper published in the journal *Science*, Northwestern University researchers in America tried to figure out what composition characteristics great creative teams in the arts, sciences and business shared.[10] Studying data on Broadway musicals since 1877 as well as thousands of journal publications in four fields of science, they found that successful teams had a mix of people who had worked together before and those who hadn't.

They point to *West Side Story* as an example of a successful Broadway production that used this old and new blood idea well. Producer and director Harold Prince and lyricist Stephen Sondheim had worked together before on *The Pajama Game*. Choreographer Jerome Robbins was experienced in the industry but hadn't worked with Prince or Sondheim before. And classical composer Leonard Bernstein was a newcomer to the Broadway scene.

The researchers found that new team members added creative spark and critical links to the experience of the entire industry. Unsuccessful teams tended to be isolated from each other whereas the members of successful teams were interconnected – in a small-world way – across a giant cluster of artists or scientists. Teams with only former incumbents, and especially incumbents who had worked together repeatedly, tended to perform less successfully.

Weak links are also important in mobilising societies. That's become apparent in the former East Germany. Since the Iron Curtain came crashing down in the early 1990s, sociologists have had a field day studying how the former communist societies have responded to the extraordinary change foisted upon them. One study has found that the fear of speaking out during the communist era caused people to stick within a close-knit social group.[11] Citizens trusted only people they knew well. They invested only cautiously in others. Extremely tightly connected networks of strong ties were formed.[12] They kept their distance from strangers. Weak links were few and far between.

It was believed that these tightly knit East German communities would adapt well to the changes posed by unification with the West. Not so. After East Germany opened itself to the West, these small, tightly knit social networks proved inadequate to address the vast changes occurring. New ideas from the outside failed to find their way into these close-knit communities and they struggled to respond to the pressures of living in a capitalist society.

Like any complex system, New Zealand society is reliant on weak links between individuals. These links ensure that New Zealand's levels of connectivity within and outside the country's geographical borders are as close as possible. Weak links ensure new ideas jump from one social cluster to another. They allow social clusters in Hokitika to exchange information and ideas with social clusters in Kaitaia. They ensure New Zealand is linked in with ideas and information in New York or Tokyo or Buenos Aires.

A large number of connections – particularly weak links – is critical to the flow of ideas in a society. It's also helped by the level of heterogeneity amongst the society's population. That's why biologist Stuart Kauffman's third characteristic of complex adaptive systems is important: diversity.

Building our diversity

In 1856 the British essayist Walter Bagehot railed against the inward-looking nature of Victorian England. He thought the homogenous nature of British society stifled excitement and innovative thinking. 'You may talk of the tyranny of Nero and Tiberius,' he wrote, 'but the real tyranny is the tyranny of your next-door neighbour.'

Put another way, Bagehot might have been saying 'Diversity rules'. At the time that was a pretty shocking idea. Today, of course, most Western societies embrace this idea . . . at least publicly. For most of us, diversity is okay, even good, for the shopping-mall side of life — we love our Thai restaurants, our Italian shoes and our reggae music. We're all about diversity in the workplace, and initiatives to build understanding across cultures. We like to think that New Zealand is significantly better for being a diverse, multicultural society.

But when it comes to the serious work of the world, suddenly diversity doesn't seem like such a good idea. That's because many of us think there is only one approach to tackling the issues that confront us – ours. We fear the unknown, and for most of us, different ethnicities remain the unknown. The controversy over Muslim women wearing full-face veils in France and Britain is a reminder of the tension between a society's tolerance of diversity and its need for social cohesiveness. In New Zealand our biculturalism constantly forces us to confront situations – the building of a highway through a sacred swamp, say, or the imposition of seating or speaking restrictions on a female prime minister visiting a marae – where cultural diversity butts heads with modern-day demands.

In those situations diversity not only seems beside the point – it could even be downright problematic. When it comes to constructing real solutions to real problems, the usual platitudes about diversity sound to many of us like obvious, well-intentioned nonsense.

The problem with diversity

Robert Putnam, a professor of Public Policy at Harvard University, is no stranger to New Zealand. He was a guest speaker at the Knowledge Wave conference held in Auckland in 2003. In 2000, he published *Bowling Alone*, a book that brought the term *social capital* into the public lexicon.

Putnam recently conducted a large-scale survey of American communities. The results suggest, uncomfortably, that levels of trust and co-operation are highest in the most homogenous communities. Putnam found trust was lowest in Los Angeles, one of the most diverse cities in the world. People living in diverse areas, it turns out, are not just more suspicious of people who don't look like them; they are also more suspicious of their own kind. In the presence of diversity, it seems, we tend to barricade the gates.

What's more, researchers at the University of Arizona have found that ties between dissimilar individuals dissolve at a higher rate than between those individuals who share more demographic similarities.[13] This principle is known as the *homophily* principle. This principle basically states that people's personal networks (including marriage, friendship, work, advice, support, information transfer, exchange, and so on) are homogeneous with regard to many demographic, behavioural and intrapersonal characteristics. Put another way, we tend to hang out with people who look, think, and act like we do.

Our homophilist tendencies appear strongest along ethnic or racial lines.[14] Sociologists have found strong homophily in race and ethnicity in a wide array of relationships, from the most intimate bonds of marriage and confiding, to the mere fact of appearing in public together or 'knowing about' someone else.[15] In a US survey, only eight per cent of adults mentioned having a person of another race with whom they 'discuss important matters'.[16] In New Zealand, I'm not sure that figure would be any higher.

Researchers at Harvard University have found that racial and ethnic homogeneity increases the propensity to participate in a variety of social activities including recreational, religious, civic, and educational groups.[17] Norway, Finland, Sweden, Denmark, and Canada – all countries with ethnically homogeneous populations – lead the rankings for civic co-operation.[18] The top five US states in social capital ranking – North Dakota, Utah, Minnesota, Wyoming, and Montana – are all very homogeneous also.[19]

The instinct to hunker down amongst our ilk is natural, and nothing new. More than two millennia ago, Aristotle noted that people 'love those who are like themselves'.[20] We fear the unknown and the unfamiliar. We're naturally more cautious when we're not surrounded by what we know and understand. Our trust in others goes down when foreigners come to us and when we go to them. Travel to a foreign land – whether it's Canada or Colombia or Chad – and chances are you'll initially be less trusting of the locals in those countries too.

The issue with us homophilists is that our social worlds become somewhat limited. The information we receive, the attitudes we form, and the interactions we experience all tend to be the same. This homophilist tendency is why we need weak links out of our circle to different groups.

Conformity in our thinking

Not only do we struggle with ethnic diversity among the people around us, we also have a hard time coping with people whose ideas are different from ours. There are natural psychological tendencies in all of us that push us away from diversity in the way we think. Deep down we want to be conformists. Society also wants us that way. As American journalist Marion McMaughon once said: 'Every society honours its live conformists and its dead troublemakers.'

Researchers have done a lot of work on how easily we are influenced in our thinking by those around us. In a famous study in 1952, the social psychologist Solomon Asch had subjects in groups of six study a line drawn on a page. They were then to say which of three lines on an adjacent page was the same length. Five of the subjects in each group were working with

Asch and purposefully gave, out loud, the same incorrect response. Asch found that after hearing the others, the sixth subject – the true focus of the experiment – was frequently swayed to give the same incorrect answer, conforming to the group rather than trusting his or her own senses. A few of the sixth subjects even reported later that they had perceived the lines differently.[21]

In the 1970s social psychologist Irving Janus explored the way groups of people come to make decisions, and concluded that often group dynamics limit the group's ability to legitimately consider alternative options. To reduce the psychological discomfort of disagreement, members of a group strive to find a consensus, and once a rough consensus is reached, it becomes difficult for dissenters to voice their ideas. They may keep quiet, not wanting to make waves. 'Concurrence-seeking,' as Janus wrote, 'becomes so dominant in a cohesive group that it tends to override realistic appraisal of alternative courses of action.'[22]

This finding appears to support the view of a University of Chicago law professor, Cass Sunstein, who argues that the Internet has abetted a culture of polarisation in which people primarily seek out points of view to which they already subscribe.[23] See only what you want to see, hear only what you want to hear, read only what you want to read. He argues that, in cyberspace, we have the ability to filter out everything but that which we wish to see, hear, and read. This creates positive feedback: we read the viewpoints we agree with – our viewpoints are reinforced.

Democracy, Sunstein maintains, depends on shared experiences and requires citizens to be exposed to topics and ideas that they would not have chosen in advance. Newspapers and broadcasters help create a shared culture. Of course, if you *only* rely on the mass media for direction on an issue, you've hardly taken a big step forward in exposure to diverse thinking either.

Because diversity can create barriers to trust in a society, and because we have to battle our innate tendency towards 'group think', we need to understand why diversity is so important. Diversity places too much strain on our societies and organisations to simply assume it's a good thing. It can't be just a concept that appeals to our moral senses. But diversity actually does work in a very practical way. And specifically, it goes a long way towards helping groups, organisations and societies generate more creative solutions to difficult issues.

Why diversity is important

As Harold Bloom points out in *Global Brain*, our bodies long ago figured out that diversity is important.[24] They use diversity as a key strategy to fight disease. Each one of us contains a flood of entities known as virus-specific T-cells. They are our front line against disease. T-cells patrol our bodies looking for the molecular signs of an invader. Each T-cell is armed with an assortment of different weapons (various types of grappling hooks). Each weapon is a piece of guesswork, preconfigured to snag the weak points of an enemy. If one antibody isn't properly shaped to lock onto an invader, another comes along to try.

Those best at snagging and disabling the invaders are heralded as champions. A formula laid out by Jesus two thousand years ago is applied: '. . . unto everyone which has shall be given, and from him that has not, even that he has shall be taken away from him.' The champions are then allowed to reproduce with explosive speed, and are given the raw material they need to increase their clones dramatically. More T-cells with the same grappling hooks are rushed to the front line. The key to success is, Bloom notes, diversity – the greater the variety of T-cell foot-soldiers, the higher the likelihood that the invading virus will be snagged.

Scott Page, a political scientist and economist at the University of Michigan, has taken the benefit of diversity and applied it to human society.[25] He has come up with the logic of diversity – a set of basic rules for explaining how diversity works in society. Page and his long-time collaborator Lu Hong, professor of finance at Loyola University, have shown that, under very general conditions, a diverse population of agents will outperform a single agent, even if that agent has a superior problem-solving ability.

Imagine diverse but inept agents taking turns at solving a problem. Each one starts from where the last one got stuck, trying an alternative approach to the problem – a bit like the T-cells with their grappling hooks. Each of the agents tends to get trapped at various stages. But, because they're diverse and have the benefit of observing the failures and successes of the other agents, they get trapped at *different* points. By using each other's work, the group avoids the trap that snagged one or other of them.

But get this: you don't necessarily get the same improvement from using a group of experts. Unlike the diverse, but inept, agents, the experts all tend to be similar to one another so tend to get stuck on the same sorts of problems. According to Page, if the best problem solvers tend to think about a problem similarly, then it stands to reason that as a group, they may not be very effective. Experts are important for solving complex problems, obviously, but so too, it would seem, is diversity.

This concept might sound familiar to you if you've come across a popular book, *The Wisdom of Crowds*, by *The New Yorker* columnist James Surowiecki.[26] Surowiecki explains how the average responses of a group of people are invariably more accurate than any single individual's answer. For example, students in psychology classes are asked to guess the number of jelly beans in a jar. Time and again, the average guess of all the students in the class is closer to the actual number than any of the individual guesses.[27]

As impressive as this is, however, it underestimates the power of diversity in problem solving. While Surowiecki's multitude of *independent* answers is powerful, Page and Hong have found that a multitude of *dependent* answers work even better.

This might seem counter-intuitive. You'd expect that if each individual's guess is strongly dependent on that of the last one, then the group would get further and further off track.

The answer to the puzzle is this: people have only a limited capacity to learn about their worlds and therefore solve their problems. When the problem or environment is too complex for any one person, you need many people making incomplete, overlapping attempts at a solution. That's because nobody, individually – not even a genius – has anything like the complete perspective; in fact, everybody's individual perspective is at best drastically incomplete.

Ability is still important. But for most jobs in the modern economy, different types of ability matter much more than pure genius. Complex problems like designing a yacht or producing a movie or developing a vaccine need teams of people with different ways of thinking. Hence, the team's performance depends as much on its members' cognitive differences as it does on their individual abilities. Two lawyers with identical perspectives and ways of thinking about issues may not be of much use to one another as partners. Neither could ever offer a strategy that the other had not already considered.

Put simply, effective groups, teams and societies need cognitive diversity. This means that the best person to hire is not necessarily the person who scores the highest on a test or has the best grades. It's the person with the most new tools to add. The most competitive and cutting-edge organisations on the planet, like Google, know this. They seek diversity. The differences in the way we see the world – whether inspired by one's ethnicity, culture, religious beliefs, sex, age, education, life experiences, golf handicap, or any other factor – all embody approaches which could prove vital for New Zealand tomorrow. In a highly uncertain future, who knows which approaches we'll need?

Building links and strengthening diversity

The question is: how can New Zealand ensure ideas are flowing around its network as effectively as possible? And how can New Zealand ensure its society is as diverse as possible? What follows are a few ideas. No doubt there are many more.

- **Grow civic participation in New Zealand.**
  This drives the level of connections between people.
- **Ensure we're plugged in around the world.**
  Our linkages with New Zealand's expatriate community will ensure we're accessing broader networks overseas, help us to gain scale, and expose our society to new ideas.
- **Appreciate the benefits of immigration.**
  This plays a critical role in helping to strengthen the diversity of our society.

Let's examine each of these in turn.

Growing civic participation

'It's not what you know, it's *who* you know.' This painful cliché sums up much of the conventional wisdom regarding what Harvard University's Robert Putnam describes as social capital. It is wisdom born of our experience that gaining membership to exclusive clubs requires inside contacts, that close competitions for jobs and contracts are usually won by those with friends in high places.

Intuitively, then, the basic idea of social capital is that one's family, friends and associates constitute an important asset, one that can be called upon in a crisis, enjoyed for its own sake, and leveraged for material gain. Anxious parents devote hours of time to the school board and to helping their kids with homework, only too aware that little Sammy's winning smile will not be enough to ensure a bright future. The absence of social ties can have an equally important impact. Office workers, for example, fear being left out of the loop on important decisions; ambitious professionals recognise that getting ahead in a new venture typically requires an active commitment to networking.

Putnam defines social capital as the 'connection among individuals – social networks and the norms of reciprocity and trustworthiness that arise from them'.[28] Networks with social capital include local neighbourhood associations, charities, religious organisations, sports teams, social clubs and civic groups. Even the weekly poker night is a social network, building social capital. Our workplaces are perhaps the most significant social networks we are involved in, given that we spend most of our waking hours during the week with work colleagues.

To assess America's social capital, Putnam set out to evaluate the level of civic participation in that country. What he found was not encouraging. Civic organisations and social clubs, from sewing circles to marching bands, were disappearing. Surveys indicate that since 1965, time spent on informal socialising and visiting is down by a quarter while time devoted to clubs and organisations has halved. Membership records of such diverse organisations as PTAs, labour unions, and even bowling clubs show participation has declined by between twenty-five and fifty per cent over the last two to three decades.

On the face of it, New Zealand's civic participation seems pretty solid.

More than one million New Zealanders are actively involved in regular volunteer work, both informally within their communities and through the sixty-thousand-plus organisations that make up the community and voluntary sector. In New Zealand each year, 2.7 billion hours of unpaid work are done by women, and 1.5 billion hours by men, together totalling 4.2 billion hours. This equates to over two million full-time jobs – larger than the size of our paid labour force.[29] A 1998 Business and Economic Research Ltd study found about twenty per cent of the adult population was involved in the physical sport and leisure sector as volunteers, contributing on average 2.7 hours a week, with an estimated monetary value of almost $2 billion per year.[30] Impressive numbers, for sure.

But who knows how impressive that really is? It's hard to figure out whether we're more engaged in clubs and groups than we were thirty years ago. We only have a few factoids.

University of Auckland political scientist Jack Vowles claims that between the early 1980s and 1999, membership of one or more types of association fell from eighty-five per cent to sixty-nine per cent.[31] Whether it was an interest group, a church, a sports group, or a social group, attendance fell. The percentage of eighteen to twenty-four-year-olds involved in one or more capacities as a volunteer in sporting activities has declined significantly from thirty-one per cent in 1997 to twenty-three per cent in 2001.

The decline of civic participation in New Zealand is not surprising. Many of the factors Putnam pointed to can be found in New Zealand. The suburban sprawl ensconces us in our cars for ever-larger chunks of the day. Mass media is far more pervasive now than in the 1970s. We're watching over two hours of TV a day each, even though women report that television is less satisfying than cleaning the house, and men that it's less satisfying than cooking.[32] More women, the traditional mainstays of the unpaid workforce, are in paid employment, limiting their time and energy for volunteer work. It's not outrageous to assume, then, that the New Zealand situation is similar to that in the US.

Our interest in social trends does not mirror Putnam's, however. He linked the decline in civic participation to declining levels of trust in society. I link it to the ability of our country to absorb new ideas – the other side of the same coin. If New Zealanders are not meeting with each other, there can't be the exchange of ideas required to adapt effectively. Weak links are not forming. In fact, no links are forming. It may not seem as though New Zealand's problems are solved over a cuppa at the bridge club (or perhaps they are), but any interaction builds the connections we have as New Zealanders. Opinions are voiced. Ideas are shared. New connections are made. The New Zealand network grows stronger.

So how do we ensure civic participation remains strong, particularly in the face of such overwhelming threats as suburbanisation and death by traffic jam? Putnam has a few suggestions for the US:

- greater individual commitment to social involvement
- programmes in schools to help build social capital in the next generation
- reforms to make workplaces more family friendly
- better public transport and the rewriting of zoning laws
- efforts to encourage voting and political involvement.

I could add two others: First, strengthening our links across cultural ties. We're a pretty segregated lot. The homophily principle (we hang out with the people who are most like us) is alive and well in New Zealand. And it invariably falls along ethnic lines. Maori predominantly mix with Maori, Pacific Islanders predominantly mix with Pacific Islanders, Koreans with Koreans, Pakeha with Pakeha, Indians with Indians, and so on.[33] There are lots of reasons why that is. Few people encourage it. Few think it is a good thing. It just seems to be human nature. And it happens in most other places around the world.

So if we're living in fairly homogenous social clusters, a sure-fire way to develop better weak links in our community must be to encourage a greater number of cross-cultural activities – particularly amongst the school-aged whose social clusters are not as rigidly fixed (or prejudices as firmly set).

Second, broadening our definition of community. The idea of social networks existing in the wider society (such as those developed through community or voluntary organisations) is a very Pakeha notion. But David Robinson, Director of the Social and Civic Policy Institute at Victoria

University, and researcher Tuwhakairiora Williams, suggest that social capital in a Maori context has a greater focus on whanau.[34] They note the cultural distinction between 'giving (European concept of volunteering)' and 'sharing (Maori concept of cultural obligation)', and suggest that New Zealand needs to support as equally valid the different organisational structures, norms, values, and aspirations of Maori communities. In other words, there isn't a standard template for what these social networks should look like, or how they should operate.

No easy wins there, for sure. Ultimately, civic participation will only increase when more New Zealanders decide to invest personally in their communities. New Zealand, like any developed country, will need to fight the ongoing drift towards social isolation, whether in the home or the workplace. The exchange of ideas won't occur if we're all merely sitting in front of our TV sets or in our offices. The seeds of a better, more dynamic, New Zealand will be sown when we all step out the door.

Ensuring we're plugged in around the world

A popular destination for those visiting Venice is the island of Murano. Murano is the heart of Venice's famous glass-making industry. Today you'll see the factories of glass-making families whose history of dipping, twisting and blowing glass into fancy goblets stretches back centuries.

Today's collection of shops and furnaces, however, is a mere shadow of the glories of Murano glass-makers in the fourteenth century. Back then, Venetian glass was highly prized, adorning the drinks cabinets of Europe's finest courts. Appropriately, the glass-makers were the toast of Venice. Not only were artisans granted the right to wear a sword, they also enjoyed immunity from prosecution (a potentially lethal combination, one would have thought). By the late fourteenth century, the daughters of glass-makers were even allowed to marry into Venice's blue-blooded families.

But those privileges came with some fairly nasty fine print. Realising that the glass-maker's secret techniques were highly valuable to the local economy, the authorities forbade glass-makers to leave the city. To ensure their elaborate glass-making secrets were never revealed, harsh sentences were meted out to individuals who leaked secrets to foreigners or left Venice without official permission – typically, hand amputations and sometimes death. At the time it was rumoured the Venetian authorities even hired assassins to track down and kill artisans who left the island.

That was the fourteenth-century approach to dealing with the departure of highly skilled workers for foreign soils (a.k.a. the brain drain). Ever since people and their skills have been transferable between societies the battle to retain talent locally has been fought. Mostly unsuccessfully. Without resorting to the Venetian tactics, most societies struggle to retain the talents of their most highly skilled. Such people are inevitably pulled to the handful of societies that can offer the greatest rewards for their labours. But their departure need not mean a loss of that individual's creative capacity. In fact, quite the reverse. In a world of social clusters and networks, one person's travels can become their home society's profit.

Take the Ancient Greeks, for example. The Greeks were renowned travellers and absorbers of ideas in the ancient world. One who was particularly so was Thales of Melitus, who lived during the sixth century BC. Thales was a one-man data-link. No one was able to connect ideas between cultures like he could. He visited the Persians and mused on Persian astronomy with such intensity that, legend says, he walked into a well while pondering the stars. He travelled to Egypt to learn their geometric and mathematical systems, and then used them to calculate the heights of the pyramids. Afterwards he brought these techniques back to Greece. Using Egyptian mathematics and Persian astronomy, he is reputed to have predicted the eclipse of May 585 BC, demystifying an event that had brought the warring Lydians and Medeans to their knees in fear.[35]

Thales was a key node in the Greek network. His travels helped expose him to ideas that were handily applied back home. New ideas – just like plagues – travelled with people. For centuries ideas (and diseases) were carried by travellers along the Silk Road, linking China and Europe. Inventions such as the spinning wheel, the windmill and the weight-driven clock recognised no boundaries. The printing press was no more a German invention than the telescope was a Dutch one or the knitting frame an English one. The clustering of interactions saw ideas for new technologies flow from country to country. European shipbuilders often travelled to see the types of ships in use elsewhere. From the fourteenth century on, sons of northern European merchants went to Italy to study the art of the merchant, including commercial arithmetic and bookkeeping. The world is full of great ideas, so we need people out there absorbing them.

That's why New Zealand's army of expats is particularly important. They are vital links between New Zealand society and the ideas of the rest of the world. And it's not a small army. According to Professor Richard Bedford of Waikato University, New Zealand has one of the highest rates of immigration and emigration in the OECD.[36] In fact, sixteen per cent of our population awakens on foreign soil. Almost twenty-five per cent of all 'highly skilled' New Zealanders live overseas.[37]

We top the OECD in this respect. A greater percentage of our educated tend to take off than anyone else's. Australia, for example, has 'lost' only about three per cent of its highly qualified population. In fact, by some estimates, New Zealand has as many expats as Australia, a country with a population five times our own. Our highly skilled people are twice as likely to emigrate compared to their counterparts in the US.[38] Forget countries in the OECD. Thailand, the Czech Republic, Venezuela, and China all have a similar or greater ability to retain their highly skilled than New Zealand.[39] That says a lot, particularly to anyone who has ever tried Czech food.

But farewelled need not mean forgotten. Our expats become vital nodes in our network, helping New Zealanders build bridges into other social clusters.[40] One of the benefits of expat networks like the Kiwi Expats Association (KEA) is that they make a very deliberate attempt at strengthening the New Zealand network globally. They allow New Zealanders, isolated geographically, to jump the thousands of kilometres of ocean that separates us from the rest of the world. They forge connections that wouldn't be made by happenstance. They ensure that the time it takes to reach the right contact – New Zealander or otherwise – is as short as possible. Say two links, instead of five. In an increasingly competitive global market, that's important.

With at least two hundred expat networks around the world, and the number climbing fast, the race is on to build the most useful one. Take India, for example. You'd have thought the Indian government has enough on its plate dealing with the needs of 1.3 billion people within its borders. Not so. Such is the importance India places on its expat community that it has created a Ministry of Overseas Indian Affairs to strengthen its connection to its Silicon Valley entrepreneurs, New York bankers and London scientists. One of the world's poorest countries, Bangladesh, has put together a multitude of expat groups in the US alone, from the Bangladeshi Medical Association of North America to the American Association of Bangladeshi Engineers and Architects.

In an increasingly diversified and specialised world, New Zealand's ability to offer the professional opportunities (not to mention the life experiences) our talented can find in larger ponds elsewhere is not getting any easier. And as the competition for talent heats up, New Zealanders will remain geographically promiscuous. Unlike fourteenth-century Venice, New Zealand can't stop people from leaving to settle elsewhere. But so long as adequate investment is made in strengthening our ties with the expat community, the New Zealand network will grow each time another New Zealander bids farewell to our fair shores. The more connected with New Zealand emigrant are, the higher the likelihood they'll return home.

It's not just the links into new networks, of course. These represent new ideas, born from interactions with foreigners in overseas environments. Small, isolated societies like New Zealand need access to different perspectives. They can help broaden our horizons. Sometimes a society needs the cutting focus of small-town single-mindedness. A society at war, for example, can't be stuck in a cycle of endless debates and musings. But more often a society benefits from pluralism, from many points of view, from carrying many arrows in its quiver. There just aren't enough new ideas in a small society, and viewpoints are too similar. As the great psychoanalyst Sigmund Freud once said, the force driving our quest for diversity should be a fear of 'the narcissism of minor difference'.[41]

Coming the other way, passing the outbound expat lugging her over-stuffed pack, is someone bidding New Zealand 'Hello' or 'Hola' or 'Talofa' or 'Ni hao'. Immigrants are the third mechanism for enhancing New Zealand's links with the wider world, and building our diversity.

Appreciating the benefits of immigration

In 2005, almost 2.5 million foreigners decided to come to New Zealand.[42] The previous year it was a few thousand more than that. In 2003, a few tens of thousands less. Most of them were visiting, but a sizeable number were also hoping New Zealand would become their new home.

To get to New Zealand you have to really want to do so. It's a long way from anywhere. In centuries past, you sailed for weeks across the ocean, risking life and limb aboard a waka or sailing ship. There were diseases, mutinies and shipwrecks. The first glimpse of New Zealand's cloud-covered shores must surely have been a sight for sore, salty eyes. Today, you also risk life and limb getting here, but these days from deep vein thrombosis. Despite the risks, millions have made the journey. New Zealand is a nation of immigrants, Maori and non-Maori alike. We, or our forebears, have all journeyed here from somewhere.

Despite the role immigration has played in bringing every New Zealander here, the immigration of others to New Zealand remains a sensitive topic, perennially ebbing and flowing in and out of the national discourse. In the mid-nineteenth century Chinese miners were welcomed when there was a shortage of labour, but anti-Chinese prejudice soon surfaced. Some politicians tried to rally popular support against immigration by claiming that a flood of Chinese threatened to overrun the country (sound familiar?). In 1881, New Zealand imposed a notorious poll tax on all Chinese immigrants. By the 1920s, it became harder for anyone who was not British to get in. Russians, Italians, Japanese, Africans – people from all over the globe faced restrictions. Pacific Islanders were welcomed with open arms during the 1960s and 1970s when economic expansion increased demand for imported labour. But conditions changed, and so did the position of the Pacific Island immigrant. Dawn raids began on Pacific Island households in Auckland during the mid-1970s.[43] Nothing says you care like dawn raids.

Despite our best attempts at homogeneity, immigrants continue to flock to these shores. The proportion of the New Zealand population born overseas rose by a third in the twenty years to 2001. In addition, the number of countries from which New Zealand has received significant migration has multiplied. The foreign-born percentage of the New Zealand population (19.5 per cent) is very high by international standards. If you take out the small European enclaves of Luxembourg and Switzerland, Australia is the only country with a higher percentage of foreign-born people. Many OECD countries have foreign-born percentages well below the ten per cent mark.

The web of connections brought by immigrants to this country strengthens New Zealand's connection to the rest of the world. Each brings links back to networks in different occupations and countries around the world. In 2003 an Azerbaijani immigrant with specialist skills as a roofer joined New Zealand's team.[44] So did two missionaries from South Korea. An acrobat from Great Britain joined up in 2004, as did a cabinet minister. In 2005, twelve Kenyans came in with a combination of skills ranging from secondary-school teaching to optometry to landscape gardening. Sixteen Bulgarians also arrived that year, including a university lecturer, a computer programmer, a fashion designer and a biologist. They were among more than twelve thousand foreigners granted residency visas in 2005. New Zealand's newest residents that year came from a hundred and ten different countries and represented more than sixteen hundred occupations. All are now part of the New Zealand network, with links back to many diverse social groups and clusters around the world.

These immigrants naturally facilitate the flow of ideas and skills from foreign lands to their newly adopted home. Throughout history, striking changes in the wealth of societies can often be traced to the importation of ideas from elsewhere. Britain, for example, was transformed from an isolated backwater of an island into the home of the world's largest empire through the importation of new ideas and skills over hundreds of years. First the Romans in ancient times and then, in later centuries, the Normans, the Lombards, the Huguenots, the Dutch, and others all brought particular skills to the British Isles that had been largely or wholly lacking there.

One of the world's most innovative regions, Silicon Valley, has a workforce among the world's most ethnically diverse. According to University of California at Berkeley professor, Annalee Saxerian, not only do Asian and Hispanic workers dominate the low-paid blue-collar workforce, but foreign-born scientists and engineers are also increasingly visible as entrepreneurs and senior management. More than a quarter of Silicon Valley's highly skilled workers are immigrants, including tens of thousands from lands as diverse as China, Taiwan, India, the UK, Iran, Vietnam, the Philippines, Canada and Israel. Far from simply replacing native workers, foreign-born engineers start new businesses and generate jobs and wealth at least as fast as their US counterparts. By the end of the 1990s, Chinese and Indian engineers were running twenty-nine per cent of Silicon Valley's technology businesses.[45] By 2000, these companies collectively accounted for more than $19.5 billion in sales and nearly seventy-three thousand jobs.

Similarly a whole raft of New Zealand industries and innovations can be tied directly to the ideas and skills of newly arrived immigrants. In Chapter Seven we met Chew Chong, the fungus-selling butter pioneer from China. New Zealand's first woman doctor, Emily Siedeberg, and first woman lawyer, Ethel Benjamin, were immigrants, not to mention those doyens of men's fashion, the Hallensteins. We can thank Dutch migrants like Suzy van der Kwast for sewing the seeds of Wellington's popular café culture. Her Dutch compatriot, Auckland restaurateur Otto Groen, challenged the conservative drinking laws that outlawed in restaurants the European custom of drinking wine with meals. Two Dutch migrants – Jo la Grouw and Johannes van Loghem – invented that very Kiwi institution, the Lockwood home, in 1951. The Dalmatian Babichs and Nobilos are stalwarts of our wine industry. The list of immigrant contributions to New Zealand is endless.

It doesn't need to be only long-term migration that builds New Zealand's networks. The revolving door of shorter-term migrants in and out of this country also provides valuable connectors for New Zealand. Take, for example, the thirty thousand Chinese students who come to study in New Zealand each year.[46] Most are trying – as part of New Zealand's English-as-a-second-language industry – to understand the past, present, and future tenses of English verbs. Contacts generated with and by this large but fluid part of our population represent some remarkable long-term possibilities. These Chinese students will be among the Chinese leaders of tomorrow.[47] New Zealand is educating a small army of Chinese who speak English with a Kiwi accent.

Immigrants, then, are great connectors – especially for small, isolated societies like New Zealand. But they serve a purpose beyond increasing our number of weak links. They also think differently. They approach problems from new perspectives. University of Michigan psychologist Richard Nisbett certainly seems to think so. Nisbett is one of the world's leading researchers on how people from different cultures approach problem solving. In his book, *The Geography of Thought: How Asians and*

Westerners Think Differently . . . and Why, he describes study after study which found that East Asians and Americans respond in qualitatively different ways to the same stimulus situation.[48]

For example, his research suggests that East Asians are more likely to attend to the whole, while Westerners focus on a particular object within the whole. In one experiment, designed to test this, Japanese and Americans viewed the same animated underwater scenes, then reported what they had seen. The very first comment from the Japanese participants was likely to be about the environment ('It looked like a pond'), whereas the Americans were three times more likely to refer to a focal fish ('There was a big fish, maybe a trout, moving off to the left.').

In another experiment described in the book, Nisbett and colleagues found that Americans respond to contradiction by polarising their beliefs whereas Chinese respond by moderating their beliefs. In still another study, the researchers found that when making predictions about how people in general could be expected to behave in a given situation, Koreans were much more likely than Americans to cite situational factors over personality characteristics as reasons for someone's behaviour.

Nisbett traces the differing cognitive approaches of the East and West to their ancient Chinese and Greek origins. Take the emphasis on logic in the West for example. The Greeks were at the trading crossroads of the world. They were constantly encountering novel and perplexing people, customs and beliefs: 'Athens would have been rather like the bar in *Star Wars*.'[49] An obvious consequence of the different practices and beliefs swirling around the Greeks would have been the necessity of dealing with contradiction. Contradiction coming from the opinions of outsiders may have forced the development of cognitive procedures, including formal logic, to deal with the dissonance.

By contrast, even today, ninety-five per cent of the Chinese population belongs to the same Han ethnic group. Nearly all of the country's more than fifty minority ethnic groups are in the western part of the country. A Chinese person living in another part of the country would rarely encounter anyone with significantly different beliefs or practices. Nisbett reasons that the face-to-face village life of China would not often require procedures to decide which of two propositions was correct, with villagers preferring instead harmony and agreed-upon norms of behaviour.

Accepting that different cultures approach problems differently, Nisbett concludes:

> Ethnic diversity has been acclaimed for all sorts of reasons, among them that educational and work environments are enriched by having people of different backgrounds. Our work does strongly support the contention that diverse views should be helpful for problem solving. The cognitive orientations and skills of East Asians and people of European cultures are sufficiently different that it seems highly likely that they would complement and enrich one another in any given setting. We would expect that for most problems one would be better off having a mix of people from different cultures than having people who are all from one culture.[50]

If cultural diversity does enrich a society's problem-solving capabilities, perhaps New Zealand needs to take more seriously the unique store of cultural problem-solving capital it sits on. Maori society has developed (and continues to improve) an extensive array of ideas and practices – from dealing with crime to educating its youth to interacting with the environment to decision-making in organisational structures, and so on. In the past, New Zealand hasn't been quick to recognise what these new (old) ideas offer.

But that's beginning to change. For example, Maori systems of restorative justice have become a successful part of the youth and family justice system. Certainly other countries see their value. They have been trialled in Britain and elsewhere in recent years to great acclaim.[51] So if we believe in the benefits of diversity, New Zealand could do a better job of integrating the unique solutions to problems stored within Maori cultural capital. That involves accepting fundamentally different (i.e., non-Pakeha) solutions to particular problems. That's tough for many to accept. Understandably. And it's tough to do. The returns from diversity are high, but they don't come without their price.

Of course, ethnic diversity is just one way of getting new skills and ideas into our society. Another source of diversity is experience. Two Maori women from Porirua, both trained as architects, may think very differently about how to design a skyscraper. Similarly the person who grew up on a farm sees the world in a different way from a suburbanite. So an acknowledgement that diversity extends beyond skin colour to include a variety of factors is equally important.

Progress, then, depends on New Zealand society maintaining its diversity. As we have seen, there *is* intrinsic merit in diversity, and few could deny the untapped potential of the many skilled, ambitious and hard-working people from around the world. Whehter that potential remains untapped depends on the conditions in which the immigrants find themselves when they arrive in this country. If the economy is robust and society is willing to employ immigrants effectively and lead them into productive work, then New Zealand will be resilient enough to handle the stress that diversity brings.

A sponge for new ideas

You could argue that one of the most creative people of the twentieth century was Walt Disney. The man who gave us Mickey Mouse and Donald Duck went on to build an empire of theme parks and a media behemoth.

Many have tried to document Walt Disney's accomplishments. One of the most popular biographies, called *How to Be Like Walt,* is by Pat Williams.[52] Williams attempts to describe Disney's creative genius by documenting many of his characteristics. According to Williams, one key to Disney's creativity, it seems, was his 'stick-to-it-ivity'. Then there was his ability 'to see tomorrow'. Another, that he was a 'sponge for ideas'.

If Walt could be a sponge for ideas, why can't New Zealand? Why can't New Zealand be great at absorbing the best ideas, whether they're generated in New Zealand or abroad? That means scouring the globe for the best solutions to our toughest problems. If someone is doing something interesting in Japan on new pre-school learning methods, we need to know about it. If a group in Mexico is trialling an innovative approach to preventative medicine for low-income households, we need to be aware of it. If someone is working on a new way to build widgets in Timbuctoo, let's try to find them and understand what's going down.

In order to do all this, New Zealanders will have to add a few more cultural qualifications to our CVs. 'Broadly connected' might be one. As a small country, New Zealand needs lots of weak links to ensure we're plugged into as many different networks locally and internationally as possible. That means ensuring the level of civic participation is as high as possible. It also means continuing to invest in strengthening the links with our expatriate community.

'Comfortable with diversity' should be another trait. Diversity is naturally painful for any community. Human instincts are such that we trust those most like ourselves. But the costs of homogeneity and the benefits of diversity are too great to risk white- or brown- or yellow-washing our society. Diversity is the salt that gives our society real flavour.

One won't work without the other. We'll need both: diversity *and* connectivity. Diversity means different relationships, many different approaches to the same problem. However, diversity is an advantage only if the community is sustained by a web of relationships. If the community is fragmented into isolated groups and individuals, diversity can easily become a source of prejudice and friction. Similarly, the benefits of being connected to others quickly disappears if we're connected only to people like ourselves.

Breaking down barriers and building communication: these are an eternal struggle for any society. But the better we become at it, the more great ideas will flow around. When great ideas are flowing around, societies become dynamic. They spark. Their creative juices flow like crazy. They become beautifully positioned to evolve and adapt even further.

12

Finding the willingness to change

Progress is impossible without change; and those who cannot change their minds, cannot change anything.

George Bernard Shaw

Across the vast South Pacific Ocean, about the only land mass of any size that stands between New Zealand and Chile is Easter Island. Spend a day wandering around Big Rapa, as the locals refer to the island, and you'll invariably bump into an enormous stone statue or two of the sort for which the island has become renowned. What you almost certainly won't bump into are any trees. That's because there are almost none on the entire island. But Easter Island wasn't always treeless. In fact, about fifteen hundred years ago when, according to legend, chief Hotu Matu'a from the Marquesas Islands stumbled across the island, it was densely covered with palm forests.

What happened to the trees, and the society that chopped them down, is rather a sad story (and a story that few anthropologists agree on). It's a story of years of growth and prosperity followed by a quick and unpleasant demise. The tale is worth recounting briefly, however, because it illustrates the third and final characteristic of highly adaptive societies: their willingness to change. The experience of the Easter Islanders shows us that all the innovation and creativity in the world won't save a society if it isn't also prepared to make hard choices and change its ways.

For over a thousand years following the arrival of Chief Hotu Matu'a, the Easter Islanders prospered. They developed an advanced civilisation, the fruits of which were more than a thousand enormous stone statues. But while the statues remind us of that civilisation, it was the wood of the abundant palm trees that were the foundation upon which this great statue-obsessed society was built. The timber was used for everything from clothing to shelter to boats. Some anthropologists believe that they even used palm tree trunks to manoeuvre and transport the statues. They were a creative people, adapting their agricultural methods to the realities of the island. For example, on the island's steep and rugged northwest coast, circular enclosures made of stacked rocks called 'Manavai' protected crops from the island's pervasive winds. They developed lithic mulching to provide sustenance to their crops.

But as the population grew and the number of trees began to dwindle, they experienced a situation that their repertoire of responses could not master. As the lifeblood of the island, the trees, ebbed away, the island descended into chaos. The islanders resorted to human sacrifice and cannibalism, war broke out and people starved. When Dutch sailors arrived at the island on Easter Day, 1722, the trees had gone. Men were sold into slavery, women taken as mistresses, and smallpox devastated the few who remained. Easter Island society had collapsed.

The tree situation wasn't helped by some of the core beliefs of the Easter Islanders. The beliefs that once played a central role in a robust society became impediments to further adaptation. As the stock of trees diminished, the islanders built more elaborate places of worship and even grander stone figures. When honouring the gods didn't succeed in renewing scare resources, religious observances became more and more extreme. Huge statues, some weighing up to fifty metric tons, were built and then toppled and decapitated to release their divine powers, their *mana*. This consumed more trees, yet their gods remained silent. Their cultural beliefs had become an impediment to their survival.

We saw in Chapter Eleven that societies need to have effective ways of absorbing ideas from the outside. The extreme isolation of the Easter Islands hardly encouraged the exchange of information with the outside world. In the hustle and bustle of everyday Easter Island life, it would have been easy to get caught up in the flow. Not enough of the islanders, one assumes, asked whether a rapidly disappearing tree population was a good thing until it was too late.

Being able to question the conventions of the day and change them if necessary is what this chapter is about. It's all very well to be great at generating new ideas and absorbing the best ones from elsewhere, but it's not enough. Societies must be willing to change themselves. Placating the gods by building more statues was a cultural practice unsuited to compensating for the rapidly deteriorating tree situation. Being great at adapting requires an *evolving* mix of values. It demands a willingness to change.

But as we'll discover in this chapter, that's not easy. As economic historian Joel Mokyr puts it, 'there is a desire for stability that exists in every society, though its intensity may vary. The sentiment 'if it ain't broke, don't fix it' is the archenemy of adaptation.' There is a tendency to stick with a strategy only because it happened to be used in a previous period. 'The pervasive influence of the status quo, trad-ition, custom, routine and adherence to precedent are powerful obstacles to change. When change occurs, it does so in the face of considerable odds.'[1]

The thing is our brains are hard-wired *against* change. So we end up exhibiting a laundry list of psychological symptoms: status quo bias, loss aversion, the endowment effect, and so on. They make us a testament to inertia. We hate change, and we curse the pain of it. For that reason, we'll do everything we possibly can to avoid it. In Bagehot's words, 'Men are too fond of their own life, too credulous of the completeness of their own ideas, too angry at the pain of new thoughts, to be able to bear easily with a changing existence.'[2]

The sheer complexity and pace of modern society can cause extraordinary anxiety about the future. Like a possum facing the lights of an oncoming car, the rapid approach of the future can daze us into a state of shock. We either end up feeling overwhelmed by the change we see around us, or we become complacent in our security. Either way, we don't tend to do anything, and as we've seen throughout this book, that's bad.

In this chapter, we'll tackle New Zealand's willingness to change in two parts. First, we'll skim through a host of factors that inhibit our willingness to change, from the way we think to the way we see the world. Then we'll offer a few ideas on how New Zealand can fight inertia – and become a society a little more willing than most to change when it needs to.

Why we hate change

Peasant societies were never going to set the world alight when it came to change. Peasants in the time of Cleopatra were living a life virtually identical to that of their ancestors when the great pyramids were built, two thousand years earlier.[3] But they resisted change for good reason. It was neither stupidity nor a love of tradition that made peasants resistant to change. Resisting change heightened their chances of survival. Peasant villagers worked out solutions to the problems of raising food, surviving in a hostile world and taking what enjoyment they could from life (not a lot). Trying new seeds or crops was a risky business. It was a case of holding to tried and tested ways. The motto was 'minimise risks to maximise lifespan'. Trying to create that bumper crop by messing around with some new-fangled crop variety – well, that was just plain lunacy.

We remain a cautious lot. Recent research in cognitive science has begun to discover why that's the case. Read some of the research into the way in which our brains make sense of the world, and you'll be wondering why we do anything in life. If we find it tough to change as individuals – from the way we think to the way we act – then it's inevitable that our society will struggle to adapt as well. We need to look at a few of the mental roadblocks scientists have discovered that lower our willingness to change.

Loss aversion and the endowment effect

In 2005 a group decided our flag needed to be hauled out of the nineteenth century and redesigned to reflect the very different New Zealand of the twenty-first century.[4] By organising a citizen-initiated referendum that would seek majority support for a new flag, their plan was to haul the old one up the flagpole to see how many people still saluted. Momentum appeared strong. Various prominent New Zealanders endorsed the idea, opinion polls suggested up to sixty per cent of New Zealanders supported a new flag, and New Zealand's largest postal and telecommunication companies agreed to distribute the petitions to most households.

In the end, only a hundred thousand of the required two hundred and seventy thousand signatures were collected and the initiative died. Strong opposition to the idea of a new flag was voiced by various groups, including many war veterans. Their opposition, when voiced as customers, shareholders or voters, put the squeeze on politicians and the executives of the companies distributing the petition, all of whom backed away, deciding there were easier battles to be fought. The Union Jack-adorned flag lived to flutter another day, its inevitable day of retirement postponed.

Sticking with the old flag may or may not have been a sound move for New Zealand in 2005. No one will ever know. But as real as the perils of changing our flag appeared to some, so too is our aversion to loss. Our struggle to confront the loss of something, even if it means gaining something better, can freeze our individual actions and those of our society. Inevitably, it is a tendency that inhibits our ability to adapt because we struggle to make choices that involve some loss. And change by definition has to involve the loss of something. Whether you favour a new flag or would rather stick with the status quo, we all have a sentimental attachment to our current flag. For everyone, then, changing the flag would require some loss, even if we were to get something better in the long run.

Trying to avoid the pain of loss is known as *loss aversion*, a very real psychological trait that hinders our willingness to change. Princeton University's Daniel Kahneman, who won the 2002 Nobel Prize in economics, has found that we prefer to avoid losses over acquiring equivalent or even greater gains.[5] For example, if you offer someone the chance of winning $1500 or losing $1000 on the flip of a coin, experiments show that most people won't take the bet. People tend to view a win of $1500 as nice to have, while losing $1000 is a disaster. This general bias will invariably make individuals less willing to change.

Closely related to loss aversion is another trait known as the *endowment effect*. The endowment effect means that we place an extra value on things we already own. Think of your favourite pair of jeans, or your house: would you swap either for something of equal market value? Probably not. What about your spouse?

Over the past decade, scientists have found support for the endowment effect in scores of experiments. In one study, half the students in a class were given pens; the others were given a token redeemable for an unspecified gift.[6] All the subjects were then given a choice between a pen and two chocolate bars. Incredibly, the pen was preferred by fifty-six per cent of those endowed with it, but only twenty-four per cent of the other subjects chose a pen. It wasn't that the pen was more attractive to those already possessing one. They just didn't want to give up what they had.

The main effect of endowment is not to enhance the appeal of the goods one owns, only the pain of giving it up. The American novelist and philosopher Ayn Rand puts it like this: 'I am the most offensively possessive man on earth. I do something to things. Let me pick up an ash tray from a dime-store counter, pay for it and put it in my pocket – and it becomes a special kind of ash tray, unlike any on earth, because it's mine.'[7] It's clear, then, why change is made more difficult by our aversion to loss and the endowment effect. If we prize what we have too highly, we'll be too reluctant to part with it in exchange for something else. Making the transition to the new will be too painful if we find it hard to release the old.

Then, on top of all that, it turns out we don't have a very good idea of measuring how happy the alternative to the status quo will make us. The outlook for change is going from bad to worse.

We don't really know what we want . . .

Mick Jagger was right. You can't always get what you want. But scientists are starting to realise he could have gone further: you don't always *know* what you want. In fact, according to Daniel Gilbert, a professor of psychology at Harvard University, we rarely know what we want. And that's a problem when it comes to being good at changing, because if we don't really know what we want it's hard to know whether we should stick with the status quo, or confront change.

Gilbert studies happiness.[8] To be more precise, he studies how people predict what will make them happy or unhappy – and then how they feel after the actual experience. His work seeks to discover how people predict they'll feel about purchasing clothes, having children, buying a new car or getting a promotion. And then he examines how they regard the outcomes after the event.

Isn't he wasting his time? After all, shouldn't people already know what will make them happy? Shouldn't they understand their future selves well enough to make the right decisions today – to find jobs and partners to love, to buy cushions for the couch to treasure for years to come? So why does what was indispensable yesterday end up being painfully embarrassing or useless today?

Well, according to Gilbert's research, it turns out we don't have a very good way of predicting what will make us happy. We're wrong to believe that a new car will make us as happy as we imagine. We are wrong to believe that a new kitchen will give us pleasure for as long as we anticipate.

In scores of experiments, Gilbert and collaborators have discovered that we falter when it comes to imagining how we will feel about something in the future. The experiments showed that, on average, good and bad events proved less intense and briefer than test participants predicted. So, for example, we are wrong to think that we will be more unhappy with a big, single setback (a broken leg, a broken heart) than with a less severe but more persistent one (a niggly knee, a tense marriage).[9]

The reason we fail to anticipate the future properly is because we underestimate how good we are at acclimatising to changing circumstances. We're highly adaptive creatures. So when bad things happen, we end up coping with them. We do eventually get over the disappointment of being dumped by our girlfriend. We find someone else or we take up pottery. The same with the job we missed out on. Even the broken leg.

Gilbert notes that the same phenomenon occurs with good things as well. The pleasure of the new BMW fades (often quicker than we'd like). It soon becomes just another vehicle with cup rings on the dashboard. We don't realise how quickly we will adapt to a pleasurable event and make it the backdrop of our lives. Whenever something happens, we make it ordinary; we lose the pleasure of the good and the pain of the bad fade more quickly than we expect.

So when we think about adopting a new national flag for the country, the pain of losing the old one is inevitably overplayed in our minds. But then, the pleasure we'll receive from the new flag, and how long it will last, is overstated too. The pleasure Auckland would have gained from a new stadium would have eroded faster than expected as the structure became a part of our everyday view of the waterfront. Thus, when we find our pleasure diminishing, we move on to the next thing or event and almost certainly make another error of prediction, and then another, ad infinitum. The way our minds distort our anticipated reaction to an event undermines our ability to make smart decisions today that will affect tomorrow.

Gilbert found that another issue with our predictive powers is our lousy ability to make the right comparisons when it comes to pleasure.[10] Real estate agents advise us to buy the most modest house in a neighbourhood of big homes rather than the biggest house in a neighbourhood of smaller homes. While that strategy will maximise value, it won't maximise happiness, because every time we drive past the magnificent houses of our neighbours and pull up outside our modest house, we'll wince.

According to Gilbert this skewed view of comparison applies to all sorts of items. Gilbert explains how the thinking behind the purchase of a stereo is often flawed. He describes the following scenario. When someone goes to the shop to buy a stereo, they'd make careful comparisons by listening to different sets of speakers. On the salesperson's prompting they might notice that the acoustic quality of the ugly, boxy speakers was slightly superior to the small, sleek ones. At the time the roomier midrange of the ugly speakers would have been clear, and their superiority to the sleek speakers, obvious. Alas, a few days after installing the ugly speakers in the middle of his living room, they would no longer be comparing them with the sleeker speakers whose acoustic benefits they could no longer quite remember. Instead he'd walk into the room every day and find themself staring at two ugly black boxes. The only comparison then would be between the ugly speakers and the rest of their otherwise sleek (and now spoiled) decor.

It isn't that making comparisons is the problem. The problem is that the comparisons we make when we purchase a product are not those we make later when we enjoy the product. Such flawed comparisons apply to new jobs and new partners as well.

Our sense, then, of which changes in our lives are worth making is horribly skewed by our apparent inability to know which ones will make us happy. If we don't really know whether a new BMW for our garage or a new flag for our country will make us happy longer term, our ability to understand what other changes are necessary in our lives won't be great.

... and become increasingly stuck in our ways

Scottish psychologist Kenneth Craik was tragically killed in a cycling accident at the age of thirty-one. Despite his early death, he had already made a series of breakthroughs about how our brains make decisions. He was the first to use the term *mental models*, an explanation of how our minds construct a model of reality it can use to anticipate events.

According to Princeton University psychologist Philip Johnson-Laird, these mental models provide important insights into how we see the world. Johnson-Laird is a leading authority on how humans perceive, reason and judge – our cognitive ability. He concludes that mental models 'play a central and unifying role in representing objects, states of affairs, sequences of events, the way the world is, and the social and psychological actions of daily life'.[11]

By definition, mental models provide simplified explanations of complex phenomena. Cognitive scientist John Holland describes human mental models as being organised into 'default hierarchies'.[12] Concepts are grouped together in hierarchical structures (for example, legless, slithery, hissing reptiles are categorised as snakes). These default hierarchies allow us to make decisions (for example, run away as fast as possible) with incomplete information (we don't need to know the type of snake, its sense of fear or level of hunger, whether it has woken up grumpy, and so on). These mental models were key to our survival as a species in earlier times, aiding our brain's reaction speed to threats of grievous bodily harm from angry tigers and angrier mammoths.

We all have significant limits on the amount of complexity we can cope with. Thus, even where we make conscious efforts to reach decisions according to a formally rational process, we often need to make simplifying assumptions and accept limits on the availability of information and the thoroughness of our analysis. That's where mental models help. We constantly use them as a way of reducing the complexity of decision-making: for example, associating a particular brand with quality rather than engaging in a detailed evaluation of the merits of different breakfast cereals at the supermarket.

Mental models are great for responding to the threat of a snake, but they hold us back when it comes to changing the way we think. They diminish our ability to change our minds. That may not matter in the case of snakes – we're always going to run – but it's an issue in a world where complexity and ambiguity require our brains to generate new perspectives on things. Our brains become conditioned to viewing things in a certain way, and it becomes harder to change these hierarchies over time.

As complexity expert Eric Beinhocker explains, when we are young and inexperienced, 'our default hierarchies are fairly shallow, so our views of the world are more general than specific'. The advantage of this is that our mental models are easily changeable: 'new experiences are readily absorbed, and reorganising the hierarchy is not very difficult, because there isn't that much to reorganise.'[13] That's why young people have a tendency to be adaptable in their thinking but also act inappropriately on occasions. They'll put fire crackers in letter boxes, but steer away from more serious offences after a warning from a policeman (in theory, anyway).

By contrast, Beinhocker adds, older people have filled up their hierarchies more thoroughly based on the experience gained with age. They have a larger collection of specific experiences ('When I was a boy . . .') and more feedback on what has worked and what has not. Their mental models 'grow into highly complex structures of categories, interlinked rules, and weightings'. They try to relate new knowledge to previous experiences.

The problem is that as our mental models become more complex, creating new hierarchies or rearranging existing ones becomes more and more difficult, says Beinhocker. There's far more structure that needs to be torn down to build a new idea. 'Our mental models thus tend to settle over time, and it takes progressively bigger and bigger shocks to shake them up'.[14]

This rigidity in thinking as we become more senior naturally affects progress in different fields. Nobel Prize-winning physicist Max Planck was credited by the Nobel committee with having made 'epoch-making investigations in physics' that brought about a whole new era in science. But he was sceptical about the ability of scientists to change their minds. In *The Philosophy of Physics* he says: 'An important scientific innovation rarely makes its way by gradually winning over and converting its opponents

. . . What happens is that its opponents gradually die out and that the next generation is familiarized with the ideas from the beginning.'[15]

The implications for a society are important. Stable mental models work well in stable environments. But as we saw in Chapter Four, the unpredictability of change in complex adaptive systems lulls our pattern-recognising, model-building minds into a sense of stability. Then we are hit with a sudden change. With the most experienced people occupying the management suites in most organisations, or the front benches of our parliament, their mental models will be best suited to execution in stable environments. But these people, so the theory goes, are, in turn, less capable of exploring new options and less likely to adapt to new environments. The result can be a frightening level of inertia. Adaptation can be stopped in its tracks.

Focus on the present

The next barrier to change is our focus on the present. Tantalus, in Greek mythology, was an earthly king but his father was Zeus, the king of the gods. And, like many who have it all handed to them by their parents, he blew it. In his case, by committing various crimes – one of which was failing to control his desire for instant gratification.

His punishment was truly one to fit the crime. He had to stand in water up to his chin with branches of trees laden with delicious fruit hanging over his head. He was hungry and desperately thirsty but each time he reached for the fruit, a wind would blow the branches up, lifting the fruit out of reach. Each time he bent down to drink, the water receded. Hence the verb 'to tantalise'.

There is an element of Tantalus's punishment in our daily existence. We seem agonisingly close to that which will fulfil us, but it always eludes us. You might have heard of the famous experiment back in the 1960s in which researchers offered marshmallows to four-year-olds.[16] One by one, each child was brought into a room and given a single marshmallow. He was told he could eat it, but if he waited five minutes until the researcher returned from an errand, he'd receive another one. About a third of the children grabbed the single marshmallow right away. Some waited a little longer, and about one-third were able to wait fifteen or twenty minutes for the researcher to return. The researchers then tracked the lives of those kids for years afterwards. Their principal finding: the kids who'd resisted eating the single marshmallow were more confident, had more friends and got better grades and better jobs.

There is no need to think about anything, including the future, if pleasure can be obtained effortlessly in a moment. This focus on the now at the expense of the future is referred to as *intertemporal choice*. This phenomenon intrigues behavioural economists such as David Laibson, professor of economics at Harvard University. 'There's a fundamental tension . . . between seizing available rewards in the present, and being patient for rewards in the future,' he says. 'If you ask people, "Which do you want right now, fruit or chocolate?" they say, "Chocolate!". But if you ask, "Which one a week from now?" they will say, "Fruit."' *Now* we want chocolate, beer, and a trashy movie. In the *future*, we want to eat fruit, to join a gym and to watch Bergman films.[17]

This focus on enjoying the present rather than preparing for the future is endemic in New Zealand if our attitude to saving is any indication. In 2005 the insurance company AXA conducted an international survey of ten thousand people across twelve countries, including six hundred and fifteen people in New Zealand. Seeking to understand attitudes about retirement, the survey found that New Zealanders were among the most optimistic about their quality of life at retirement, but among the lowest savers. New Zealanders' spending binge has made them the worst savers in the OECD. In 2005, the net savings rate was *negative* 6.3 per cent of disposable household income.[18] The response to the findings of AXA New Zealand's CEO: 'While the [New Zealanders'] optimism is to be applauded, I am concerned that it reflects a somewhat blasé, 'she'll be right' attitude.'[19]

Overly-optimistic about our abilities

This attitude is also indicative of another constraint to change: we're generally overly positive about our ability to handle the future and therefore unwilling to prepare for it. You'll see this optimism in our abilities the next time you sit down to a board game involving the throwing of dice. Watch to see whether the other players throw the dice with different intensities depending on the number they're hoping for. Chances are, they'll shake up the dice more and throw them harder if they want a higher number than if they're seeking a lower number.[20] It's illogical, of course. The number that does come up is random, regardless of how we roll the dice. But our brains trick us into believing we can exert just a tiny bit of control over something as random as throwing dice.

We tend to overestimate our control over an outcome, a cognitive condition psychologists refer to as *over-optimism bias*. In a groundbreaking study in 1975, psychologist Ellen Langer found that under some circumstances, people have even been induced to believe that they could affect the outcome of a purely random coin toss. Subjects in experiments she conducted who guessed a series of coin tosses more successfully, began to believe that they were actually superior guessers and that their guessing performance would deteriorate if they were distracted.[21]

This bias towards over-optimism affects us all the time. It's the emotion that makes us annoyed when we see someone driving erratically while talking on a cellphone, even if we've done the very same thing, that very same day. We tell ourselves we're different, because our call was shorter or our driving ability while talking is superior to others. What optimism bias comes down to, however, is the convenient belief that risks that apply to other people don't apply to us.

In other words, we see ourselves as a lot better than we actually are. According to Dan Lovallo, a researcher at the Australian Graduate School of Management, and Nobel Prize-winner Daniel Kahneman of Princeton, the bias toward over-optimism is part of a deep-rooted human desire to believe in ourselves and our abilities.[22] Syndicated columnist Dave Barry was more spot-on than he realised when he observed that, 'the one thing that unites all human beings, regardless of age, gender, religion, economic status or ethnic background, is that, deep down inside, we *all* believe that we are above-average drivers.'[23]

It's a dangerous mix. The tendency we have is to focus on today at the expense of preparing for tomorrow. Why? Because we're driven by an overly optimistic estimation of our ability to handle whatever tomorrow brings. 'She'll be right' ends up becoming our national excuse to avoid preparing today for our future tomorrow. No need to push our politicians for a solution to the looming superannuation crisis, we reason, because we'll personally be okay (we'll downsize our housing through some clever timing of the real estate market, or we'll luck out on a few stocks, or our unique combination of Lotto numbers will come up). Never mind that everyone else is banking on the same turn of events.

Not everyone thinks like that, of course. Some are diligent in preparing for tomorrow, even at the expense of today. But most of us imagine that we'll cope with whatever the future brings, when the future arrives. Let's eat the marshmallow now, because, who knows, perhaps the rules will change when the researcher returns. That reasoning erodes the motivation to change today. That's problematic for New Zealand if adapting to an uncertain future requires a willingness to change *today*.

Helplessness about the future

There is a further nuance to our view of the future. We may be overly optimistic about our ability to handle the future, but we're pessimistic about everyone else's. If we're all thinking we're above-average drivers, we must all be looking down on the driving ability of our fellow citizens. And that's the other side of the optimism coin. We're pretty confident we'll be able to handle our own situation, but we have severe doubts about everyone else. We can handle our vehicle, but we're certain we'll get rammed from behind as a result of the incompetence of everyone else.

American journalist David Whitman has termed this the 'Optimism Gap' or the 'I'm OK– They're Not' syndrome. His 1998 book *The Optimism Gap* talks about the widespread perception among Americans that their country is deteriorating. He cites 1996 polls which showed that only fifteen per cent of Americans believed their country was getting better.[24] In similar polls, about half said the nation was worse off compared to the way it was when their parents were growing up, and sixty per cent believed the US in which their children would live, would be worse off still. Though most Americans are today healthier, better housed, better fed, better paid, better educated, better defended, freer, and distracted by a cornucopia of new entertainment products and services, they've managed to convince themselves their grandparents had it better during the dust-bowl era of the 1930s.[25]

Part of the reason for this distorted perception of the world we live in is our extraordinary dependence on the media for interpreting the world for us. As we've seen, the fact that we live more isolated lives than we used to (we sit alone in our cars rather than sit with others on the bus;

we watch TV at home rather than hang out at the rugby club or pub), combined with the increase in the time and money we have to spend on media entertainment, has heightened the mass media's role in our lives.

There's nothing wrong with our increasing use of the mass media, except that it begins to play too big a role in shaping our views of the world. There's nothing wrong with that, either, except that the media interprets the world in a way that will drive sales of newspapers and magazines, boost TV ratings, and fill movie theatres. A key way of doing all of that is by the use of fear.

Fear, one could argue, has become the dominant currency of public life. Our airwaves and newspaper columns are filled with fearful phenomena, from obesity to dodgy chicken-legs. Some may be true, but it is our inability to grasp the nature of the risk they pose that is the issue. Despite the prosperity that ephemeralisation has brought us – we live for longer and are less vulnerable to absolute poverty than any previous generation of human beings – we're more fearful than ever.

Some have asked, why? In 2004, the BBC screened a controversial documentary called *The Power of Nightmares* that looked at the pervasiveness of fear in Western society. It argued that while politicians once offered dreams of a better future, they now offer to protect us from nightmares. Fear has become a political resource to be mined to boost politicians' own legitimacy and authority, argues the documentary's maker, Adam Curtis.

Bill Durodié, director of the International Centre for Security Analysis at King's College, London, is an expert on risk and the political society, and he agrees with Curtis. At least in part. He has argued that while fear has often been used as a political tool in history, we are particularly vulnerable to it now because of how isolated and fragmented our lives are.[26] He points to World War II, when panic was more prevalent in places where people were isolated. It turns out that fear, like any other problem, is halved when it's shared.

Without the moorings of social connectedness to political and religious institutions, community groups, sports clubs and neighbourhoods, we have no reality-check on our own fears. Without gossiping across the fence to the neighbour, how do we build up any mutual assessment of risk to, say, the well-being of our children? Is it safe to put them on the school bus? Are there any houses they should avoid when they set out to sell Girl Guide biscuits?

If we can't ask our neighbour about the safety of our own street, then our perceptions will inevitably be shaped (and probably distorted) by the news report of the child who got into trouble in some distant town. The news report shows us that there is risk involved in allowing your child to door-knock up and down your street. There is. But it doesn't help us assess just how big a risk it is. Without another data point or two (for example, the neighbour across your fence who actually knows the people in your street), our sense of the risk will be disproportionately skewed by our reliance on the media.[27]

Furthermore, Durodié suggests that our profound sense of insecurity is fuelled not so much by the speed with which the world is changing, but rather by our collective inability to shape that change. Television crime coverage in particular seems pitched to cause civic anxiety, while movies and general entertainment programming depict violence as far more pervasive than it actually is.

TV dramas have become so realistic it's easy to become excessively alarmed about life. As Christopher Jencks, a professor of Government at Harvard University, notes: 'When I was growing up there was violence on TV, but it was cowboys having shootouts. I never worried that rustlers would come over the hill into my neighborhood. Now the violence on television is presented as if it's about to get you personally. Every screen you look at, at home or in [cinemas], has something disastrous on it. No wonder people think [we are] out of control.'[28]

The most common way to manage our anxieties about what the future holds is simply to switch off: don't bother voting, watching the news, or thinking about the future. Toffler saw future shock as a disease of change – the stress and disorientation induced in people who are subjected to 'too much change in too short a time'. Twentieth-century composer John Cage once said that paralysis often comes from not knowing where to begin.[29]

According to Johns Hopkins University psychiatrist Anthony Reading, apathy is an amotivational state caused by the lack of hope, not the loss of it.[30] It is characterised by settling for one's present lot, rather than trying to improve it by investing one's energy in future-oriented activities. It affects people who live their lives in the present without any hoped-for future to motivate them. Samuel Johnson got it right over two hundred years ago: 'When there is no hope,' he said, 'there is no endeavour.'

So there we have it. Our overblown fears can lead to a sense of anxiety about the future. It's easy to feel overwhelmed by what appears to be a mountain of problems confronting us. It's natural to throw up our hands in despair if these problems feel beyond our control, to hunker down, to do nothing.

Building a New Zealand more willing to change

After all of that, it's easy to see why change is so difficult. We confront a bunch of cognitive barriers our minds erect when it comes to change. As a society we struggle to change because we're similarly focused on maximising the moment, even at the expense of the future. We're over-optimistic about our ability to control our own lives, but overly pessimistic about the wider world. It's no wonder changing is so difficult – for us both as individuals and as a society.

Faced with these barriers to change, one could reasonably ask if there is any hope at all that we can construct a society good at changing. Well, yes there is. While we can't rewire the cognitive processes of the brain, there are a few things we can do. And they all have to do with how we think about our country and its future.

... and reclaiming control of how we see the future

The late Fritz Roethlisberger, professor at Harvard Business School and a pioneer in the field of organisational behaviour, observed that most people think of the future as the end and the present as the means, whereas, in fact, the present is the end and the future the means. What he meant was that the future forms and alters what people do now. In that respect, the future is the *means* to alter behaviour today.

That's why I think we need to rediscover hope for a better future. Hope energises us to engage in projects we believe will improve our future, even though they are of no immediate value to us. Without hope driving our aspirations we become captive to whatever is happening in the present. Hope gives us a vision that things can be better, rather than just continuing as they have been. For that reason, according to Reading, it has been the driving force behind all of humanity's great achievements through the ages.[31]

As individuals, we are able to rise above the present and create a world partly of our own making. It's the same with our society. According to Stanford University economist Paul Romer, only a failure of imagination – the very one that might lead someone to suppose that everything has already been invented – leads us to think that all of the relevant institutions have been designed and that all of the policy levers have been found.[32] And only that failure can prevent any society from taking the lead in the twenty-first century. To take up the opportunities of a dynamic, turbulent world, New Zealand will need to embrace bold new ideas and ignore those who say they can't work.

Our newspapers and televisions may be filled with stories of crime, violence, gangs and prison; of negative economic news; of health scares and mishaps in our hospitals; of troubled schools. We have all of that, just as every country does. But these stories don't represent the full canvas of New Zealand life. They don't represent the vast number of quiet accomplishments, unheralded breakthroughs, inspired ideas, courageous risk-taking, and countless acts of selfless generosity that pull New Zealand forward each day. That's the true picture of New Zealand, but it doesn't make for gripping television. It's too easy to forget that. And when we do forget it, we shake our heads in despair and we book our tickets to Australia.

Robert Kennedy once said, 'The future does not belong to those who are content with today, apathetic toward common problems and their fellow man alike, timid and fearful in the face of bold projects and new ideas.' He was right. We need to be a nation that kicks apathy about our future to the curb and embraces bold projects and big ideas. We need leaders who aren't afraid to define an ambitious future, to occasionally lift our vision above the petty and mundane.

Ralph Waldo Emerson, the great nineteenth-century American writer, once summed up the inherent distinction between two views of the world like this: 'Mankind,' he said, 'is divided between the party of Conservatism and the party of Innovation, between the Past and the Future, between Memory and Hope. Neither Memory nor Hope provides by itself an entirely persuasive basis for political action. But the distinction expresses a deep contrast in human temperament and purpose. Some people resent change and others welcome it. Some are satisfied with what we have; others think we can do better.'[33] I think it's important that we're a nation filled with fewer of the former and more of the latter. Not just because it would make for more uplifting talkback radio, but because the spirit in which we take on the future will go a long way towards determining how successful we are at it.

To some, this might sound like a head prefect's high-school valedictory speech. And I admit it does have that ring to it. But even the most cynical among us – and let's face it, as a nation we can do cynicism better than most – can't deny that big accomplishments only come from bold ideas and ambitious goals. Winning the America's Cup showed that. So did countless Oscars for *The Lord of the Rings*. Accomplishments of that magnitude are as much a reflection of attitude as they are of ability.

Confronting the hard choices

In mid-2006, protestors gathered on the lawns outside Hungary's parliament.[34] They were there to demand the resignation of Hungary's deeply disliked Prime Minister, Ferenc Gyurcsany. A week earlier, in an amazingly honest speech to his party, the Hungarian Socialist Party, Gyurcsany had admitted that his government had made a mess of Hungary's economy, and that 'We lied, morning, noon and night'. Now the crowds outside his office demanded he go.

One man summed up the feelings of the crowd. For more than two years he said, 'we had an economic boom and everybody believed him and voted for him. Now it turns out the opposite was true. If he'd told us we were in trouble and it was going to be difficult for a few years, we would have accepted it.'

The frustration of the Hungarians raises a difficult question that confronts modern democracies like New Zealand: why do politicians struggle to confront us with the truth? Part of the problem is that most politicians don't think people would vote for the unvarnished truth. But there is more to it than that.

A society is best able to confront necessary change when it has not only honest politicians but also an honest electorate. It needs voters willing to face the fact that sometimes there is only a choice between unpalatable options. As the leadership guru Max De Pree once said, the first responsibility of a leader is to define reality. We need politicians honest enough to tell us how it is, but as a society we also need the courage to accept it.

New Zealand has skirted tough choices before. The changes wrought in the 1980s and early 1990s to the economy and our public institutions are still fresh in the minds of many New Zealanders. As a society, we had settled into the post-World War II mindset of cradle-to-grave welfare, shipping all our butter to Britain, and taxing, regulating and subsidising everything that moved. But then Britain decided to throw its lot in with Europe rather than the Commonwealth, OPEC decided to ping us hard for our oil, some massive public-works schemes emptied the government's coffers, and suddenly the world changed. New Zealand had let itself drift to the brink of bankruptcy before the resuscitation paddles were applied to jolt the economy back to life. And we still have the scars to prove how much it hurt.

But those scars need not be for nothing. Lessons can be learned. And it's for this reason that the parallels that I've made throughout the book between the evolution of a society, and that of species come to an end. In Chapter Five we saw that the New Zealand giant penguin didn't have the foresight to comprehend that it wasn't ready to cope with changes in its environment. But humans are different. Unlike the penguin, New Zealand can learn from the mistakes of the past, anticipate some challenges in the future and try to alter its course in an intelligent way.

Doing so involves being realistic about what can and cannot be accomplished. In his book, *The Good Life and Its Discontents*, economic journalist Robert Samuelson addresses the sense of entitlement that pervades western societies like New Zealand.[35] His thesis may be summarised as 'You never had it so good'. We complain so much, he argues, because we expect too much from the prosperity we achieved in the twentieth century. We demand the impossible: economic growth without business cycles, easy credit without property bubbles, and – everyone's perennial favourite – benefits without taxes. Samuelson argues that if we are to restore faith in our institutions, we must return to a realistic sense of what the economy and, in particular, the government can deliver – we need 'responsibility, not entitlement'.

As a small nation, we can't afford to vote for politicians who promise what they can never actually deliver. Instead of looking for saviours, we must always look for leadership that will challenge us to face problems for which there are no simple, painless solutions – problems that require us to change our own behaviour.

Tom Bentley, the former head of UK democracy think tank Demos, and now executive director for policy and cabinet for the premier of Victoria, Australia, points out that in the 2004 British election more people abstained than voted Labour, the party that won power.[36] He sees this as a sign that voters no longer trust politicians and the political process. He suggests that a new generation of political leaders will only regain trust if they start being honest with the electorate about the scale of the problems facing society and the inability of governments to solve them alone. He argues that the real task of future leaders will be to tell voters that they have to change their own behaviour and attitudes if issues such as climate change and superannuation shortfalls are to be solved.

We're in the same boat. To meet the extraordinary challenges of tomorrow, we need a different idea of leadership and a different set of expectations about what the government can and cannot do. Improving our willingness to change requires that New Zealand's most pressing challenges of the future – like how we build an economy able to compete in a rapidly globalising world or how we deflate the rising levels of distrust and marginalisation in modern-day New Zealand – aren't glossed over with the usual political platitudes. Instead they need to be framed by our politicians in a realistic way that acknowedges that solving them requires some tough choices without which some tougher times are ahead. Once that happens, these challenges require an electorate prepared to accept that changes to the way they think and act may be necesary.

Peering into the rear-vision mirror

In the 1970s, sociologist Richard Sennett co-wrote a book about working-class life in modern times.[37] In the course of writing that book he interviewed Enrico, a cleaner. Enrico's work was predictable, his life routine. He knew exactly where he would work and how much he would earn throughout his life until he retired. It was a common narrative for the lives of many.

Twenty-five years later, Sennett had a chance encounter with Enrico's son at an airport. Unlike his father, the son was a wealthy professional. His work was interesting. He earned a lot more money than his father. Enrico's son had, by the metrics of today's society, made it. But unlike Enrico, his son faced an unpredictable future. He wasn't sure where he would be working the following year or living the year after that.

This encounter inspired Sennett to write *The Corrosion of Character*.[38] In this book he examines the effect of the rapidly changing world on the people who work in it. He describes how workers feel pressured to change jobs frequently. If they stay still they are often seen as failures. So they move, but without calculating whether it makes sense to or not. They gamble on their next move without knowing what the odds are.

This frequent shuffling of the workforce disrupts relationships. In times of change, such as those New Zealand struggled through in the 1980s and 1990s, there is inevitably disruption to communities, and the severing of deep relationships. In a world (and in a book) praising flexibility and change, what people achieved yesterday can end up seeming of little value today.

But adaptation is not simply a matter of casting aside old baggage. It also means learning how to mitigate the costs. Toffler suggests that there must be balance 'not merely between rates of change in different sectors, but between the pace of environmental change and the limited pace of human response'.[39] It is when the rates of change within a society are uneven, argues the sociologist William Ogburn, that social stresses emerge.

Today's fast-moving world threatens to create divisions in New Zealand. Arising from the opportunities and risks of globalisation, it is a division between those enfranchised by the fast-paced, high-skilled, market-driven society and those at risk of being left behind. It's a division between those who have faith in the social and economic changes of the 1980s and 1990s, and those who hold on to an earlier vision of New Zealand with a mix of fear and pride.

We've seen in this book that we cannot keep redundant institutions or ideas for the sake of convenience. We need the creativity that comes from letting them go. But it would be wrong to imagine that is all there is to it. Because it isn't.

Unless we can ease the pain of disruption for those hardest hit by change, fierce resistance will inevitably follow. Unless we can help others bear the consequences of change, we'll undermine our ability to change again when it's required in the future. Charging headlong into the future, therefore, requires frequent glances over our shoulders to ensure we're not leaving segments of society behind in our rush to change, grow and move on.

Glancing behind is also necessary to avoid losing sight of where we've come from. It's too easy to discount the lessons or ways of the past as outdated and irrelevant to modern times. Mark Twain was right when he said, 'The altar cloth of one generation is the doormat of the next.'

Shaping our future does not mean ignoring the past out of which the future evolved. It doesn't mean throwing away all that we love about our country. Nor does it mean turning ourselves into a society we don't want to be. Indeed, it can't. The past and future are inextricably connected and progress is only ever incremental, made possible by what has come before. We seek to improve on the legacy of the past, but it is from that legacy that any improvement must start. This sense of continuity is vital.

Our responses to the future, whatever it holds, will be linked to the choices we've made as a nation in the past. The economist Thomas Sowell once said, 'To seek to look ahead into the future is to seek to understand the momentum of the past and the choices available to us in the present. We live in a world of options constrained by decisions already made and actions already taken – many before we were born.'[40]

Edmund Burke once said, 'society is a partnership not only between those who are living, but between those who are living, those who are dead, and those who are [yet] to be born.'

As a nation we can't walk away from the choices we've made in the past, any more than future generations will be able to undo the choices we make today. They'll pick up from where we left off, tearing down and rebuilding, retaining some ideas, improving others and casting aside some more. The historian and philosopher of science Stephen Toulmin puts it like this: 'The belief that, by cutting ourselves off from the inherited ideas of our cultures, we can "clean the slate" and make a fresh start, is as illusory as the hope for a comprehensive system . . . that is capable of giving us timeless certainty and coherence . . . All we are required to do is use our experience critically and discriminatingly, *refining and improving* our inherited ideas.'[41]

New Zealand's cultural legacy is that of the many ethnicities that comprise our nation. We celebrate our diversity because we have a lot of it to celebrate. A Samoan captained the All Blacks, while his compatriot carried the New Zealand flag at the opening ceremony of the Olympics. Hundreds of thousands of New Zealanders from every sphere of life wander along to cultural festivals such as the Chinese New Year, the Pasifika festival, St Patrick's Day, Matariki and Diwali.

But New Zealand's story is primarily of two peoples – Maori and Pakeha. For millennia they lived half a world apart. Each culture represents, in a sense, the ideas and ways of living and prospering handed down from generation to generation, moulded to the conditions of, in the one case, the North Atlantic and, in the other, to the South Pacific. Theirs are the ideas and ways shaped, in each case, by a long journey, by starting from nothing, by isolation, by having only a small part to play on a big stage. They represent, individually and together, strategies for succeeding in New Zealand's unique context.

Dr Pita Sharples, co-leader of the Maori Party, says that nationhood is 'learning how to understand and speak from a position of strength in knowing our own background; our history, and our traditions . . . a powhiri, a marae, a Pakeha, are unique to this land, unique to Aotearoa, to New Zealand; and we must celebrate that, not shy away from it.'[42] So in adapting to an unknown future, New Zealand's ideas and ways of the past should not necessarily be cast aside. Instead, they should be refined, updated and improved upon. To put it another way, adapting to the future doesn't mean turning the kiwi into kangaroo or a lion. Instead it involves growing bigger wings or faster legs. The challenge is to build, enhance and improve the uniquely New Zealand way of doing things.

The future

Time magazine had this to say about New Zealand a few years back: 'New Zealand is in the vanguard of a dynamic world – its human diversity, open spaces, wit, flexibility and sheer tenacity have taken a rugged isolated country and positioned it on the cutting edge of adventure, knowledge and creativity.'[43] Not bad for a country that was the last to be settled by mankind.

That said, we're a country that has as yet come nowhere near pushing the envelope of what is possible. To do so means confronting the challenges of an unknown future, the instability of which is heightened by the fluidity of contemporary life. Ours is a magnificently dynamic era. But that dynamism produces change, and change can be uncomfortable.

Undoubtedly many of the solutions needed to address the problems and capture the opportunities of these times will require input from political, social and business leaders. But ultimately the outcome lies with the rest of us. No individual, organisation, or government can plan, control, or supervise the creative, dynamic New Zealand jigsaw envisaged in this book. It will simply have to continue assembling itself through the decisions each of us make each day. The ways in which we approach difficult choices, how we spend our time and money, for whom we cast our votes and work for, and what we speak up for – these will determine the New Zealand of tomorrow.

How we feel about the evolving future tells us who we are as a society. Do we value sameness, or change and learning? Do we think that progress requires a return to past ways of thinking, or do we see it as infused with new ideas? Do we pine for a country comprised of people just like us, or can we appreciate the value of diversity, despite its challenges? Do we consider mistakes disasters, or the inevitable by-product of risk and experimentation? Do we crave predictability, or accept uncertainty? This book has tried to show that New Zealand's answers to these questions will define its response to the future.

Formulated at this level of abstraction, tackling the turbulence of tomorrow seems almost too easy. It won't be. What's more, this book certainly doesn't come close to filling in all the blanks. Bertrand Russell once said that he didn't pretend to start with precise questions, and I haven't pretended to end this book with precise answers.

Some will find that frustrating. Yet such imprecision is appropriate. Because what we've been discussing is not really what New Zealand should do, but how it should be, how we think and act, how we see ourselves and our country, how we make decisions as individuals and on what basis. These aren't quick-fix solutions. They're more fundamental than that. They go to the heart of who we are as a people.

It's for that reason that navigating New Zealand through the unknown, dragon-filled future needs to involve lots of people – from all walks of life – coming into the ring, discussing, disagreeing, imagining, and experimenting. And that seems right. Because each of us is a part of the New Zealand story. And we each have a role to play in shaping its next chapters.

Endnotes

Introduction

1 Sowell, T., *The Economics and Politics of Race: An International Perspective*, Quill, New York, 1985. 243, 257

Part I The end of certainty

1 A complex, crazy world

1 To read more about the motor vehicle's colourful beginnings in New Zealand, see Graham Hawkes' book *On the Road: The Car in New Zealand*, GP Books, Wellington, 1990.

2 1966 Encyclopedia of New Zealand website: www.teara.govt.nz/1966/en.

3 Quoted in Waldrop, M., *Complexity: The Emerging Science at the Edge of Order and Chaos*, Simon and Schuster, New York, 1992, p. 119.

4 Beinhocker, E., *The Origins of Wealth*, Harvard Business School Press, Cambridge, 2006, pp. 8–9.

5 Landes, D., *Prometheus Unbound: Technological Change and Industrial Development in Western Europe from 1750 to the Present*, Cambridge University Press, Cambridge, 1960, p. 5, quoted in Beinhocker, E., *The Origins of Wealth*, Harvard Business School Press, Cambridge, 2006, p. 11.

6 Flynn, J., 'Massive IQ gains in 14 nations: What IQ tests really measure', *Psychological Bulletin*, 101, No. 2, 1987, pp. 171–191.

7 New Zealand's increase was not as substantial as some other countries, but when you're starting from a high base . . .

8 Johnson, S., *Everything Bad is Good for You*, Riverhead Trade, New York, 2006.

9 Fixmar, R., 'Internet Insight: Moore's Law & Order', www.eWeek.com.

10 *World Resources 1998–99*, World Resources Institute, Oxford University Press, New York, 1998.

11 Taken from Heylighen, F., 'Complexity and Information Overload in Society: Why Increasing Efficiency Leads to Decreasing Control', draft paper, version: April 12, 2002, to be submitted to: The Information Society, p. 3.

12 Shermer, M., *Why People Believe Weird Things: Pseudo-science, Superstition, and Bogus Notions of our Time*, MJF Books, New York, 1997.

13 Merry, U., *Copying with Uncertainty*, Praeger Publishers, Westport, 1995.

14 Gleick, J., *Faster: The Acceleration of Just About Everything*, Pantheon Books, New York, 1999, p. 9.

15 *Around the Clock:Findings from the New Zealand Time Use Survey 1998–99*, Statistics New Zealand, and Ministry of Women's Affairs, Wellington, 2001.

16 Gleick, J., *Faster: The Acceleration of Just About Everything*, Pantheon Books, New York, 1999.

17 *Around the Clock:Findings from the New Zealand Time Use Survey 1998–99*, Statistics New Zealand, and Ministry of Women's Affairs, Wellington, 2001.

18 Helprin, M., 'The Acceleration of Tranquility,' *Forbes*, December 2, 1996.

19 Brand, S., *The Clock of the Long Now: Time and Responsibility*. Basic Books, New York, 1999.

20 Shenk, D., *Data Smog: Surviving the Information Glut*, Harper, San Francisco, 1997.

21 Miller, G., 'The Magical Number Seven Plus or Minus Two: Some Limits in our Capacity for Processing Information', *Psychological Review*, 1957, pp. 63–97.
22 Csikszentmihalyi, M., *Flow: The Psychology of Optimal Experience*, Harper and Row, New York, 1990.
23 Quoted in Seven, R., 'Life Interrupted', *Seattle Times*, November 28, 2004.
24 'Majority in International Poll Feels Stress Daily', *International Herald Tribune*, 20 December, 2006.
25 Kirsh, D., 'A Few Thoughts on Cognitive Overload', *Intellectica*, 2000/1, p. 30.
26 Toffler, A., *Future Shock*, Random House UK, London, 1970.
27 *ibid*, p. 19.
28 Twenge, J. M. 'The Age of Anxiety? Birth Cohort Change in Anxiety and Neuroticism, 1952–1993.' *Journal of Personality and Social Psychology*, 2000, 79, pp. 1007–1021.
29 Twenge, J. M., Zhang, L., & Im, C., 'It's Beyond My Control: A Cross-temporal Meta-analysis of Increasing Externality in Locus of Control, 1960–2002.' *Personality and Social Psychology Review*, 8, 2004.
30 Zweibel, J., '"Generation Whatever" Growing Gloomier', www.sdsuniverse.info/story.asp?id=19297.
31 'Majority in International Poll Feels Stress Daily', *International Herald Tribune*, 20 December, 2006.
32 UMR survey commissioned by NZQA, 2006 *National Business Review* Phillips Fox poll.
33 Perry, P. & Webster, A., *New Zealand Politics at the Turn of the Millennium: Attitudes and Values about Politics and Government*, Alpha Publications, Auckland, 1999.
34 Barnes, C., & Gill, D., 'Declining Government Performance? Why Citizens Don't Trust Government', Working Paper 9, State Services Commission, 2000. This report lists a multitude of possible explanations for the fall in confidence in government, from the role of the media to the greater expectations we have in government policy.
35 'Americans Distrust Government, But Want It To Do More.' National Public Radio, The Henry J. Kaiser Family Foundation, and Harvard University John F. Kennedy School of Government, 2000.
36 'America Unplugged: Citizens and Their Government.' Council for Excellence in Government /Hart-Teeter. Washington DC, 1999, www.npr.org.
37 Freeman, D, *From Eros to Gaia*, Pantheon Books, New York, pp.242–243.
38 Speech at the Harvard Club of Singapore's 35th anniversary dinner. 6 January, 2004.
39 Hayek, F, *Constitiution of Liberty*, University of Chicago Press, Chicago, 1978, p112.

2 New Zealand's unknown future

1 'Standing on the Edge of a New Frontier: The World in 2031', Panel Discussion, Kennedy School of Government, Harvard University, 30 September, 2006.
2 'IBM Owes Me A Rematch' by Garry Kasparov, *Time*, May 26, 1997.
3 Lengauer, C., Diaz, L.A., and Saha S., 'Cancer drug discovery through collaboration.' Nature Reviews Drug Discovery. May 2005, pp.375–385.
4 US Department of Health and Human Services, Center for Medicare & Medicaid Services. National Health Expenditures Tables. Table 3: National Health Expenditures by Source of Funds and Type of Expenditure: Selected Calendar Years 1997–2002 (US Department of Health and Human Services, CMS, Washington, DC, 2004).
5 Corey, P.N.,Lazarou, J., & Pomeranz B.H., *Journal of the American Medical Association*, 1998, 279, pp. 1200–1205.
6 Evans, B., Flockhart, D., & Meslin,

E., 'Creating Incentives for Genomic Research to Improve Targeting of Therapies', *Nature Medicine*, 2004, pp. 10, 1289–1291.

7 The task of sequencing the individual genome – in this case, scientist Craig Venter's – cost about $6.5 billion and took about 10 years. Already the same could now be done at a mere fraction of the time and cost (about $16 million) and in any number of locations. Source: Adams M. D., Venter, J. C., et al. 'The Sequence of the Human Genome.' *Science*. Vol 291, 16 February 2001, p.1305.

8 Caspi, A., McClay, J., Moffitt, T.E., et al. 'Role of Genotype in the Cycle of Violence in Maltreated Children', *Science*, Vol. 297, 2 August 2002; p. 851.

9 P. Danzon, A Towse. 'The Economics of Gene Therapy and of Pharmacogenetics', *Value Health*, Vol 5, 2002, pp. 5–13.

10 Bozdech Z., Coppel, R.L., Roos, D.S., 'The Genomics of Malaria Infection', *Trends Parasitol*, 2004; 20:553–557. As cited by Guttmacher, A.E., Collins, F.S., 'Realizing the Promise of Genomics in Biomedical Research.' *Journal of the American Medical Association*. 21 September, 2005. Vol 294, No. 11.

11 Arendt, H., *The Human Condition*, University of Chicago Press, Chicago, 1958.

12 'A Meaty Question', *Economist*, 21 September, 2006.

13 'Architect of Life', *Forbes*, 2 October, 2006.

14 *ibid.*

15 *ibid.*

16 'Nanotechnology – Size Matters' white paper, 3i and the Economist Intelligence Unit, July 2002.

17 'Standing on the Edge of a New Frontier: The World in 2031', Panel Discussion, Kennedy School of Government, Harvard University, 30 September, 2006.

18 'Non-Tear Plastic Film Increases Glass Strength,' *New Materials Japan*, 1 Nov, 2003.

19 'Business: Clever Stuff', *Economist*, London, 29 March 2003, Vol. 366, Iss. 8317, p. 68.

20 Brown, C., 'Nanotech Goes to War', *Electronic Engineering Times*, 25 August 2003, p. 18.

21 In order to build the product on a human scale, these auto-assemblers would have to be able to reproduce themselves – also using raw material from the natural world – in massive numbers. 'Grey goo' is what would happen if one of the auto-assemblers went haywire and the self-replication never stopped. In just ten hours an unchecked self-replicating auto-assembler would spawn sixty-eight billion offspring; in fewer than two days the auto-assemblers would outweigh the earth.

22 Sperber, S. H., 'A Small World: Shelly Scott–Star Scientist', *North and South*, August 2005, p.41.

23 www.stuff.co.nz/stuff/0,2106,3235164a13,00.html

24 Schwartz, P., & Koselka, R., 'Quantum Leap: Brain prosthetics. Telepathy. Punctual Flights. A Futurist's Vision of Where Quantum Computers Will Take Us', *Fortune*, 1 August 2006.

25 Borin, E., 'New Memory That Doesn't Forget', *Wired Magazine*, July 2003.

26 Swarup, A., 'Einstein's "Spooky Action" Seen on A Chip', www.newscientist.com/article.ns?id=dn8568.

27 Herper, M., Biotech Report. *Forbes*. June 6, 2005, p. 28.

28 Giles, J., 'Blue Brain Boots Up to Mixed Response', *Nature*, Vol.. 435, 9 June 2005, p. 720.

29 Herper, M., 'IBM Aims to Stimulate a Brain', *Forbes*, 6 June 2005.

30 Schwartz, P., *Inevitable Surprises*, Gotham, New York, 2003, p. 177.

31 Kurzweil, R., 'Long Live AI', *Forbes*, 15 August 2005, p. 30.

32 Kurzweil, R., *The Age of Spiritual Machines: When Computers Exceed Human Intelligence*, Penguin Books, New York, 2000, pp. 103–105.
33 'The Future of the Internet II', Pew Internet and American Life Project, September 2006.
34 Chelminksi, R., 'This Time It's Personal', *Wired Magazine*, October, 2001.
35 Hoffman, P., 'Who's Best at Chess? For Now, It's Neither Man Nor Machine', *New York Times*, 8 February 2003.
36 Adapted from Pink, D., *A Whole New Mind: Why Right-Brainers Will Rule the Future*, Riverhead Books, New York, 2006, pp. 40–41.
37 *Tough Choices or Tough Times: The Report of the New Commission on the Skills of the American Workforce*, National Center on Education and the Economy, John Wiley, San Francisco, December 2006.
38 'The Best and the Brightest', *Esquire*, December 2002.
39. Kessler, A., *The End of Medicine*, Harper Collins, New York, 2006, p. 323.
40. Blass, E., 'Robots Continue Their Quest to Take Over Entire Hospitals', www.engadget.com/2006/10/29/robots-continue-their-quest-to-take-over-entire-hospitals, 28 October 2006.
41 The robots in hospitals situation has become even more bizarre in South Korea where medical students are resorting to robots to practise bringing babies into the world. Student regularly crowd around 'Noelle' as she gives 'birth'. They take turns at monitoring her vital signs and at pulling the 'baby' out of her body. The newborn, also a robot, is equipped with lights on its hands and cheeks to indicate its health – blue lights mean problems while pink lights signal all is okay. Sounds highly realistic.
42 Fishman, T., *China, Inc*, Scribner, New York, 2005.
43 *ibid.*
44 External Trade Statistics, 2006, New Zealand Department of Statistics.
45 Leong, M., 'The Parallel Universes of China', *The World of Harvard*, Winter 2007.
46 Fishman, T., *China, Inc*, Scribner, New York, 2005.
47 *ibid.*
48 Farrell, D. & Grant, A., 'China's Looming Talent Shortage', in *The McKinsey Quarterly*, 2005 Number 4.
49 Statistics quoted from Pink, D., *A Whole New Mind: Why Right-Brainers Will Rule the Future*, Riverhead Books, New York, 2006, p. 39.
50 Davis, I. & Stephenson, E., 'Ten Trends to Watch in 2006', *McKinsey Quarterly*, January 2006.
51 External Trade Statistics, 2006, New Zealand Department of Statistics.
52 CIA World Factbook, 2005 estimate.
53 *ibid*, 2003 estimate.
54 Fishman, T., *China, Inc*, Scribner, New York, 2005.
55 Schwartz, P., *Inevitable Surprises*, Gotham, New York, 2003, p. 193.
56 'Three Gorges Dam Wall Completed', BBC, http://news.bbc.co.uk/2/hi/asia-pacific/5000092.stm, May 2006.
57 Fishman, T., *China, Inc*, Scribner, New York, 2005.
58 Population Division of the Department of Economic and Social Affairs of the United Nations Secretariat, *World Population Prospects: The 2004 Revision and World Urbanization Prospects: The 2003 Revision.*
59 'Demographic Aspects of New Zealand's Ageing Population', Statistics New Zealand, March 2006.
60 A New Zealand Treasury report on this very issue concluded that this dependency ratio issue was not as much of a problem for the workforce at the time, as productivity improvements would mean that

the future worker in 30 years time' would be enjoying real incomes more than 50 per cent higher than at present. Creedy, J., and Scobie, G., 'Population Ageing and Social Expenditure in New Zealand: Stochastic Projections', New Zealand Treasury, Working Paper 02/28; 'Demographic Aspects of New Zealand's Ageing Population', Statistics New Zealand, March 2006.

61 But don't get too alarmed. New Zealand has 'been there, done that' on this problem before. If you include the other bunch of dependents – those ungrateful whipper-snappers under the age of 14 (who also don't pay a ton of tax beyond GST on lollies and arcade games) – then New Zealand's 'dependency ratio' in 2050 will be about the same as it was when the baby boomers were children in the 1950s and 1960s. In 1960, for example, our dependency ratio (number of dependents to those in working age population) was 71. In 2004 it was 51. In 2050 it will be at 73. So if you plotted New Zealand's dependency ratio from 1950 to 2050, you'd see that we're currently at the bottom of a big U shape. This is our prime earning time as the baby boomers move through their highest earning stage in their careers. Revenues need to build the reserves necessary for the impending slope upwards in the dependency curve. Source: 'Demographic Aspects of New Zealand's Ageing Population', Statistics New Zealand, March 2006.

62 Of course, if Alzheimer's strikes, 70 becomes the new. A tragic footnote to a health system that is getting better at keeping bodies functioning, but that still struggles to stave off ailments that affect the mind.

63 An International Monetary Fund study found that the average person aged 65 or older costs New Zealand's public health system five times as much as the average person under 65. Source: Bryant, J., Audrey T., Martin T., Jit, C., and Mhairi, M., 2004, 'Population Aging and Government Health Expenditures in New Zealand,' Working Paper No. 04/14, New Zealand Treasury. Bryant, J., Sonerson, A., 'Gauging the Cost of Aging' *Finance and Development*, Volume 43, No. 3, September 2006; Creedy, J., & Scobie, G., 'Population Ageing and Social Expenditure in New Zealand: Stochastic Projections', New Zealand Treasury, Working Paper 02/28.

64 Creedy, J., and Scobie, G., 'Population Ageing and Social Expenditure in New Zealand: Stochastic Projections', New Zealand Treasury, Working Paper 02/28.

65 Rand Study Finds Advancing Medical Technology Likely To Greatly Increase Future Medicare Costs', Rand Corporation, 2005.

66 2002/03 *New Zealand Health Survey*, Ministry of Health, Wellington, 2003.

67 *ibid.*

68 'Trends in Participation in Sport and Active Leisure 1997–2001', Sport and Recreation New Zealand, 2003.

69 'Submission to the Health Select Committee of Inquiry Into Obesity and Type 2 Diabetes', Diabetes New Zealand Inc, April 2006.

70 'All the Right Moves', *Fast Company*, Issue 24, April 1999, p. 192.

71 These enhancements made Deeper Blue the world's 259th most powerful computer at that time.

72 That's 9,000,000,000,000,000,000, or, if you prefer, nine quintillion, moves. American mathematician and Nobel Prize-winner Claude Shannon has calculated that the possible paths through the maze of a typical chess game could number 10^{120}.

73 Chess masters are thought to analyze two moves per second, based mainly on pattern recognition. Source: Leakey, D., 'Artificial Intelligence', *Van Nostrand Scientific Encyclopedia*, Ninth Edition, Wiley, New York, 2002.

3 A world of uncertainty

1 Petzinger, T., *The New Pioneers: The Men and Women Who Are Transforming the Workplace and Marketplace*, Simon & Schuster, 1999, p. 18.
2 Quoted in Brian Arthur, W., *'The End of Certainty in Economics'* in Clippinger, J., (ed.), *The Biology of Business*, Jossey-Bass, San Francisco, 1999.
3 Prigogine, I., & Stengers, I., *Order out of Chaos*, Bantam, New York, 1984, p. xii.
4 Weinberg, S., *Dreams of a Final Theory: The Scientist's Search for the Ultimate Laws of Nature*, Vintage, New York, 1994.
5 Jeans, J., *The Mysterious Universe*, Longmans, Green & Co, London, 1950.
6 Petzinger, T., *The New Pioneers*, Simon & Schuster, New York, 1999, p. 122.
7 *ibid*, pp. 122–123.
8 Metaphor taken from Beinhocker, E., 'Strategy at the edge of Chaos' in *The McKinsey Quarterly*, No. 1, 1997.
9 The presumption of predictability is why we get headlines like this: 'Fickle Kiwi's Likely Moves Baffle Experts' *NZ Herald*, 15 January, 2007.
10 Merry, V., *Coping with Uncertainty*, Praeger, Westport, 1995, p. 25.
11 Gleick, J., *Chaos: Making a New Science*, Penguin, New York, 1987, p. 15.
12 Story from Beinhocker, E., *The Origin of Wealth – Evolution, Complexity and the Radical Remaking of Economics*, Harvard Business School Press, Boston, 2006, p. 326.
13 One can only speculate that Phoebe's drinking late into the night prior to a performance must have caused some level of tension in her relationship with Frank.
14 That said, an exciting new technology developed by a Taranaki company, MetOcean, uses high-resolution modelling to predict different wave heights 100 metres apart, up to seven days ahead.
15 Anderson, P., 'More is Different', *Science*, 1972, p.177.
16 Beinhocker, E., *The Origin of Wealth: Evolution, Complexity and the Radical Remaking of Economics*, Harvard Business School Press, Boston, 2006, p. 141.
17. *ibid*.
18 Beinhocker, E., *The Origin of Wealth: Evolution, Complexity and the Radical Remaking of Economics*, Harvard Business School Press, Boston, 2006, p. 450.
19 Waldrop, M., *Complexity: The Emerging Science at the Edge of Order and Chaos*, Simon and Schuster, New York, 1992, p. 81.
20 *Science*, 284, 2 April, 1999.
21 Dyson, F., *From Eros to Gaia*, Pantheon, New York, 1992, p. 242.
22 'The Relentless Contrarian', *Wired Magazine*, August 1996.
23 Postrel, V., *The Future and its Enemies*, The Free Press, New York, 1998, p. xv.
24. *ibid*.
25 Wheatley, M., *Leadership and the New Science*, Berrett-Koehler, San Francisco, 1992, pp. 21–22.

Part 2 How to build a successful society

4 Entropy, energy, and rats

1 See Rhonda Bartle's article, 'A Plague of Rats', located on Puke Ariki's website, www.pukeariki.com/en/stories/scienceandmedicine/plaguerats.asp.
2 'The End of the World' by J. Acocella, *The New Yorker*, March 21, 2005, p. 83
3 In what must have been perceived as divine disapproval of this appointment, the new Archbishop of Canterbury, John Bradwardine,

became a victim of the plague a mere week after arriving from France to take up his post in 1348. In August of the same year, King Edward III's daughter, Princess Joan, contracted, and ultimately succumbed to, the plague while docked at the port of Bordeaux on her way to Spain to marry Prince Pedro, heir to the kingdom of Castile.

4 A more fertile recruiting age it turned out, given the average fifteen year old male didn't know what celibacy meant.

5 Delemeau, J., *Sin and Fear*, St Martins Press, New York, 1991.

6 Herlihy, D., *The Black Death and the Transformation of the West*, Harvard University Press, Cambridge, 1999, p. 49.

7 *ibid*, p. 10.

8 *ibid*, p. 48.

9 Dols, M., *The Black Death in the Middle East*, Princeton University Press, Princeton, 1977, pp. 270–272.

10 Waldrop, M., *Complexity: The Emerging Science at the Edge of Order and Chaos*, Simon & Schuster, New York, 1992, p. 33.

11 Alternatively, you might find the following explanation from the chemist P.W. Atkins more helpful: 'There are Four Laws. The third of them, the Second Law, was recognized first; the first, the Zeroth Law, was formulated last; the First Law was second; the Third Law might not even be a law in the same sense as the others.'

12 Wright, R., *Nonzero: the Logic of Human Destiny*, Vintage, New York, 2000, p. 244.

13 Schneider, E.D., Kay, J.J., 'Life as a Manifestation of the Second Law of Thermodynamics', *Mathematical and Computer Modelling*, Vol. 19, No. 6–8, 1994, pp. 25–48.

14. Wright, R, *Non Zero: the Logic of Human Destiny*, Vintage, New York, 2000, pp. 245–246.

15 Schneider, E.D., Kay, J.J., 'Life as a Manifestation of the Second Law of Thermodynamics', *Mathematical and Computer Modelling*, Vol. 19, No. 6–8, 1994, pp. 25–48.

16 Cited in Beinhocker, E., *The Origin of Wealth: Evolution, Complexity and the Radical Remaking of Economics*, Harvard Business School Press, Boston, 2006, p. 301.

17 Waldrop, M., *Complexity: the Emerging Science at the Edge of Chaos* Simon & Schuster, New York, 1992, p. 33.

18 *ibid*.

19 When Hurricane Katrina swept through New Orleans in 2005, many in America were surprised by how quickly civil disorder broke out. The institutions that maintain civic stability collapsed. Almost a fifth of the police force abandoned their posts. National Public Radio in the US investigated reports that patients were either abandoned or euthanised at some hospitals (February 16, *All Things Considered*). Looting and vandalism were widespread. Chaos reigned.

20 Wright, R, *Non Zero: the Logic of Human Destiny*, Vintage, New York, 2000, p. 246.

21 Wright, R., *Nonzero: the Logic of Human Destiny*, Vintage, New York, 2000, p. 246.

22 Boccaccio, G., *Decameron*.

23 Description of the properties of open and closed systems modified from Beinhocker, E., *The Origin of Wealth:Evolution, Complexity and the Radical Remaking of Economics*, Harvard Business School Press, Boston, 2006.

24 Kelly, K., *Out of Control*, Basic Books, New York, 1994, p. 12.

25 *ibid*, p. 13.

26 The economist Paul Krugman has developed a mathematical model that simulates the emergence of the plum-pudding pattern of the modern metropolis. In his book, *The Self-Organizing Economy*, (Blackwell Publishers, Oxford, 1996), Krugman says: 'any initial distribution of

businesses across the landscape, no matter how even (or random), will spontaneously organize itself into a pattern with multiple, clearly separated business centers.' (p. 25).

27 Of course some governments (e.g., Cuba, North Korea) do try to dictate the lives of their citizens, but history has shown that they are unsustainable models. Curbing the freedoms of the individual to an excessive degree appear to be a great way to kill off a society.

28 Pagels, H., *Dreams of Reason: The Computer and the Rise of the Science of Complexity*, Bantam Books, New York, 1989, p. 53.

5 Two laws and adaptation

1 In this section, I relied heavily on examples from Buchanan, M., Nexus: *Small Worlds and the Groundbreaking Theory of Networks*, WW Norton, New York, 2002, pp. 138–155.

2 This story is taken from Buchanan, M., *Nexus: Small Worlds and the Groundbreaking Theory of Networks*, WW Norton, New York, 2002, p. 146.

3 For those of you who are interested in such things, the total number of marine species that we know about in New Zealand is around 15,450, there are approximately 4,000 freshwater species and about 33,500 species on the land. Source: Gordon, D., 'Species 2000: New Zealand', *Water and Atmosphere*, Vol. 12., No. 3, September 2004.

4 Sole, R., and Jose, M., 'Complexity and Fragility in Ecological Networks', working paper 00–11–060, Santa Fe Institute, Santa Fe, New Mexico, 2000. Available at www.santafe.edu/sfi/publications/00wplist.html.

5 Gulli, A., and Signorini, A., of the University of Pisa and the University of Iowa calculated the size based on the indexable Web. Including the non-indexed pages would bump this number up considerably. See 'The Indexable Web is More than 11.5 billion pages' at www.cs.uiowa.edu/~asignori/web-size/size-indexable-web.pdf.

6 Barabasi, A. L., *Linked: How Everything is Connected to Everything Else and What It Means for Busienss, Science, and Everyday Life*, Penguin, New York, 2003, p. 34

7 Buchanan, M., *Nexus: Small Worlds and the Groundbreaking Theory of Networks*, WW Norton, New York, 2002, p. 184.

8 Bak, P., *How Nature Works: The Science of Self-Organized Criticality*, Springer-Verlag, New York, 1996; Buchanan, M., *Nexus: Small Worlds and the Groundbreaking Theory of Networks*, WW Norton, New York, 2002.

9 Buchanan, M., *Nexus: Small Worlds and the Groundbreaking Theory of Networks*, W.W.Norton & Co., New York, 2002, p. 184.

10 The technical dimensions of the pyramid are taken from Socrates Taseos' fascinating book *Back in Time, 3104 B.C. to the Great Pyramid: Egyptians Broke Their Backs to Build It: How the Great Pyramid Was Really Built*, S.O.C. Publishers, Charlotte NC, 1990.

11 Taseos, S., *Back in Time, 3104 B.C. to the Great Pyramid: Egyptians Broke Their Backs to Build It: How the Great Pyramid Was Really Built*, S.O.C. Publishers, Charlotte NC, 1990

12 www.uni.uiuc.edu/departments/SocialStudies/flowchart/hyper_flow/eg_flood.html.

13 *ibid.*

14 Grimal, N., *A History of Ancient Egypt*, Blackwell, Oxford, 1988, p. 139.

15 *ibid*, p. 139.

16 For an in depth look at the effect on fish living in the sea and in fishbowls, see *Finding Nemo*.

17 Swerdlow, J., 'Biodiversity: Taking Stock of Life', and Moreli, V., 'The Variety of Life', in *National Geographic*, February 1999.

18 Quoted in Buchanan, M., 'Power Laws and the New Science of Complexity Management', in *Strategy + Business*, Issue 34, 2004.
19 Between 1976 and 1981, Packard joined some other graduate students from the University of California to develop a strategy for beating the roulette wheel using a toe-operated computer. The computer was designed to predict where a roulette ball would land on a wheel, allowing the operator to play almost risk-free. When they had difficulties shrinking the computer small enough to fit inside a shoe (this was the 1970s, after all), the project was disbanded.
20 Lewin, R., *Life at the Edge of Chaos*, MacMillan, New York, 1992, pp. 52–54.
21 Wright, R, *Non Zero: the Logic of Human Destiny,* Vintage, New York, 2000, p. 270..
22 *ibid*, p. 265.
23 Simon, H., *The Sciences of the Artificial*, MIT Press, Cambridge, 1981, pp. 189–190.
24 Wright, R, *Non Zero: the Logic of Human Destiny,* Vintage, New York, 2000, p. 248.
25 Braudel, F., *A History of Civilizations*, Penguin Books, 1994, p. 22.
26 Random House, New York, 1974.
27 *Psychology Today*, October, 1978, pp. 88–94.
28 Sowell, T., *Migrations and Cultures: A World View*, Basic Books, New York, 1996, p. 380.
29 Landes, D., *The Wealth and Poverty of Nations,* WW Norton, New York, 1998, p. xix.
30 Sowell, T., *Migrations and Cultures: A World View*, Basic Books, New York, 1996, p. 381.
31 *ibid.*

6 What Peter the Great learnt from the Dutch

1 Cited in Landes, D., *The Wealth and Poverty of Nations*, WW Norton, New York, 1999, p. 137.
2 Schama, S., *The Embarrassment of Riches: An Interpretation of Dutch Culture in the Golden Age*, Vintage, New York, 1997.
3 Cited in Landes, D.,*The Wealth and Poverty of Nations*, W.W.Norton, New York, 1999, p. 443.
4 *ibid*, p. 137.
5 Horrox, R. and Ormrod, W., *A Social History of England, 1200–1500*, Cambridge University Press, Cambridge, 2006, p. 27 and www.tacitus.nu/historical-atlas/population/westeurope.htm.
6 Cited in Landes, D., *The Wealth and Poverty of Nations*, WW Norton, New York, 1999, p. 137.
7 Cipolla, C., *Guns, Sails, and Empires*, Sunflower University Press, Kansas, 1965, p. 93.
8 To test the effectiveness of an earlier, smaller version, Mehmed decided to fire at a Venetian galley that had been travelling in the straits of the Bosphorus nearby. One huge stone ball fired from the gun was sufficient to crack the ship and sink it.
9 Barbaro, N., *Diary of the Siege of Constantinople, 1453*, trans. John Melville-Jones, Exposition Press, New York, 1969.
10 Nofi, A., and Dunnigan, J., *Medieval Life and The Hundred Years War*, DENO Partnership, 1994, found at www.hyw.com/Books/History/Evolutio.htm.
11 Examples taken from Wright, R., *Nonzero – the Logic of Human Destiny*, Pantheon, 2000.
12 Florida, R., *The Rise of the Creative Class: And How It's Transforming Work, Leisure, Community and Everyday Life*. Basic Books, New York, 2002, p. 56-66.
13 *ibid*. p. 56
14 As described in Florida, R., 'The World is Spiky', *The Atlantic Monthly*, October 2005.
15 Saxenian, A., 'Brain Circulation: How High-Skill Immigration Makes Everyone Better Off', *The Brookings*

Review, Vol.20, No.1, Winter 2002.
16 Harrison, L., *Underdevelopment is a State of Mind*, Madison Books, Lanham, 1985, p. 2.
17 The Anglo-Saxons would have had even greater numbers had King Harold not ridden so quickly to catch the Norman invaders by surprise. In so doing he left half his army scattered behind him, unable to keep up.
18 White, L., *Medieval Technology and Social Change*, Clarendon Press, Oxford, 1962, p. 37.
19 *ibid*, p. 78.
20 *ibid*, p. 2.
21. Kessler, A., *How We Got Here*, Harper Collins, New York, 2005, pp. 128–131.
22 *ibid*.
23 Wright, R., *Nonzero: the Logic of Human Destiny*, Vintage, New York, 2000, p. 158
24 *ibid*.
25 Landes, D., *The Wealth and Poverty of Nations – Why Some Are So Rich and Some So Poor*, WW Norton, New York, 1999, pp. 94–95.
26 Wright, R., *Nonzero: the Logic of Human Destiny*, Vintage, New York, 2000, p162.
27 Landes, D., *The Wealth and Poverty of Nations – Why Some Are So Rich and Some So Poor*, WW Norton, New York, 1999, p. 96.
28 Wright, R., *Nonzero: the Logic of Human Destiny*, Vintage, New York, 2000, p163.
29 Landes, D., *The Wealth and Poverty of Nations – Why Some Are So Rich and Some So Poor*, WW Norton, New York, 1999, p. 92.
30 Bray, F., 'Agriculature', in *Science and Civilization in China*, Vol. 6, Part 2, ed. Joseph Needham, Cambridge University Press, Cambridge, 1984, p. 569.
31 Toynbee, A., *A Study of History*, from the abridgement by D.C.Somervell, Oxford University Press, London, 1946, p. 90.
32 Quoted in Olson, M., *The Rise and Decline of Nations*, Yale University Press, New Haven, 1982, p. 155.
33 Cipolla, C., *Guns, Sails, and Empires*, Sunflower University Press, Kansas, 1965, p. 81.
34 Mokyr, J., *The Lever of Riches*, Oxford University Press, Oxford, 1990, pp. 178–179.
35 Bagehot, W., *Physics and Politics: Or Thoughts on the Application of the Principles of 'Natural Selection' and 'Inheritance' to Political Society*, Kegan Paul, Trench, Tubner & Co, London, 1900, p. 53.

Part 3 New Zealand's DNA

7 Maori I – a crash course in survival

1 Over the ensuing four pages I have relied heavily on one source for the description of the battle at Ohaeawai. James Belich's *The New Zealand Wars*, Penguin, Auckland, 1987, pp. 47–54.
2 This non-historian's skim through the historical record is heavily reliant on a couple of key sources, most notably James Belich's *Making Peoples: A History of the New Zealanders from Polynesian Settlement to the End of the Nineteenth Century*, (University of Hawai'i Press, Honolulu, 2001), and Michael King's *The Penguin History of New Zealand* (Penguin, Auckland, 2003). For those interested in diving deeper into the historical topics covered in the following three chapters, there are many great books, from Anne Salmond's *Two Worlds: First Meetings of Maori and Europeans, 1642–1772*, (University of Hawai'i Press, Honolulu, 1991) to Hazel Petrie's recent *Chiefs of Industry: Maori Tribal Enterprise in Early Colonial New Zealand* (Auckland University Press, Auckland, 2006).
3 Ferguson, N., *Empire: The Rise and Demise of the British World Order and the Lessons for Global Power*, Allen Lane,

London, 2002.
4 Belich, J., *The New Zealand Wars*, Penguin, Auckland, 1987, pp. 53–54.
5 *ibid*, p. 54.
6 'Senior Reptiles', *Time*, 27 October, 1952.
7 King, M., *The Penguin History of New Zealand*, Penguin Books (NZ) Ltd, Auckland, 2003, p. 22.
8 Belich, J., *Making Peoples: A History of the New Zealanders from Polynesian Settlement to the End of the Nineteenth Century,* University of Hawai'i Press, Honolulu, 2001, p. 69.
9 Salmond, A., *Two Worlds: First Meetings of Maori and Europeans, 1642–1772*, University of Hawai'i Press, Honolulu, 1991, p. 39.
10 Belich, J., *Making Peoples: A History of the New Zealanders from Polynesian Settlement to the End of the Nineteenth Century,* University of Hawai'i Press, Honolulu, 2001, pp. 64–67.
11 Nicholas, J.K., *Narrative of a Voyage to New Zealand*, Vol. 1, London, 1817, p. 307.
12 Fitzpatrick, J. 'Food, Warfare and the Impact of Atlantic Capitalism in Aotearoa/New Zealand', a paper presented to the Australasian Political Studies Association Conference, University of Adelaide, 29 September – 1 October, 2004, p. 8.
13 Belich, J., *Making Peoples: A History of the New Zealanders from Polynesian Settlement to the End of the Nineteenth Century,* University of Hawai'i Press, Honolulu, 2001, p. 70.
14 King, M., *The Penguin History of New Zealand*, Penguin Books (NZ) Ltd, Auckland, 2003, p. 89.
15 His work is often cited in Raymond Firth's extensive study, *Economics of the New Zealand Maori* (R.E. Owen, Wellington, 1959), which I refer to extensively during this section.
16 Firth, R., *Economics of the New Zealand Maori*, R.E. Owen., Wellington, 1959, p. 58.
17 *ibid*, p. 73.
18 *ibid*, p. 292.
19 *ibid*. p. 89.
20 King, M., *The Penguin History of New Zealand*, Penguin, Auckland, 2003, p. 25.

8 New Zealand and the crazy 1870s

1. An 1866 New Zealand Herald article suggested that the departing imperial troops legacy was 'a large number of dancing saloons attended by large numbers of loose women!'
2 Belich, J., *Making Peoples: A History of the New Zealanders*, University of Hawai'i Press, Honolulu, 2001, p. 448.
3 *ibid*, p. 449.
4 It is little wonder, then, that of the six years spent leading the government from 1870 to 1876, Vogel spent almost two of them travelling overseas . . . presumably stumping for cash.
5 Their concern was not entirely groundless. While *Dunedin* made approximately sixteen subsequent voyages between New Zealand and Britain, in 1890, after departing from Oamaru with a crew of thirty-four, she disappeared without trace while rounding Cape Horn.
6 It was not an uneventful voyage however. According to Gordon McLauchlan's *Great Tales from New Zealand History* (Penguin, Auckland, 2005) the captain had to contend with a fire in the sails ignited by the machinery. He also had problems with the freezer as they sailed through the tropics. When the captain crawled below to cut air ducts, he was overcome by the cold and would have died had it not been for the first officer crawling down, attaching a rope to his leg and pulling him free.
7 When the war ended, the producers were left with 180,000 tonnes of frozen stock, which they dumped on the UK market, causing a minor meltdown.

8 Rae, A., Strutt, A., & Mead, A., 'New Zealand's Agricultural Exports to Quota Markets', Agricultural Policy Discussion Paper No. 21, Massey University, September 2006.

9 www.tawahistory.wellington.net.nz/projects/best_article_porirua_war.html

10 Belich, J., *Making Peoples: A History of the New Zealanders*, University of Hawai'i Press, Honolulu, 2001, p. 442.

11 *ibid*.

12 Of course, what is progress to one is another's slide to hell in a handbasket. Premier Richard Seddon later said: 'By granting the franchise to women, Parliament plunged into an abyss of unknown depth.' Given that one of Sheppard's primary motivations for seeking universal suffrage was to achieve a national majority able to prohibit the sale of alcohol, we can perhaps forgive at least a certain level of resistance from some segments of the New Zealand electorate.

13 Belich, J., *Making Peoples: A History of the New Zealanders*, University of Hawai'i Press, Honolulu, 2001, p. 450.

9 Maori II – a new world

1 Jarman, R., *Journal of a Voyage to the South Seas in the* Japan *Employed in the Sperm Whale Fishery Under the Command of Capt. John May*, Beccles, England, 1838, p. 149, quoted in Petrie, H., 'Colonisation and the Involution of the Maori Economy', paper presented to XIII World Congress of Economic History, Buenos Aires, July 2002.

2 Bayly, C.A., *The Birth of the Modern World, 1780–1914*, Blackwell, Oxford, 2004, p. 100; Barthorp, M., *To Face the Daring Maoris: Soldiers' Impressions of the First Maori War, 1845–47*, Hodder & Stoughton, London, 1979, p. 188.

3 Fitzpatrick, J. 'Food, Warfare and the Impact of Atlantic Capitalism in Aotearoa/New Zealand', paper presented to the Australasian Political Studies Association Conference, University of Adelaide, 29 September – 1 October 2004, p. 13.

4 Cowan, J., *A Trader in Cannibal Land; the Life and Adventures of Captain Tapsell*, quoted in Parsonson, A., 'The Expansion of a Competitive Society', *The NZ Journal of History*, 14(1), p. 55.

5 Petrie, H., 'Colonisation and the Involution of the Maori Economy', Paper for Session 24, XIII World Congress of Economic History, Buenos Aires, 2002, p. 2.

6 *ibid*.

7 During Hongi Hika's voyage he met a Charles Philippe Hippolyte, Baron de Thierry. The baron was captivated by the promise of land in New Zealand, and promptly gave Hongi Hika £1100, a fortune in those days, in return for the promise of a huge estate. Hongi Hika used the cash to buy muskets. Furious attempts by the baron to retrieve his money, or his land, proved futile. By the time he arrived in Tahiti in 1835, Hippolyte was calling himself 'Sovereign Chief of New Zealand'. Despite this claim, he spent his last years as a music teacher in Auckland.

8 Petrie, H., *Chiefs of Industry: Maori Tribal Enterprise in Early Colonial New Zealand*, Auckland University Press, Auckland, 2006, p. 7.

9 Parsonson, A., 'The Expansion of a Competitive Society', *The NZ Journal of History*, 14(1), p. 54.

10 Petrie, H., 'Colonisation and the Involution of the Maori Economy', paper presented to XIII World Congress of Economic History, Buenos Aires, July 2002.

11 Petrie, H., *Chiefs of Industry: Maori Tribal Enterprise in Early Colonial New Zealand*, Auckland University Press, Auckland, 2006, p. 7.

12 *ibid*.

13 *ibid*, p. 9.

14 Fitzroy, R., *Remarks on New Zealand in February 1846*, London, 1846, p. 67, quoted in Petrie, H., 'Colonisation and the Involution of the Maori Economy', paper presented to XIII World Congress of Economic History, Buenos Aires, July 2002.
15 Te Ara Encyclopedia of New Zealand, www.teara.govt.nz.
16 From Brittan, S. J. and Grace, A. V., eds, *A Pioneer Missionary Among the Maoris 1850–1879, Being Letters and Journals of Thomas Samuel Grace,* Palmerston North, 1928, pp. 62–63, quoted in Petrie, H., 'Colonisation and the Involution of the Maori Economy', paper presented to XIII World Congress of Economic History, Buenos Aires, July 2002.
17 Petrie, H., *Chiefs of Industry: Maori Tribal Enterprise in Early Colonial New Zealand*, Auckland University Press, Auckland, 2006, p. 63.
18 *ibid*, p. 13.
19 Rough, D., *Narrative of a Journey Through parts of the North Island of New Zealand*, London, 1852, p. 9, quoted in Petrie, H., *Chiefs of Industry: Maori Tribal Enterprise in Early Colonial New Zealand*, Auckland University Press, Auckland, 2006, p. 13.
20 Gorst, J., *The Maori King*, London, 1864, quoted in Petrie, H., *Chiefs of Industry: Maori Tribal Enterprise in Early Colonial New Zealand*, Auckland University Press, Auckland, 2006, p. 14.
21 Petrie, H., *Chiefs of Industry: Maori Tribal Enterprise in Early Colonial New Zealand*, Auckland University Press, Auckland, 2006, p. 47.
22 Fortesque, J. W., *History of the British Army*, Macmillan, London, 1930, p. 516.
23 Darwin, C., *The Voyage of the Beagle (1839)*, London, 1959, pp. 402–403.
24 One of the many innovations Maori adopted to counteract the threat of heavy bombardment was to create false targets. At Puketakauere, they placed their main firing trenches well in front of virtually unmanned stockades, and the British shells passed harmlessly overhead.
25 Belich, J. *The New Zealand Wars and the Victorian Interpretation of Racial Conflict*, Penguin, Auckland, 1988, pp. 294–298.
26 Davidson, J., 'The Paa Maaori Revisited', in *Journal of the Polynesian Society*, 96, p. 13.
27 Te Ara Encyclopedia of New Zealand, www.teara.govt.nz.
28 Quoted in *Te Whānau: A Celebration of Te Whānau o Waipareira*, Te Whānau o Waipareira, Waitakere City, 2001, p. 12.
29 *Te Ao Hou*, no. 36 (September 1961), p. 29.
30 King, M., *The Penguin History of New Zealand*, Viking, Auckland, 2004, p. 475.
31 Metge, J., *A New Maori Migration*, Melbourne University Press, 1964, p. 251.
32 King, M., *The Penguin History of New Zealand*, Penguin, Auckland, 2004, p. 478.
33 Ministry of Health, New Zealand. *Reducing inequalities in health*, Ministry of Health, Wellington, 2002.
34 Hefford, M., Crampton, P., & Foley, J., 'Reducing Health Disparities Through Primary Care Reform: The New Zealand Experiment', in *Health Policy*, 72 (2005), pp. 9–23.
35 Rich, M., *Census of Prison Inmates 1999*, Strategic Analysis Section, Department of Corrections, Wellington, 2000.
36 Ministry of Health. *Our Health Our Future: the Health of New Zealanders*, Ministry of Health, Wellington, 1999.
37 Life expectancy for Maori males was 69 years in 2000–2002 compared with 64.9 years in 1985–1987. For females it was 73.2 years compared with 70.5 years. The percentage of Maoris smoking cigarettes had dropped from 51 percent in 1990 to 47 percent by 2004. Source:

The Social Report, Ministry of Social Development, 2006.

38 Maori unemployment rate was 11.3 percent in 1986. It rose steadily to peak at 25.4 percent in 1992, but was 8.6 percent in 2005. Source: *The Social Report*, Ministry of Social Development, 2006.

39 *The Social Report*, Ministry of Social Development, 2006.

40 *ibid.*

41 *ibid.*

42 Snedden, P., *Pakeha and the Treaty: Why It's Our Treaty Too*, Random House, Auckland, 2006, p. 179.

43 Global Entrepreneurship Monitor, Report on High-Expectation Entrepreneurship, 2005, www.gemconsortium.org.

44 Global Entrepreneurship Monitor, 2006, www.gemconsortium.org.

45 Snedden, P., *Pakeha and the Treaty: Why It's Our Treaty Too*, Random House, Auckland, 2006, p. 182.

46 Park, R., Burgess, E., & McKenzie, R., *The City*, University of Chicago Press, Chicago, 1925, p. 40.

47 King, M., *The Penguin History of New Zealand*, Viking, Auckland, 2004, p. 478.

48 *ibid*, p. 47.

49 See also Walker, R., *Tradition and Change in Maori Leadership*, Research Unit of Maori Education, University of Auckland, 1993.

50 Metge, J., *A New Maori Migration*, Melbourne University Press, 1964, p. 259.

51 Whina Cooper's work culminated in the famous 30,000-strong land march that travelled literally the length of the North Island to Parliament, to protest against the ongoing loss of Maori land. Not only was this event instrumental in raising national awareness of the land grievances of Maori, it must also be one of the most impressive acts of physical endurance by a then 80-year-old woman.

Part 4 A few ideas for a more adaptive New Zealand

10 Unstoppable creativity

1 McLauchlan, G., *Great Tales from New Zealand History*, Penguin, Auckland, 2005, p. 226.

2 *ibid*, p. 226.

3 See, for example, Langley, P., Simon, H., Bradshaw, G., and Zytkow, J., *Scientific Discovery: Computational explorations of the creative process*, MIT Press., Boston, 1987; Boden, M., *The Creative Mind: Myths and Mechanisms*, Basic Books, New York, 1992; Smith, S., Ward, T., and Finke, R. (eds.) *The Creative Cognition Approach*, MIT Press, Boston, 1995.

4 Florida, R., *The Rise of the Creative Class: And How It's Transforming Work, Leisure, Community and Everyday Life*, Basic Books, New York 2002, p. 68.

5 Florida, R., *The Flight of the Creative Class: The New Global Competition for Talent*, Collins, 2005.

6 See, for example, a paper by four academics from Massey University and Victoria University: Prichard, C., Boon, B., Bill, A. & Jones, D., 'Creativity and Class', Ephemera, www.ephemeraweb.org/journal/6-4/6-4prichard-etal.pdf, or Jacobs, K., 'Why I Don't Love Richard Florida', MetropolisMag.com, February 2005, which says that Florida's distillation of creativity 'into the kind of prescription routinely proffered by management consultants makes me fairly sure that what he's selling is not the virtues of creativity but rather the ingredients of a formula'.

7 Harrison, L., *Underdevelopment is a State of Mind*, Madison Books, Maryland, 1985, p. 2.

8 *ibid*.

9 Breen, B., 'The 6 Myths Of Creativity', *Fast Company*, Issue 89, December 2004.

10 Romer, P., 'Economic Growth', from Henderson, D., (ed) *The Concise*

Encyclopedia of Economics, Liberty Fund, 2007.

11 Paraphrased from Postrel, V., *The Future and Its Enemies*, The Free Press, New York, 1998, p. 64.

12 *Tough Choices or Tough Times: The Report of the New Commission on the Skills of the American Workforce*, National Center on Education and the Economy, December 2006.

13 *WIPO Patent Report: Statistics on Worldwide Patent Activity (2006)*, World Intellectual Property Organization.

14 For the US Patents Office to issue a patent, the invention must be novel, non-obvious, and 'useful'. Useful does not necessarily mean commercially viable. A 'Smoker's Hat', which is pretty much like wearing the exhaust hood for a stove on your head, has a patent. There's a beerbrella – an umbrella for your beer can – that qualifies for a patent. An electrified table cloth that zaps flies is patent-protected. And my personal favourite: a tricycle lawnmower.

15 Statistics from US Patent and Trademark Office.

16 According to the OECD, New Zealand is also a patent laggard when it comes to the number of patents granted by the three large patent offices (the US, Europe and Japan), coming in around 24th place in the OECD for both patents per GDP and patents per capita. *Compendium of Patent Statistics*, OECD, 2005.

17 Description of the properties of open and closed systems modified from Beinhocker, E., *The Origin of Wealth:Evolution, Complexity and the Radical Remaking of Economics*, Harvard Business School Press, Boston, 2006, p. 149.

18 *ibid*.

19 There are certainly highly innovative New Zealand companies in our primary product industries. Compac, for example, is a company that produces machines that scan the insides of produce for imperfections. But these sorts of products are just a fraction of the industry's total output.

20 Frederick, H., *The Unitec Global Entrepreneurship Monitor*, 2003/2004.

21 Statistics New Zealand, www.statistics.govt.nz.

22 Frederick, H., *The Unitec Global Entrepreneurship Monitor*, 2003/2004.

23 *ibid*.

24 Mokyr, J., *The Lever of Riches: Technological Creativity and Economic Progress*, Oxford University Press, New York, 1992.

25 OECD, 2006.

26 Investment in knowledge is defined as the sum of expenditure on research and development, on total higher education (public and private), and on software. OECD, 2006.

27 This was one of the supposed benefits of the failed waterfront stadium option in Auckland in late 2006.

28 'Government may ditch Eden Park in favour of a new stadium', *New Zealand Herald*, 3 November, 2006.

29 *Tough Choices or Tough Times: The Report of the New Commission on the Skills of the American Workforce*, National Center on Education and the Economy, December 2006.

30 *ibid*.

31 Whitehead, A., *The Aim of Education*, Free Press, New York, 1967.

32 Land, G. and Jarman, B., *Breakpoint and Beyond: Mastering the Future Today*, Leadership 2000 Inc, 1998.

33 This programme is designed and coordinated by the New Zealand Enterprise Trust.

34 In other words, teachers do have knowledge to impart. They are more than just 'facilitators' of learning, a criticism often levelled at outcome-based education.

35 Foster, R., and Kaplan, S., *Creative Destruction*, Doubleday, New York,

2001.

36 Christensen, C., *The Innovator's Dilemma: When New Technologies Cause Great Firms to Fail*, Harvard Business School Press, Boston, 1997.

37 Peters, T., & Waterman, R., *In Search of Excellence: Lessons from America's Best-Run Companies*, Warner Books, New York, 1982.

38 Harris, P., Harvey O., & Huddart, A., 'Being More Like Ourselves – Smart New Zealand Enterprises', Growth and Innovation Advisory Board, January 2005.

39 *ibid*, p. 49.

40 *ibid*, p. 48.

41 John-Steiner, V., *Creative Collaboration*, Oxford University Press, New York, 2000.

42 Burt, R., 'Structural Holes and Good Ideas', *American Journal of Sociology*, 2004.

11 A sponge for ideas

1 Example taken from Bloom, H., *Global Brain: The Evolution of Mass Mind from the Big Bang to the 21st Century*, John Wiley, New York, 2000, pp. 45–46.

2 *ibid.*

3 Beinhocker, E., *The Origin of Wealth: Evolution, Complexity and the Radical Remaking of Economics*, Harvard Business School Press, Boston, 2006, p. 276.

4 Socio-biologists contend that humans have evolved a social disposition which has advantaged the *Homo sapiens* species. Palaeontologists have argued that it was the enhanced capacity of Cro-Magnon humans to communicate beyond their immediate 'tribe'. This helped them deal with rapid climatic changes. The more solitary *Homo erectus* in Africa and Neanderthal in Europe couldn't figure out how to cope, and perished. Source: Wilson, E., *Sociobiology: the New Synthesis*. Harvard University Press, Cambridge, MA, 1975.

5 Kauffman, S., *The Origins of Order: Self-organisation and Selection in Evolution*, Oxford University Press, Oxford, 1993.

6 Buchanan, M., *Nexus: Small Worlds and the Groundbreaking Theory of Networks*, W W Norton, New York, 2002, p. 14.

7 Buchanan, M., Nexus: Small Worlds and the Groundbreaking Theory of Networks, WW Norton, New York, 2002, pp. 138–155.

8 *ibid*.

9 Granovetter, M., 'The Strength of Weak Ties', in *American Journal of Sociology* 78, pp. 1360–1380. Granovetter had tremendous difficulties getting his paper published, with one publication claiming that his manuscript should not be published for 'an endless series of reasons that immediately come to mind'. Since publication, however, it has become one of the most cited articles in sociology.

10 Guimerà , R., Uzzi, B., Spiro, J., & Nunes Amaral, L., 'Team Assembly Mechanisms Determine Collaboration Network Structure and Team Performance', *Science*, 308, 29 April 2005.

11 Volker, B., & Flap, H., 'Weak ties as a liability: the case of East Germany', *Rationality and Society*, 2001, 13(4): pp. 397–428.

12 In fact, the average size of an East German's personal network was only about 11 persons. Comparable studies in the United States and the Netherlands found larger personal networks (18.5 in California and 22 in the Netherlands). Source: studies quoted in Volker, B., & Flap, H., 'Weak ties as a liability: the case of East Germany', *Rationality and Society*, 2001, 13(4): pp. 397–428.

13 Miller McPherson, M., Smith-Lovin, L., & Cook, J., 'Birds of a Feather: Homophily in Social Networks', *Annual Review of Sociology*, Vol. 27, August 2001, pp. 415–444.

14 See, for example, Leigh, A., 'Trust,

Inequality and Ethnic Heterogeneity' in *The Economic Record*, Vol. 82, No. 258, September 2006.

15 Miller McPherson, M., Smith-Lovin, M., & Cook, J., 'Birds of a Feather: Homophily in Social Networks', *Annual Review of Sociology*, 2001, Vol. 27: pp. 415–444.

16 *ibid.*

17 Alesina, A., and La Ferrara, E., 'Participation in Heterogeneous Communities', *Quarterly Journal of Economics*, 2000, v115, pp. 847–904.

18 Knack, S., and Keefer, P., 'Does social capital have an economic payoff?' *Quarterly Journal of Economics* 112, 1997, pp. 1251–73.

19 Alesina, A., and La Ferrara, E., 'Participation in Heterogeneous Communities', *Journal of Economics*, 2000, v115, pp. 847–904.

20 Aristotle, *Rhetoric. Nichomachean ethics*. In *Aristotle in 23 volumes*, Rackman transl., Harvard University Press, Cambridge, 1931, p. 1371.

21 Asch, S., 'Effects of Group Pressure upon the Modification and Distortion of Judgment,' in Guetzkow, H., ed., *Groups, Leadership and Men*, Carnegie Press, Pittsburgh, 1951, cited in Buchanan, M., *Nexus: Small Worlds and the Groundbreaking Theory of Networks*, W W Norton, New York, 2002, p. 115.

22 Janus, I., *Groupthink*, Houghton Mifflin, Boston, 1982.

23 See Sunstein, C., *Republic.com*, Princeton University Press, 2001.

24 Example modified from Bloom, H., *Global Brain: The Evolution of Mass Mind from the Big Bang to the 21st Century*, John Wiley, New York, 2000, p. 9.

25 I relied on the helpful discussion of Page's work in Shalizi, C., '*The Logic of Diversity: the Complexity of a Controversial Concept*" at http://cscs.umich.edu/~crshaliz/bulletin/logic-of-diversity.html

26 Surowiecki, J., *The Wisdom of Crowds*, Anchor, 2005.

27 There's nothing magic about it, though. A principle of statistics known as the Central Limit Theorem explains this phenomenon

28 Putnam, R., *Bowling Alone: The Collapse and Revival of American Society*, Touchstone, New York, 2000.

29 'Around the Clock Findings from the New Zealand Time Use Survey 1998–99', Statistics New Zealand, and Ministry of Women's Affairs.

30 'Volunteers and Volunteering Policy Project: Paper One – Recognition and Valuing of Volunteering', Office for the Community and Volunteering Sector, December 2002.

31 Vowles, J., 'Civic Engagement in New Zealand: Decline or Demise?' Inaugural professorial address delivered at the Conference Centre, University of Auckland, 13 October 2004.

32 Robinson, J., & Godbey, G., *Time for Life: The Surprising Ways Americans Use Their Time*, Pennsylvania State University Press, 1998.

33 Only 14 percent of the adult population had been to an ethnic community activity in the previous 12 months. (Source: *A Measure of Culture*, Statistics New Zealand, 2001).

34 Robinson, D., & Williams, T., 'Social capital and voluntary activity: Giving and sharing in Maori and non-Maori society', *Social Policy Journal of New Zealand*, 17, 2001.

35 Bloom, H., *Global Brain: The Evolution of Mass Mind from the Big Bang to the 21st Century*, John Wiley, New York, 2000, p. 128.

36 www.keanewzealand.com/news/eoc-summary.html

37 Dumont, J.-C., & Lemaître, G., 'Counting Immigrants and Expatriates in OECD Countries: A New Perspective', Directorate for Employment Labour and Social Affairs, OECD, 2005.

38 Hansen, W., et al, 'The Brain-Drain – Emigration Flows for Qualified

Scientists, Part 6, Flows Across the Ocean – New Zealand', United Nations University, 2003.

39 World Competitiveness Report, 1999.

40 Trade and Enterprise New Zealand runs a 'Beachheads' programme specifically designed to help New Zealand exporters link into overseas markets through New Zealand expats living in those markets.

41 Freud, S., *Civilization and Its Discontents*, WW Norton, New York, 1989.

42 New Zealand Immigration Department statistics, found at: www.immigration.govt.nz/migrant/general/generalinformation/statistics.

43 A study carried out in 1985–86 showed that while Pacific Island people comprised only a third of overstayers, they made up 86% of all prosecutions for overstaying. Overstayers from the United States and the United Kingdom also made up almost a third of those overstaying, and yet they represented only 5% of prosecutions. Source: Te Ara New Zealand Encyclopedia, www.teara.govt.nz.

44 NZ Immigration Department statistics, found at: www.immigration.govt.nz/migrant/general/generalinformation/statistics

45 Saxenian, A., 'Brain Circulation: How High-Skill Immigration Makes Everyone Better Off', *The Brookings Review*, Vol.20, No.1, Winter 2002, pp. 28–31.

46 Xinhua News Agency; www.chinaview.cn, 16 October, 2006.

47 Britain, which takes over 60,000 students from China each year, allows each student to spend a year working in Britain following the completion of their studies, further cementing their ties to that country.

48 Nisbett, R., *The Geography of Thought: How Asians and Westerners Think Differently . . . and Why*, Free Press, New York, 2003.

49 *ibid*, p. 31.

50 *ibid*, p. 217.

51 For an account of the trial in Britain, see 'Traditional Maori ways translate to a new style of justice in Britain', *The Independent*, 25 August, 2003.

52 Williams, P., *How To Be Like Walt*, HCI, 2004.

12 Finding the willingness to change

1 Mokyr, J., *The Lever of Riches: Technological Creativity and Economic Progress*, Oxford University Press, New York, 1992, p. 154.

2 Bagehot, W., *Physics and Politics: Or Thoughts on the Application of the Principles of 'Natural Selection' and 'Inheritance' to Political Society,* Ivan R. Dee, p. xzz.

3 Chirot, D., *How Societies Change*, Pine Forge Press, Thousand Oaks, 1994, pp. 37–38.

4 The author is a biased commentator on events to the extent that he is an enthusiastic supporter of a new flag for the country.

5 Kahneman, D., Slovic, P., & Yversky, A., *Judgement Under Uncertainty: Heuristics and Biases*, Cambridge University Press, Cambridge, 1982.

6 Lowenstein, G., & Kahneman, D., 'Explaining the Endowment Effect,' working paper, Department of Social and Decision Sciences, Carnegie Mellon University, 1991.

7 Rand, A., *The Fountainhead*, Bobbs-Merrill, Indianapolis, 1943.

8 I relied on Gilbert's 'Shall I Compare Thee to a Summer Sausage' article on Forbes.com, February 2006, for the description of his research.

9 For example, one experiment of Gilbert's had students in a photography class at Harvard choose two favourite pictures from among those they had just taken and then relinquish one to the teacher. Some students were told their choices were permanent; others were told they could exchange their

prints after several days. As it turned out, those who had time to change their minds were less pleased with their decisions than those whose choices were irrevocable. The photography experiment challenges our common assumption that we would be happier with the option to change our minds when in fact we're happier with closure.

10 Examples taken from Gilbert, D., 'Shall I Compare Thee To A Summer's Sausage?' Forbes.com, February 2006.

11 Johnson-Laird, P., *Mental Models: Towards a Cognitive Science of Language, Inference, and Consciousness*, Harvard University Press , Cambridge, 1983, p. 397.

12 Holland, J., Holyoak, K., Nisbett, R., and Thagard, P., *Induction: Processes of Inference, Learning, and Discovery*, MIT Press, Cambridge, 1986.

13 Beinhocker, E., *The Origin of Wealth: Evolution, Complexity and the Radical Remaking of Economics*, Harvard Business School Press, Boston, 2006, p. 359–360.

14 *ibid.*

15 Quoted in Jennings, J., and Haughton, L., *It's not the Big that Eat the Small . . . It's the Fast that Eat the Slow*, HarperCollins, New York, 2002, p. xviii.

16 Shoda, Y., Mischel, W., & Peake, P.K., 'Predicting adolescent cognitive and self-regulatory competencies from preschool delay of gratification', *Developmental Psychology*, 1990, 26 (6).

17 Quoted in Lambert, C., 'The Marketplace of Perceptions', *Harvard Magazine*, www.harvardmagazine.com/on-line/030640.html, March 2006.

18 And to fix this problem, finance minister Michael Cullen employed fire to fight fire by using apathy as a weapon. He estimated – probably correctly – that most New Zealanders would find it too much bother to quit the Kiwi Saver programme during the six-week opt-out period, leaving them locked into a savings programme until they turn 65.

19 www.scoop.co.nz, February 2006.

20 Studies have in fact confirmed that when people at a casino roll dice in craps, they tend to throw harder for high numbers and softer for low numbers. Henslin, J., 'Craps and Magic', *American Journal of Sociology*, 73, 1967.

21 Langer, E., & Roth, J., 'Heads I win, tails it's chance: The illusion of control as a function of the sequence of outcomes in a purely chance task', *Journal of Personality and Social Psychology*, 1975, p. 34.

22 Lovallo, D., & Kahneman, D., 'Delusions of Success: How Optimism Undermines Executives' Decisions', *Harvard Business Review*, July 2003, pp. 56–63.

23 A study in the early 1980s actually confirmed Dave Barry's hunch. Ole Svenson in 'Are we all less risky and more skillful than our fellow drivers?' (*Acta Psychologica*, 47,1981), found that 80% of respondents rated themselves in the top 30% of all drivers.

24 Whitman, D., *The Optimism Gap: The I'm Ok – They're Not Syndrome and the Myth of American Decline*, Walker & Company, New York, 1998.

25 *ibid.*

26 Durodié, B., 'The Timid Corporation – Why Business is Terrified of Taking Risk' book review, *Risk Analysis*, Vol. 24, No. 1, February 2004.

27 This is not a criticism of the media. Their job is to provide content that will compel the reader or viewer to stick around and read or view more (including their advertising). The observation I'm making here is more about the growing reliance we have on the media to shape our perspective of the world.

28 Quoted in Easterbrook, G., 'America

the OK', *The New Republic*, 11 January, 1998.
29 This is the very same John Cage who composed *4'33'*, a towering work whose three movements are performed without playing a single note. Known as the 'four and a half minutes of silence', it's a moving piece of great depth.
30 Reading, A., *Hope and Despair: How Perceptions of the Future Shape Human Behavior*, The Johns Hopkins University Press, Baltimore, 2004.
31 *ibid.*
32 Romer, P., 'Economic Growth', in Henderson, D., (ed) *The Fortune Encyclopedia of Economics*, Time Warner Books, New York, 1993.
33 Quoted in Schlesinger, A.M., Jr., *The Politics of Hope*, Houghton Mifflin, Boston, 1949.
34 Story and quotations taken from 'Europe Diary: Political Lies', BBC, 21 September, 2006.
35 Samuelson, R., *The Good Life and Its Discontents: The American Dream in the Age of Entitlement: 1945 to 1995*, Vintage, New York, 1995.
36 Winter, D., 'Demos chief warns of crisis', *The Guardian*, May 31, 2005.
37 Sennett, R., *The Hidden Injuries Of Class*, Alfred A. Knopf, 1973.
38 Sennett, R., *The Corrosion of Character: The Personal Consequences of Work in the New Capitalism*, WW Norton, 1998.
39 Toffler, A., *Future Shock*, Random House, London, 1970, p. 13.
40 Sowell, T., *The Economics and Politics of Race: An International Perspective*, Quill, New York, 1983, pp. 243, 257.
41 Toulmin, S., *Cosmopolis: The Hidden Agenda of Modernity*, Free Press, New York, 1990, pp. 178–179.
42 Budget 2006 : National identity – whose identity?, Dr Pita Sharples, Co-leader, Maori Party, 24 May, 2006.
43 *Time*, 18 August, 2003.

Index

adaptation 88, 143–5, 267
  Athenian society 141–2
  China 136–8
  companies 227–9
  Egypt 109–10, 143
  Europe, in response to Black Plague 88–92, 96, 100–1
  India 142
  Maori 145, 149–65, 180, 185–6, 189–92, 195–201, 258
  mitigating costs of 282–3
  Netherlands 125
  New Zealand 82, 119–20, 145, 152, 167, 172, 177–9, 200–1, 210, 231, 232, 249, 277–86
  Venice 142
  See also change; complex adaptive systems
Africa 48, 137, 138, 142, 150, 164
ageing population, New Zealand 63–4, 290–1 nn.60–63
agriculture 30, 90–1,
agriculture, New Zealand 129, 206, 218
  impact of Britain's membership of EEC on 171–2
  impact of refrigeration on 170–1
  Maori 185–6, 187, 191
  threat of bio-sciences to 49
  See also dairy industry
Air New Zealand 60
Aizu Central Hospital 57
Amabile, Teresa 211
America's Cup yacht design 229
American Chopper (television programme) 31–2
Anderson, Philip 77
Anglo-Saxons 130–2
Anglo-Zulu War 150
anxiety 36–7
Appligenics 56
Arawa 182
Arendt, Hannah 47
Aristotle 242
artificial intelligence 43, 55
Asch, Solomon 242–3
Asia 34, 164. See also specific countries
Athenian society 141–2, 257
Atkins, P.W. 293 n.11
ATMs 41, 57
Attica 141–2
attitudes 39, 82, 119
Auckland 27, 28, 94, 99–101, 172, 174, 175, 185, 220, 238, 254, 256, 267
Australia 36, 48, 73, 111, 130, 166, 173, 173, 176, 178, 180, 182, 186, 189, 209, 215, 216, 252, 255, 278. See also New South Wales; Tasmania; Victoria
Austria 150
automation 41–3, 55–8
AXA New Zealand 272

Babich family 256
Bagehot, Walter 143, 144, 240, 263
Bangladesh 253
Barabasi, Albert-Laszlo 107
Barbaro, Nicolo 127
Barry, Dave 273, 305 n.20
Bartle, Rhonda 292 ch. 4, n.1
Bay of Islands 149, 163, 182, 186
Bayley, Christopher 181
Beagle 113
Bedford, Richard 252
Beinhocker, Eric 27, 78
Belgium 124
Belich, James 151–2, 156, 176, 191
Bell, Alexander Graham 231
Ben-Jacob, Eshel 233
Benjamin, Ethel 256
Benjaminson, Maurice 48
Bentley, Tom 281
Bernstein, Leonard 239
Best Elsdon 159
bi-culturalism 241, 284

biomachines 49
Black Plague 87–92, 96, 100–1, 137
Bletchley Park 132–3
blogs 35
Blue Brain Project 42–3, 54
Boccaccio 96
Bolivia 34
bombardier beetle 114, 115, 128
Bombay 135–6, 138
bounded rationality 35
Bourke, Sir Richard 184
Bradshaw's Act (1973) 176
'brain drain' 251, 252, 260
brain power, human 54
Brand, Stewart, The Clock of the Long Now 30, 33
Braudel, Ferdinand 117
Brazil 27, 122, 183
Britain, see United Kingdom
British Patent Office 215
Brydone, W.S. 170
Buchanan, Mark 108, 236
Buck, Sir Peter 193
Buffalo Bill's Wild West Show 74
Burke, Edmund 285
Burt, Ronald 230
Busby, James 184
Business and Economic Research Ltd 248
butterfly effect 75–6
'Buy New Zealand Made' campaign 59
Byzantine Empire 125–7, 130

Caffa 87–8
Cage, John 276, 305 n.24
call centres 34, 59–60
Canada 34, 36, 65, 216, 242, 256
cars 25–7, 30, 32, 38
castles, inability to withstand cannon fire 125–8
Catholic Church 89–90, 96, 175
cause and effect 69, 72–3, 76, 91
Cayley, Sir George 140
Cedar Creek Natural History Area, Minnesota 104
cell automation 234
cellphones 30, 34, 58
certainty 69–70, 72–3
change 36–7, 38–9, 41, 82, 89–94, 100–1
  consequences of not adapting to 261–3
  continuous, companies' difficulty with 227–9
  knowing what we want 266–9
  mitigating the consequences of 282–3
  necessity for 109–13
  resistance to 264–77
  uneven rates of 282
  willingness to allow 141–5, 145, 263, 277–86
  See also adaptation
chaos 73–6, 95, 96, 112. See also complexity; uncertainty
  edge of 112–3, 235
chaotic systems 234
Chartered Semiconductor 217
chess 40, 41–3, 55, 66–7, 77
Chew Chong 166–7, 256
China 41, 48, 65, 81, 129, 135, 164, 214, 252, 255, 256, 257–8
  economic growth 61–2, 63
  GDP 59, 61
  manufacturing economy 58–9, 62
  New Zealand exports to 60, 61, 181, 183
  overseas Chinese 117–8
  relationship with Europe, 14th century 136–8, 139, 251
  students from 256, 304 n.43
  workers in 58–60
  Chinese in New Zealand 100, 166–7, 254, 256
choices, hard 279–81
Christchurch 173, 174, 175, 224
Christensen, Clayton 227
Ciompi Revolt (1378) 90
cities 99–100
civic participation 247–50
  New Zealand 248–9, 260
Clinton, Bill 44
closed systems 97, 164
Colossus computer 133–4
Combinations 213
communications 30
  New Zealand 173–5, 176, 177
  See also information; Internet; railways; shipping; telegraph lines; telephones; text messages
Compac 301 n.17
complex adaptive systems 98–101, 102, 103–4, 231

Rule One 104–8
Rule Two 109–13
weak links in 236–8, 239–40, 249
complexity 27–9, 36, 37, 38–9, 67, 77–83, 88, 91, 95, 97, 102, 218, 269–70. See also chaos; uncertainty
complexity science 83, 98, 99, 105, 106, 107, 234
computer chess 40, 41–3, 55, 67
computer games 40–1
computer software 56
computers
American 52–4, 55–6
British 133–4
programming 56
quantum 53–5
rise of 40–3, 56–8
super 52–5
super-small 51
See also electronic entertainment; Internet
computing power 29, 52–5, 56
conformity in thinking 242–4
Congo, Democratic Republic of 95
connectivity 235–8, 240, 249, 260
global 250–3, 256–7
See also superconnectors
Constantine XI, 126, 127, 130
Constantinople, fall of 125–7, 130
consumers
China 60–3
New Zealand 59, 62
spending power of 60
consumption 28, 31, 32, 60
control, personal 37
Cook, James 180–1, 182
Cooper, Dame Whina 199, 300 n.53
Craik, Kenneth 269
creative capital 221
creativity 112, 124, 125–35, 143–4, 206
applying 130–2
collective 230–1
creative class 208–11
definitions of 211, 212
description of 207–8
importance of 212–5
institutional support for 217, 219
investment in 220–1, 229, 301 n.24
looking for 211–2
New Zealand 209, 210, 211, 212, 213–4, 215–7, 219–21, 229, 285
See also ideas; innovations
Crick, Francis 94
Cullen, Michael 305 n.15
cultural capital 116–9, 258
culture 117, 118
Holland 124
New Zealand 116–7, 119, 120, 240–1, 258, 284
Curtis, Adam 275
Czech Republic 252

Da Vinci, Leonardo 139, 140
dairy industry, New Zealand 167, 171–2, 185, 188
Danzig 144
Darling, Ralph 184
Darwin, Charles 113–4, 188–9
Davis, Wade 115
Dawkins, Richard 116
De Long, J. Bradford 27–8
De Pree, Max 280
De Thierry, Charles Philippe Hippolyte, Baron 298 n.7
decentralised systems 224
decision-making 269–70
Declaration of Indepence (Confederation of United Chiefs) 184
Deeper Blue computer 42–3, 56, 67
democracy 243
Demos 281
Denmark 216, 242
dependency ratio, New Zealand 290–1 nn.60–61
Descartes, René 124
Despard, Henry 149, 150, 151
developing nations 62
digital technology 228–9
disequilibrium 97
Disney, Walt 259
dissipative structures 97
divergent thinking 223
diversity 124, 125, 235, 240–6, 253, 255–6
ethnic 241–2, 249, 255–6, 257–9, 284
importance of 244–6
New Zealand 240–1, 258–9, 260, 284, 285
problem with 241–2
DNA 44, 45, 70, 94, 116

Driver HMS 172
Drucker, Peter 79–80
drug discovery and development 45–6, 47
Dunedin 45, 166, 174, 175
Dunedin (ship) 169, 170, 171, 297 nn.4–5
Durodié, Bill 275, 276
Dutch East India Company 122
Dying for Information 36
dynamics 91, 99, 124
Dyson, Freeman 38, 79

East Coast 196
Easter Island 261–3
economic benefit 221
economic choices 27, 32
economic core 219
economic equilibrium 70–2
economic growth
 China 61–2, 63
 New Zealand 62, 212–3, 281, 290 n.54
ecosystems 103, 104–8, 111, 129, 153
Eden Park 220, 301 n.25
education 222–5
Education Act (1877) 176
Egypt 109–10, 143, 251, 264
Einstein, Albert 53, 70, 79
electricity 32, 34
email 29, 30, 34–5
emergence 77–8, 80
Emerson, Ralph Waldo 279
endowment effect 264–6
Endy, Drew 48–9
energy 93–4, 95–6, 97, 101, 116
England 41, 121, 123, 125, 128, 130–2
ENIAC computer 52, 53
Enigma codes 132–3
entertainment, electronic 28, 29, 41, 58
entropy 94, 95, 97, 104
environmental influences on human body 45
ephemeralisation 29–31, 33, 34
epidemics 34
equilibrium 93–4, 109–13
 economic 70–2
 maximum entropy 97
Ericsson 217
Escherichia coli 232–3
ethics, and genomics 47
ethnic groups 241–2, 249, 255–6, 257–8
Europe 60, 63, 75, 121, 122, 129, 135, 136, 164, 182, 304 n.44
 and the Black Plague 87–92, 96, 100–1
 explorers and explorations 138, 139, 142–3
 relations with China, 14th century 136–8, 251
 See also specific countries
European Economic Community 171
European Union 207
evolution 94, 128
 Darwin's theory of 113–4
 of society 114–9
exercise 65, 291 n.69
expatriate New Zealanders 251, 252, 260
exports, New Zealand 60, 61, 170, 171–2, 177, 181, 183
extinctions 103, 105, 107, 111, 156

Fayol, Henri 71
fear 275–7
Feynman, Richard 49, 51–2
Fiji 60
Finland 119, 209, 216, 217, 242
Fisher & Paykel 217
Fitzroy, Robert 113, 186, 189
flag, New Zealand 184, 264–5
flax 160–1
 trade in 181–2, 184, 185
Florida, Richard 129, 208–9, 221, 300 n.6
flour mills, Maori 185
Flynn, James 28
food supply 30
Footprints Waipoua 196
Forbes magazine, 100 largest US companies list 227
Formigny, Battle of 128
Forrester Research 60
Foster, Dick, Creative Destruction 227
Fox, William 168
France 36, 71, 121, 123, 128, 183
Frederick the Great 69
Frederick Wilhelm II, Prince 74
French peasants' Revolt (1358) 90
Freud, Sigmund 253
friction 31–4

frozen accident 75
frozen meat, export of 171–2
frozen systems 234
Fuller, Buckminster 29–30
fungus 166–7
future
  connection with the past 283–4, 285
  helplessness about 274–7
  New Zealand's 40–67, 76, 79, 81–2, 102, 277–9, 283–6
  over-confidence in ability to handle 272–4
  prediction of 69–70, 76, 79–82
future shock 36–7

Galapagos Islands 113
Gardner 30
GDP, see gross domestic product
General Electric 227
General Motors 61
genetic engineering 47–9
genetic screening 46–7
genomics 44–9, 217–8
George III, King 182
George IV, King 183
Georgescu-Roegen, Nicholas, The Entropy Law and the Economic Progress 95
Germany 36, 59, 60, 74, 130, 132–3, 144, 215, 216, 302 n.10
Germany, East 239–40
giant magnetoresistive effect (GMR) 53
Gilbert, Daniel 266–7, 304 n.8
Gleick, James 33, 73
globalisation 58, 62, 137, 207, 209, 282
Gondwana 153
Gorst, John 188
government
  control by 100, 293 n.23
  loss of confidence in 37–8,
  New Zealand 176, 177–8, 229, 280–1, 285
  role of 39, 82, 100
Grace, T.S. 187
Granovetter, Mark 238, 302 n.7
Great Pyramid, Giza 109
Greece 251, 257. See also Attica
Greenfield, Jeff 35
Grey, Earl 186
Grey, George 186, 189
Groen, Otto 256
gross domestic product (GDP) 27–8
  China 59, 61
  distribution as power law 108
  India 61
  New Zealand 63
'group think' 243
groups, power of 232–3, 243, 244–6
Growth and Innovation Advisory Board 229
Gutenberg, Johann 90
Gyurcsany, Ferenc 279–80

Hadfield, Octavius 187
Hallensteins 256
Halley, Edmond 68
Hann, Otto 79
happiness 266–9
harakeke, see flax
Harold, King 130, 131
Harris, Marvin 117
Harrison, Laurence 210
Harvard Business School, Entrepreneurial Management Unit 211
Hastings, Battle of 130–2
Hawai'i 111, 180
Hawke's Bay 187
Hayek, Friedrich 39
healthcare
  and ageing population 64
  and genomics 43–7, 49
  and nanotechnologies 50–1
  and obesity 64–6
  automation of 56–7
  Maori services 196, 199
Heke, Hone 149
Helprin, Mark 33
Henry, John 55–6, 57
Hewlett-Packard 53, 119
Hobart 181
Hobbes, Thomas 95
Hobson, William 186, 189
Holland, see Netherlands
Holland, John 269
Homo sapiens 302 n.4
homophily principle 241–2, 249
Hong Kong 36, 207
Hong, Lu 244, 245
Hongi Hika 182–3, 185, 298 n.7
hope 277–8, 279
Hotu Matu'a 261, 262

Hotunui (meeting house) 162
Hungary 279–80
Hurricane Katrina 293 n.17
Huxley, Aldous, Music at Night 34
Huygens, Christiaan 124

IBM 42, 129
ideas 39, 82, 111, 119, 124
  absorption of 141–5, 249
  dispersal of 275
  encouragement of 143, 219–20
  generation of 125–35, 141, 206, 210, 211–4, 216–7, 220–1
  novel and incremental, distinction between 226–9
  openness to 139, 140–1, 145
  thirst for 135–41
  See also creativity
identity, New Zealand 116–7
immigration to New Zealand 169, 173, 176, 179, 254–9
imports, New Zealand 58–9, 62–3
income 27, 60
  distribution as power law 108
India 40, 48, 58, 59, 60, 61, 62, 63, 117, 122, 129, 136, 137, 142, 164, 181, 189, 252–3, 255, 256
Indonesia 62, 122, 164
industrial revolution 41, 136
information
  collection and processing of 30–1, 35–6, 38, 116
  genetic 116
  low-quality 34–5
  overload of 35–6, 38
  transmission of 30, 108
  See also communications
initial conditions, sensitive dependence on 73, 75–6, 97
innovations 31, 39, 82, 112, 113, 114, 115, 119, 128–30, 143–4, 145
  applying 130–5
  China 136, 164
  Dutch shipbuilding 123–5
  gradual process of 139–40
  in big organisations 217–20
  Maori 159, 161, 163–4, 185, 215, 299 n.24
  New Zealand 134, 167, 177, 216–7, 219–20, 229, 301 n.17
  See also inventions
intelligence
  artificial 43, 55
  increase in 28–9
International Centre for Security Analysis 275
Internet 28, 29, 30, 33, 35, 55, 224, 243. See also World Wide Web
intertemporal choice 271–2
inventions 134–5, 251–2
  China 136, 139
  Europe 139
  Germany 144
  incremental improvements in 226–9
  new concepts 226
  New Zealand 134, 139–40
  See also innovations
investment in research and development 220–1, 229, 301 n.24
IQ, see intelligence
Ireland 119, 209
isolation
  and fear 275–6
  impact on innovation 140, 163–4, 262–3
Israel 216, 256
IT jobs, future of 60
Italy 36, 59

J Paul Getty Trust 207
Janus, Irving 243
Japan 50, 57, 63, 129, 215, 216
Jarman, Beth, Breakpoint and Beyond 223
Jarman, Robert 180
Jeans, Sir James 70
Jencks, Christopher 276
John-Steiner, Vera, Creative Collaborations 230
Johnson, Samuel 277
Johnson, Steven, Everything Bad Is Good For You 29
Johnson-Laird, Philip 269
Jouvenal, Bertrand de 80

Kahneman, Daniel 265, 273
Kamen, Dean 41
Kaplan, Sarah, Creative Destruction 227
Kasparov, Garry 42–3, 55, 67
Kauffman, Stuart, The Origins of Order 234, 235

Kawiti 149–50, 151, 191
Keely, Mr 87
Kelly, Kevin, Out of Control 99
Kelvin, Lord 92
Kennedy, Robert 278
Kessler, Andy, How We Got Here 133
Kimberley, Lord 168
King Country 174
King, Michael 153, 194, 198
King, Philip 182
Kirsh, David 36
Kiwi Expats Association 252
Kiwi Saver programme 305 n.15
kiwis 94, 105, 106, 235
knowledge 116
Koa 182
Kodak 227
Korea, North 95
Korea, South 36, 129, 215, 216
Kororareka 181
Krugman, Paul 293 n.22
Kurzweil, Ray 54
Kuwait 65

La Grouw, Jo 256
labour costs 59–60
Laibson, Dabid 272
Land George, Breakpoint and Beyond 223
Landes, David 28, 118, 122
Langer, Ellen 273
Laplace, Pierre-Simon 69
Latin America 164. See also South America
Law of Requisite Variety 110
Lawrence Livermore National Laboratory 52
Laws of Motion (Newton) 68–70
Learning Discovery Trust 224
Lee Hsien Loong 39
Leeghwater, Jan 124
leisure 96. See also entertainment, electronic; physical activity
Leonardo da Vinci 139, 140
Liverpool Institute for Performing Arts 207
Lollards 89
L'Oréal 50
Lorenz, Edward 75, 76
Los Angeles 241
loss aversion 264–6
Lovallo, Dan 273
Luxembourg 255

MacDiarmid Institute for Advanced Materials and Nanotechnology 51
machines, replacement of human activities by 41–3, 55–8
magnetoresistive random access memory (MRAM)
mail service, New Zealand 168, 174–5
Maketu 181, 182
malaria treatment 46
Malaysia 119
management 71
Mangakahia, Mere 193
Maori 65, 115, 249, 284
- adaptive society 145, 149–65, 180, 185–6, 187–8, 189–92, 195–201, 258
- carved meeting houses 162–3
- entrepreneurs 196
- food production 156–8, 159
- growing complexity of society 158–9
- impact of colonisation 164–5
- inter-tribal competition 160–2, 189
- moa hunting 154–6
- network effect on 197–8
- new beginning 193
- population decline 192–3
- pragmatism and flexibility 187–8
- renaissance 195–7
- social capital, context of 250
- social statistics, early 21st century 195, 299 n.37
- social statistics, mid-1990s 194–5
- trading 180–2, 183–6, 192
- travel, 19th century 182–3
- urbanisation 193–4, 197–200
- warfare 149–52, 188–92, 299 n.24
- See also Treaty of Waitangi

Maori Language Act (1987) 199
Maori Women's Welfare League 199
marae, urban 198, 199
Mark, Gloria 36
Marshall Plan 304 n.44
mass media 243, 248, 274–5, 278, 305 n.23. See also television
Massachusetts Institute of Technology 48, 50, 66, 75, 224
Matara 182
Matatua (meeting house) 162

McCartney, Sir Paul 207
McCracken, Grant 115
McLean Motor-car Act 1898 26
McLean, William 25–6
McMaughon, Marion 242
mechanical principles 69–72
media, mass 243, 248, 274–5, 278, 305 n.23. See also television
medicine, see healthcare
Mediterranean 142–3
Mehmed II 125–7, 140–1
melting systems 234, 235
Melville, Herman 237
meme pool 116
memory
  computer 53
  human 35
mental models 269–71
Messina 87–8
Metge, Joan 198
MetOcean 292 n.11
Michelangelo 230
Middle East 91
Miller, George 35
moa 153, 154–6
Mokyr, Joel 129, 143
Mongol (steamship) 173
Mongols 173
Montoya, Jose 107
Moore's Law 29, 52
Morgan, Sam 230
Moses, Phoebe 74, 228
motor vehicles, custom-made 31–2. See also cars
Muldoon, Robert 168
multitasking 36
Munro, Burt 215
Murano 250–1
Murdoch, Colin 134
Musket Wars 183, 190

Nano Cluster Devices Ltd 51
nanotechnologies 49–52, 81, 222
Napier 171, 174
nationhood, New Zealand 174–9
nature/nurture 45
Nehru, Jawaharlal, The Discovery of India 142
Nelson 167, 174
Netherlands 48, 121–5, 145, 183, 302 n.10
network theory 106, 107–8
  and Maori renaissance 197–8
  See also social networks
New Commission on the Skills of the American Workforce 214
New Plymouth 166–7
New South Wales 182, 183, 184. See also Sydney
New York 27, 122
New Zealand and Australia Land Company 170
New Zealand Enterprise Trust 301 n.30
New Zealand Wars 149–52, 189–92, 299 n.24
Newton, Sir Isaac 68–70, 139
Nga Tau e Waru (meeting house) 162
Ngata, Sir Apirana 193
Ngati Toa 172–3
niches 115
Nile River 109–10
Nisbett, Richard, The Geography of Thought 256–258
Nobilo family 256
Nokia 217
Normans 130–2, 255
norms 111, 119
North America 63, 164, 182. See also Canada; United States
Norway 88, 216, 242
Nuremberg 144

obesity 64–6
OECD 219, 220, 252, 272
off-shoring work 60
Ogburn, William 282
Ohaeawai pa 149–52, 191
open systems 97–8
Orban 126–7, 140–1
order
  from disorder 92–4, 95–6
  from order 94
organisations
  large 217–8, 233
  small 218–9, 229
Otago Peninsula 103
Ottawa Conference 1932 171
Ottoman Empire 125–7, 130, 135, 140–1
over-optimism bias 272–4

pa, modified for use with firearms 190–

2, 299 n.24
Pacific Island peoples 64, 65, 100, 249, 254, 291 n.69
Pacific Islands 180. 181, 182. See also specific islands
Packard, Norman 112
Page, Scott 244, 245
Pagels, Heinz 102
Palo Alto research centre 118
Papua New Guinea 164
Pareto, Vilfredo 108
Park, Robert 197
patents 129–30, 134, 215–7, 300–1 n.14
  New Zealand 215, 216–7, 301 n.16
Patuone 184
Pearce, Richard 140
Peasants' Revolt (1381) 90
penguin, New Zealand giant 103, 104, 280
Peter the Great 121–2, 123
Peters, Tom 56, 228
Petrie, Hazel 182, 185, 187
Pew Institute 55
pharmaceuticals, discovery and development 45–6, 47
Philippines 65, 164, 256
physical acitvity 65, 291 n.69
Pink, Dan, A Whole New Mind 60
plague 87–92, 96, 100–1, 137
Planck, Max, The Philosophy of Physics 270–1
Polaroid 228–9
Pomare, Sir Maui 193
popular culture 29
population, New Zealand 63–4, 290–1 nn.60–63
Port Chalmers 170
Port Taranaki 167
Portugal 122, 123, 124, 136, 138–9, 143, 183
positivism 69–70
Postrel, Virginia, The Future and its Enemies 80
power law 107–8, 113
The Power of Nightmares (BBC documentary) 275
present, focus on 271–2
prices 31, 32
Prigogine, Ilya 96, 97
Primary Enterprise Program (PrEP) 223–4, 225
Prince, Harold 239
printing, and dissemination of idea 175
production costs 31, 32, 59–9
products, accumulation of 28, 31
public works projects, Vogel's 168–9
Puketaukauere 299 n.24
purchasing power 27, 61
Putnam, Robert 241, 247–8, 249

quantum computing 53–5
quantum theory 70

railways, New Zealand 169–70, 177
Rand Corporation 64
Rand, Ayn 266
Rangitihi (meeting house) 162
Reading, Anthony 276–7
reductionism 70, 78, 96
refrigeration 167, 170–2
Resnick, Mitchel 224
restorative justice 258
retirement savings, New Zealand 272
rigidity in thinking 269–71
Robbins, Jerome 239
Robinson, David 249
Robinson, Sir Ken, All Our Future 207–8, 212, 225
robots 51, 56, 57, 290 n.39
Roethlisberger, Fritz 277
Roman Empire 118, 127, 255
Romer, Paul 129, 213, 278
Roosevelt, Theodore 79
Rosetta Stone 45–6
Rotorua 174, 85
Rough, David 188
rugby 167–8, 173, 220–1
Russell, Bertrand 285
Russia 59, 60, 74, 121. See also Soviet Union
Rutherford, Ernest 79

Sahelian climate 110
Salmond, Anne 156
Samuelson, Robert, The Good Life and Its Discontents 280–1
savings rate, New Zealand 272
Saxenian, AnnaLee 129
Schama, Simon 122
Schrödinger, Erwin 92, 93, 94, 96
Schumpeter, Joseph 26

scientific and technical literature 30–1
scientific management 71
scientific research 31, 35
Scimitar 173
sealers, trade with 181
Second Law of Thermodynamics 92–4, 95, 100, 110
Seddon, Richard 297 ch. 8, n.10
self-employment, New Zealand 219
self-organisation 97, 99–101
Sennett, Richard, The Corrosion of Character 281–2
sensitive dependence on initial conditions 73, 75–6, 97
Shapiro, Robert 93
Sharples, Pita 193–4, 284
Shaw, George Bernard 205–6
SheepGenomics 48
Sheppard, Kate 175, 297–8 n.10
shipbuilding, Dutch 122, 123–5
shipping, New Zealand
  Maori coastal shipping 183–4
  refrigerated 167, 170–2
  steamships 172–3, 177
Siedeberg, Emily 256
Silicon Valley 118–9, 129, 255–6
Simon, Herbert 115
Simpson, George Gaylord 103
Singapore 36, 39, 119, 123, 207, 209, 214, 216, 217
Sir George Murray 184
small business, New Zealand 218–9, 229
small world systems 106, 108, 235, 236, 237, 239
Smith, Adam, The Wealth of Nations 71–2
Snedden, Patrick, Pakeha and the Treaty 196, 197
Snowden, David 111
social capital 241, 242, 247, 249, 250
social networks 234–8, 239–40, 302 nn.4, 10
  global 250–3
  New Zealand 235, 240, 246–59, 260
society/societies 78, 82–3
  decentralised 124
  divisions in 282–3
  order in 95–6, 98–101, 293 n.17
  reasons for success of 117–9
  See also adaptation
Sole, Richard 107
Sondheim, Stephen 239
South Africa 122, 150
South America 182. See also Latin America; and names of specific countries
South East Asia 63, 207, 214. See also specific countries
Soviet Union 133, 135, 226. See also Russia
Sowell, Thomas 118, 283
Spaichl, Hans 144
Spain 122, 123, 124
Spinoza, Baruch 124
Sport and Recreation New Zealand 65
Stafford, Edward 168
standard of living, New Zealand 62, 212
Stanford University 118
State Services Commission (NZ) 37
Stegeman 48
stirrups, invention of 131–2, 295 n.19
stock-keeping units 27
Strassman, Fritz 79
stress 36
students, Chinese 256, 304 n.43
suffrage 175–6, 297–8 n.10
Sunstein, Cass 243
supercomputers 52–5
superconnectors 107, 108, 113, 236. See also connectivity
Surowiecki, James, The Wisdom of Crowds 245
Svenson, Ole 305 n.20
Sweden 216, 217, 242
Swiss Federal Institute of Technology 54
Switzerland 255
Sydney 173, 180, 181, 183
synthetic biologists 49
systems 77–8
  chaotic 234–5
  frozen 234
  melting 234, 235
  open and closed 96–8
  small world 106, 108, 235, 236, 237, 239

T-cells 244
Tahiti 180, 183
Taiwan 216, 255
Taiwhanga, Rawiri 185

Tantalus 271
Taonui 184
Tapsell, Peter 182
Taranki 185
Taranaki Coolstores 167
Tasman, Abel 145, 164
Tasman Vaccine Ltd 134
Tasmania 183. See also Hobart
Te Pahi 182
Te Rauparaha 172–3, 184
Te Wheherua 182
team building 239–40
technical and scientific literature 30–1
technologies, new 31, 38, 39, 128, 227–9. See also automation; computers
Telecom 217, 233
telegraph lines 169, 173, 177
telephones 30, 173–4
television 28, 29, 31–32, 50, 57, 58, 60, 248, 275, 276
termites 98–9
text messages 30, 225
textiles, of nano particles 50–1
Thailand 65, 252
Thales of Mellitus 251
Thames 174, 181
thermodynamics 96–7
  Second Law of 92–4, 95, 100, 110
thinking
  conformity in 242–4
  divergent 223
  entrainment of 111
  rigidity in 269–71
Three Gorges Dam 62
timber trade, New Zealand 181
time
  and quantum theory 70
  compression of 33–4
  New Zealand Standard Time 175
Tindall, Stephen 230
Tizard Brothers 186
Toffler, Alvin, Future Shock 36–7, 276, 282
Toray Industries 50
tornadoes 97
Total Early-Stage Activity (TEA) index 218–9
Tough Choices or Tough Times 214, 222
Toulmin, Stephen 283–4
Toynbee, Arnold 118, 142
trade deficits, New Zealand 31
transport, see railways; shipping
Treaty of Waitangi 40, 186, 197
Tuhoe people 159
Tunisia 65
Turing, Alan 132–3
Twain, Mark 283
Twenge, Jean 37

uncertainty 70, 77–83. See also chaos; complexity
United Kingdom 28, 36, 37, 59, 60, 117, 118, 132–3, 150, 181, 255, 258, 281, 304 n.43. See also England
  and New Zealand 150–2, 164, 167, 168, 170, 171–2, 174, 175, 177–8, 181, 184, 189–91, 280
United States 30, 34, 36, 48, 74, 75, 183, 214, 215, 216, 241–2, 253
  and Marshall Plan 304 n.44
  and New Zealand 168
  civic participation in 247–8
  computers in 52–4, 55–6
  healthcare in 43–4
  innovation in 117, 118–9, 129, 133
  IQ scores in 28
  perception of Americans that US is deteriorating 274
  public opinion about government 37–8
  social networks in 302 n.10
  workforce in 56, 59, 60
  See also Los Angeles; New York, Silicon Valley
United States Patent and Trademark Office 215, 300–1 n.14
University of California 129
Unlimited paenga tawhiti school 224–5

Van der Kwast, Suzy 256
Van Loghem, Johannes 256
variety, cultivation of 110–1
Venezuela 252
Venice 142–3, 250–1
Venter, Craig 289 n.7
Vest, Charles 66
Victoria, Australia 281
Vietnam 59, 255
Vinge, Vernor 56
viruses
  digital 34

human 34, 51
Vogel, Julius 168–9, 177
Voight, Christopher 49
Volkswagen 60
Vowles, Jack 248

Waiapu meeting house 162
Waikato 185, 191
Waitangi Tribunal 196, 197
Wal Mart 59
Wallace, William E. 230
Warehouse 58–9
Waterman, Bob, In Search of Excellence 228
Watson, James 94
weak links 236–8, 239–40, 249
wealth 28, 117
weather forecasting, long-range 75–6, 97
Weinberg, Steven, Dream of a Final Theory 70
well-being 266–9
Wellington 25–6, 172, 174, 176, 209, 256
West Indies 122
West Side Story production of 239
Westminster parliamentary political system 71
Weta Workshop 209
whalers, trade with 181, 183, 184
Whalewatch Kaikoura 196
Wheatley, Margaret 81
Whitehead, Alfred 223
Whitman, David, The Optimism Gap 274
Wiesel, Torsten 54
William IV, King 184
William, Duke of Normandy 130–1
Williams, Pat, How to be Like Walt 259
Williams, Stan 53
Williams, Tuwhakairiora 250
women, New Zealand
employment 176
Maori 195–6, 199, 299 n.42
suffrage 175–6
wool production, genomic techniques 48
work, future of 41, 55–60, 282
workforce, New Zealand 63–4, 290–1 nn.60–61
World Health Organization 65–6
World Intellectual Property Organization 129, 215
World Trade Organization 59
World War I 168, 171
World War II 132–3, 168, 275
World Wide Web 57, 77, 107–8. See also Internet
Wycliffe, John 89

yacht design 229
Yanomamo tribe 27, 31
Yodzis, Peter 105–6

Zaandam 121, 122
Zheng, Admiral 136–7